THE *COMPLETE* BOOK OF
SEA
FISHING

THE *COMPLETE* BOOK OF
SEA
FISHING

INTRODUCTION BY TREVOR HOUSBY

CollinsWillow

An Imprint of HarperCollins*Publishers*

First published in 1993 by
Collins Willow
an imprint of HarperCollins Publishers
London

Based on The Art of Fishing
© Eaglemoss Publications Ltd 1993

A CIP catalogue record for this book is
available from the British Library

ISBN 0 00 218514 8

Printed and bound in Hong Kong

Contents

Introduction

When I first had a chance to do some sea fishing, as a boy from London enjoying an unforgettable holiday in Cornwall, the sport was very much a hit-and-miss affair. In those days the sea angler had to learn from his mistakes. Books on sea fishing were a rare commodity, and most of those that young anglers like me came across were long out of date. The only thing for it was to experiment with new ideas, improvising tackle and set-ups to suit the water and the types of fish we were after.

Since those times the face of sea fishing has changed dramatically. It is now an exact science, and today's sea angler is a specialist dedicated to the pursuit of certain species or particular areas of the sport – bass, maybe, or jigging. What has also changed, along with the ever-greater technical sophistication, is that nowadays many of the best anglers not only catch fish but want to share the secrets of their success by writing about it. Some of the top names in the field – anglers like Mike Millman, Alan Yates, Mick Toomer, John Darling and Bob Gledhill – have come together in *The Complete Book of Sea Fishing* to produce a definitive guide to the sport as it is practised now – and even to give some glimpses into the future.

All the essential equipment is discussed in the first chapter, which concentrates on shore fishing and includes detailed instruction on beachcasting. The next chapter, devoted to boat angling, explains the main techniques and looks at fishing over different types of ground. Baits, natural and artificial, are the subject of the third chapter, which offers ▶

invaluable advice on this crucial area. The last chapter, covering the habitat, characteristics and breeding patterns of all the popular species as well as many less familiar fish, is a mine of information and full of practical value. For the successful sea angler is the one who learns as much about his quarry as possible.

The Complete Book of Sea Fishing is a short cut to the knowledge it has taken me 40 years to acquire. So read it and then go out and put the know-how it contains to good use. But at the same time as learning from the experts, join your local club if you haven't already done so. In that way you can put something back into the sport by helping junior members and newcomers. They are, after all, the sea anglers of the future, and the way forward for our wonderful sport.

Trevor Housby

CHAPTER ONE

SHORE FISHING

Hooks

The best rod, reel, line and bait in the world are wasted with the wrong hook, advises top Southern sea match angler Tony Kirrage.

The golden rule is always to match the size and type of hook to the size and type of fish you are seeking and the size and type of bait you are using.

It's largely a matter of common sense – a small, fine wire hook suitable for dabs is clearly not up to the job of landing a shark, while even the greediest dab would be hard pressed to get a huge, forged hook designed for shark fishing into its mouth.

Equally, a small, fine wire hook cannot be expected to hold a whole mackerel bait, nor a large, forged hook a tiny harbour ragworm.

Yet many anglers – some of them quite experienced – too often choose the wrong hook for the job. They still catch fish, of course, but they would catch many more if they gave a little more thought to their choice of hooks.

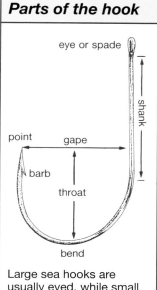

Parts of the hook

eye or spade

shank

point

gape

barb

throat

bend

Large sea hooks are usually eyed, while small ones sometimes have spade-ends.

▲ *Aberdeen hooks are best for delicate baits such as these sandeels as they do little damage to the bait.*

◄ *Long shank, fine wire Aberdeen hooks and fresh lug are the perfect combination for small-mouthed flatfish such as this plump 3lb (1.4kg) summertime plaice.*

Basic hook types

Aberdeen

Needle-sharp, this fine wire hook has a long shank and a round bend. It is ideal for delicate baits, such as worms, sandeels and prawns, as it does little damage to the bait.

Limerick

This is a medium wire hook with a short shank and a wide gape. It is excellent for bulky baits such as peeler crab, as the wide gape prevents the bait from masking the point.

Uptide

Also with a short shank and a wide gape, this hook is forged for greater strength. It is excellent for fishing large, bulky baits such as peeler crab for cod and bass.

O'Shaughnessy

Made of thick, stainless steel, this medium shank and medium gape hook is ideal for strong fish such as conger. It is also used when you have to heave out smaller but still hard-fighting fish like wrasse.

▶ *The strikingly coloured wrasse is not a big fish but it fights well, has a bony mouth and lives among rocky and often kelp-infested shores – all of which means you must use a strong hook such as an O'Shaughnessy.*

Hook types

Five main types of hook cover the sea angler's needs, not counting freshwater hooks for mullet fishing or treble hooks attached to pirks, spinners and trolling lures. The five are: Aberdeen, Limerick, Uptide, O'Shaughnessy and Seamaster.

The hook for the job

Below are the recommended hook sizes and types for most of the popular fish sought in the seas around Britain.

Mullet are wary, small-mouthed and hard-fighting fish. Use short shank, forged, size 8 and 6 freshwater hooks when fishing with small, delicate baits such as bread and harbour ragworm.

Dabs, plaice and flounders For these small-mouthed fish, choose size 4 and 2 Aberdeens when fishing with worm baits in calm seas. These hooks can also land bonus codling and bass. In choppy seas use a larger and stronger size 1/0 Aberdeen. When fishing for flounders with peeler crab, use a size 4 or 2 Limerick.

Sole Small hooks are essential as sole have very small mouths. Size 6 and 4 Aberdeens are best for worm baits.

Tip   Use offset hooks

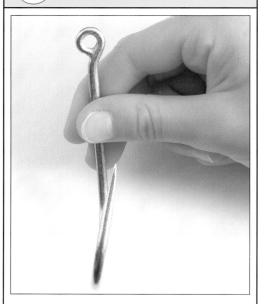

For some reason, you hit more bites when using hooks with offset points. Some hooks come with their points already offset. If not, you can offset the points with pliers.

Eels Use size 4 and 2 Limericks for shore fishing with peeler crab as bait.

Whiting A bold biter that rattles and thumps your rod tip, this is nevertheless one of the hardest fish to hook. Use an extra sharp size 1 Aberdeen.

Bass When fishing over rocks, large hooks are essential to land hard-fighting bass. A size 6/0 Uptide is favourite for crab baits, a size 6/0 Kamasan B940 Aberdeen – a stronger, thicker wire Aberdeen – for worm and sandeel baits. When fishing over sand, a size 2/0 is big enough.

Wrasse A strong, sharp hook is needed when fishing off rocks for these hard-fighting, bony-mouthed fish. A size 1 O'Shaughnessy is ideal.

Cod Use size 1/0 and 2/0 Uptides for shore fishing. In these sizes Uptides are also small enough to hook any smaller fish

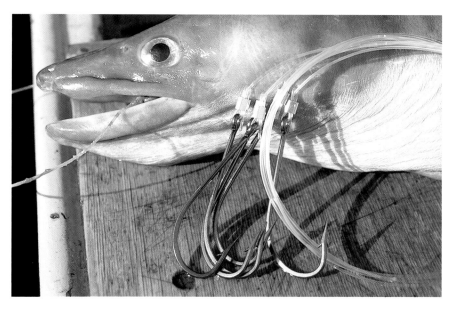

▼ A wide range of hook sizes is used in sea fishing around Britain, reflecting the different fish you can catch and the variety of baits you can use. The basic range, in ascending order of size, is: 8, 6, 4, 2, 1, 1/0, 2/0, 3/0, 4/0, 5/0, 6/0, 7/0, 8/0, 9/0, 10/0, 12/0 and 14/0.

about, such as whiting, dabs and flounders. When boat fishing for cod you need a larger, stronger hook – a size 5/0 or 6/0 Uptide or O'Shaughnessy.

Pollack and coalfish Use size 3/0 and 4/0 O'Shaughnessy hooks with artificial eels and fish baits. For delicate baits such as

▲ Congers are all muscle. To have any chance of hauling one from its lair you need a strong rod, strong line, a large, strong O'Shaughnessy hook – and last but not least, a strong back.

Hook sizes (reproduced actual size)

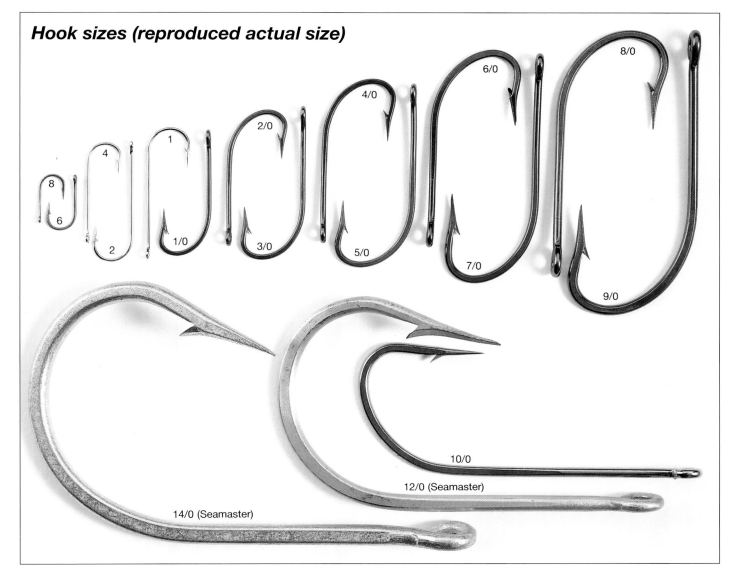

▶ *A dogfish from the deep is brought alongside the boat. Size 2/0 or 3/0 Kamasan B940 Aberdeens are ideal for this hard-mouthed fish. They are made from thicker and stronger wire than normal Aberdeens.*

Tip Twin-point hooks

Twin-point Aberdeens are a recent and very effective innovation for shore fishing with worm baits, because the bait stays on the hook so well. Squeeze the two points together and push a baiting needle on to the single point formed. Thread the worm up the needle on to the shank and line. Remove the needle and the two points spring apart, stopping the worm sliding off the hook.

king ragworm and live sandeels, choose Kamasan B940 Aberdeens in the same sizes as the O'Shaughnessy hooks.

Dogfish and smooth hounds Extra sharp size 2/0 and 3/0 Kamasan B940 Aberdeens are ideal for these hard mouthed fish.

Conger, ling and tope You need a big, strong hook when fishing with large baits such as whole mackerel for these large, hard-fighting fish. Use size 7/0, 8/0, 9/0 and 10/0 O'Shaughnessy hooks.

Sharks The recommended hooks for boat fishing with very big baits for these very large and powerful fish are size 10/0, 12/0 and 14/0 Seamaster hooks. A Seamaster is a short shank, medium gape hook made of even thicker and stronger wire than the O'Shaughnessy.

Care of your hooks

Keep your hooks sharp or you will miss bites and lose fish. One retrieve over rough ground is enough to blunt any hook. For small hooks, buy a sharpening stone and touch up the point every cast. For large O'Shaughnessy and Seamaster hooks, use a metal file to sharpen the point and the edge from the point to the barb.

When you pack up, never put used hooks back in with unused ones – the salt water will rust them all in days. If you decide to throw your used hooks away, wait until you get home before doing so. If you decide to keep and re-use them, rinse in fresh water, dry thoroughly, wipe with an oily rag and store in a dry place.

 Bait-holder hooks

The popular bait-holder hook has barbs cut into the outside of the shank. The idea is that these barbs stop the bait sliding down on to the bend. In fact, all they do is weaken the hook. Bait-holders also tend to be made from brittle metal, so avoid using them.

Leads and booms

Lead weights and booms are the basis of most saltwater terminal rigs. John Holden explains the when, why and how of using the huge variety available.

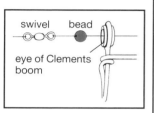
S altwater tackle relies heavily on weights and booms to get the bait to where the fish are feeding in a way they find attractive. There is a large and often confusing variety of both kinds of terminal tackle – much of it designed to do a fairly specialized job. Knowing when to use each item of tackle can save you time and hassle and make your fishing more satisfying.

Weights for saltwater

Choosing the right lead weight is important in both beach and boat fishing. Many beginners make the mistake of thinking that size is all that matters – the deeper the water and the bigger the waves, the heavier the lead should be.

Simply increasing weight to overcome tide, waves and so on seems a logical plan and, for lowering baits straight down into deep water, it works. That is why an egg or cone-shaped lead, weighing between 6oz-2lb (170-900g), has become the usual choice for general boat angling.

For bottom fishing over very deep marks swept by powerful currents, experienced anglers use wire line instead of Dacron or monofilament. Wire line is much thinner than nylon of the same breaking strain and so presents much less resistance to the current. This means that less lead is needed to hold bottom.

Wire line has the added advantage that it does not stretch like nylon, so bites are much more positive in deep water. To be effective, line and weight must be chosen as a team. Always ask the skipper's advice, otherwise your baits may never reach the bottom.

Wired leads

For surfcasting and uptide boat fishing, there are other considerations besides

▶ In a boat you can reach marks well offshore, but away from the shelter of the coast, tides can be very strong. This requires the use of heavy weights to reach the sea bed. If the tide is not too strong, light tackle such as this pirking gear is much more sporting and more fun.

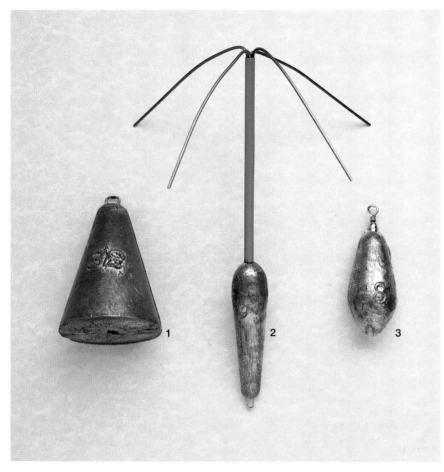

▲ *A selection of boat leads for a variety of situations: A 2lb (900g) conical lead for general boat use (1), a 6oz (170g) wired uptide lead for boat casting (2) and an 8oz (227g) bomb (3) for fishing in light tides.*

weight. Long casting – essential in many cases – requires the use of bomb or torpedo-shaped leads. Also, few fishermen, or their rods, can handle more than 6oz (170g). Besides, even a massive chunk of lead alone cannot possibly anchor tackle against strong lateral tides. If you were to use a plain lead on most cod or bass beaches, the tackle would be swept back ashore within a few minutes. The answer is to use a wired lead. These are available in weights of between 3-8oz (85-227g) and in fixed or breakaway forms.

A fixed-wire lead has wires sprouting from the nose which act as mini grapnels, anchoring the tackle to the sea bed almost regardless of wind and tide. An 8oz (227g) wired lead sits tight where a 24oz (680g) plain weight rolls uncontrollably. The only drawback is that the wires sometimes get caught up on the retrieve. They are supposed to bend out of the way of snags but, as every angler knows, rocks and weeds can be remarkably clever when it comes to stealing tackle.

The breakaway lead is designed to overcome problems with the retrieve. The wires are fixed during the cast and while the bait lies on the sea bed, but they swivel free to trail behind when you recover your tackle. This combination of high grip and easy handling has made the breakaway the standard choice for beachcasting and uptiding. The best weight for long distance casting is 5¼oz (150g) and it copes well with most conditions and bait sizes.

Other weights

Heavyweight eggs and wired bombs are the main weapons against water depth and tide. Often the angler has no choice but to use them even though they require heavier tackle than the fish themselves deserve. Sometimes though, the sea lies calm with little or no tide. This is the time to let your tackle roll slowly along the sea bed. For this you'll need a 2-6oz (57-170g) plain torpedo or bomb for beach and uptide fishing, and 4-10oz (113-284g) for boat fishing in deeper water.

For spinning the weights must lie close to the line to minimize water resistance during the retrieve. The best weights for this are Jardine spirals which you can change without cutting the line, or Wye leads which help to reduce line twist. Pierced barrels are also used for spinning, though as they slide freely on the line they need to be held in place with beads and stop knots. This freedom of movement makes them a good weight for float fishing as you can easily change their position.

Sea booms

The boom has been the foundation of successful terminal tackle in sea fishing for

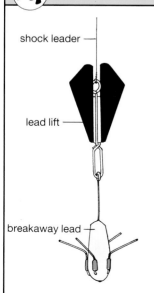

▼ You've often got to cast a long way to reach the fish from the beach, which means streamlined leads and rigs. A bait clip can be useful to hold the snoods in flight.

For beachcasting in strong surf, you need a wired lead. A wired torpedo (**1**) has soft brass wires which can be bent with a tug. A breakaway lead (**2**) has rigid wires which swivel when retrieved. A plain torpedo and clip-on plastic breakaway (**3**) – used with another breakaway, they increase grip more.

and hold them in place with stop knots.

Fold-flat booms work on the same principle but have the advantage of lying alongside the leader for casting. Casting distances improve and baits are less liable to damage as they aren't left to flap during the cast. Once underwater, the boom swings out at right angles to the leader once more. You need a bait clip to hold the baited hook in position and it is important that you assemble the whole rig accurately to ensure clean disengagement.

Weight-carrying booms are key components of sliding rigs for boat and heavy beach fishing. One of the best sliding booms for light tackle is a link swivel with a short length of rigid plastic tube pushed tightly into the eye. This tube carries the reel line. Booms like this can be bought, or made at home from plain swivels and a short length of plastic sleeve – the tube from a ballpoint-pen for example.

These DIY booms are excellent for light boat work of all kinds, but they should not be used for long range casting unless the line running through the tube is at least 50lb

many years. There are two separate types of boom – one to carry weights and one to carry hook snoods. Nowadays most are made of tough plastic, though you can certainly still get metal ones as well.

Snood booms are stiff extenders which link the hooklength to the main line while preventing tangles by holding the two lines apart. French booms are based on the traditional wire paternoster, but more modern plastic booms and 'bait arms' do the same job. Thread them on to the line

Breakaways

The breakaway lead ready for casting (**1**). The rollers sit in grooves on the lead, holding the wires rigid for grip. When retrieved, the wires swivel out of the way (**2**). In really rough conditions some anglers increase the tension needed to break the grip by looping an elastic band around the wires before casting.

(22.7kg) breaking strain. You would perhaps be wiser to avoid the sliding boom arrangement altogether for long range work.

Short range congering and tope fishing from the shore, deep water fishing and heavy uptiding call for a weight boom that is tough and which protects the line running through it. The traditional Clements and Kilmore booms are of brass or stainless steel wire with one or two ceramic-lined eyes for the line. They work well, but are quite expensive and have now been largely superseded by nylon bodied booms with stainless steel weight clips.

Booms with two eyes should always be attached with the 'tail' (the eye which is not directly above the weight) pointing towards the hook. This helps ensure greater running smoothness and prevents tangles, which is after all, the purpose of the rig.

The variety of booms and leads available is supposed to make fishing easier and more effective, not to make things difficult, so select your terminal tackle with an eye to the fish you are after and where you are fishing. But remember, simplicity is the key – if something is not doing a useful job in your rig, get rid of it.

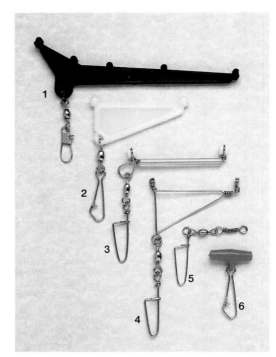

▲ A selection of weight carrying booms: the Eddystone boom (1), Clements booms (2-4), a Kilmore boom (5), and a more modern type of plastic boom (6).

▲ A circular watch grip (left) and a pierced coffin (right) are useful over soft muddy ground as they are flat and do not sink into mud very easily. However, they are no good for long casting and the watch grip is prone to twisting over and over in a strong tide.

▲ The banana shaped Wye lead (1) is ideal for spinning, as is the Jardine spiral (2), which can be moved easily. The pierced barrel (3) can also be used for spinning, or for float fishing and the pierced bullet (4) is perfect for fishing with a heavy float.

Fold-flat boom and bait clip

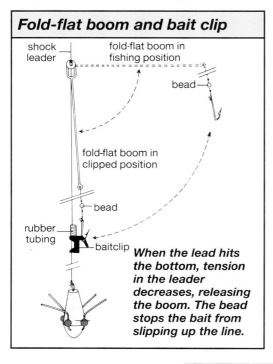

shock leader
fold-flat boom in fishing position
bead
fold-flat boom in clipped position
bead
rubber tubing
baitclip

When the lead hits the bottom, tension in the leader decreases, releasing the boom. The bead stops the bait from slipping up the line.

A sliding boom rig

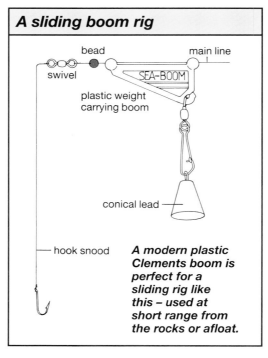

bead
main line
swivel
SEA-BOOM
plastic weight carrying boom
conical lead
hook snood

A modern plastic Clements boom is perfect for a sliding rig like this – used at short range from the rocks or afloat.

▶ Sliding bait booms (1-3) are easily repositioned. Plastic booms (4-5) are held in position with beads and stop knots. A metal version of the plastic boom (6). A three way swivel with beads (7) is an inexpensive way of attaching a snood. The French boom (8) is held in place by twisting the line around the central projecting loop, making it very easy to reposition.

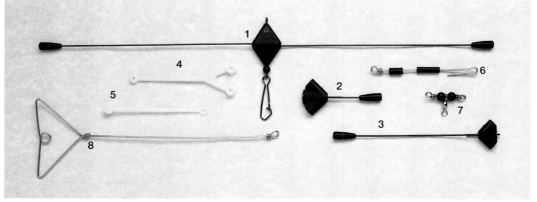

Six essential knots

Many knots used in sea angling have only very specialized uses. For general shore and boat fishing the beginner need actually know very few, says Mike Thrussell.

L earn to tie the following half dozen knots – they are essential components of safe, secure and trouble-free tackle set-ups.

Tucked half blood knot The standard half blood knot can come undone under pressure. By tucking the tag end through the knot a second time before drawing it tight you greatly increase the knot's reliability.

This is a simple and effective knot for tying hooks, swivels, lead links and so on to your main line or traces.

Uni knot This is an alternative to the tucked half blood knot. It is more complicated but is good for tying on hooks when threading worms up the shank and on to the line; the tag end lies flush against the line and does not burst the worm.

Use the same knot to tie an effective stop knot/slider knot on your main line with a separate length of lighter line.

Spool knot Tying line to the spool of a multiplier reel with a bulky knot can make the spool empty unevenly when you cast, cut-

▶ *A conger eel takes the mackerel bait and battle is joined. The strain imposed on your tackle when heaving a big fish away from a wreck and up through the water is immense. Therefore you cannot afford the slightest weakness in your tackle. Not in your hooks, not in your line – and certainly not in your knots.*

ting distance and increasing the risk of a bird's nest. With a badly tied spool knot there is also always the possibility, however remote, of a fish stripping all the line from the reel. A well tied, reliable spool knot gives you added confidence when a big fish takes a lot of line.

Tied correctly, the spool knot illustrated overleaf never comes undone and, more importantly, sits flat on the spool, allowing the line to wind on and come off evenly for

▼ *Well tied knots can mean the difference between punching your lead smoothly out into the deep blue yonder or having it crack off at the point of maximum compression and bury itself deep in the skull of some unfortunate bystander. And remember the leader rule – 10lb (4.5kg) of breaking strain per ounce of lead.*

Mike Thrussell's six essential sea knots

1. Tucked half blood Use instead of the standard half blood knot for tying on hooks and swivels.

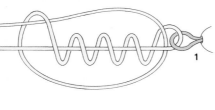

2. Uni knot A harder knot to tie than the tucked half blood but a better choice when using worms, as the tag lies flush with the line and doesn't damage the bait.

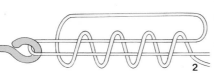

Knots **1** and **2** are both more secure if you double the line through the eye of the hook or swivel.

3. Spool knot A simple but secure knot for tying line to the spool of a multiplier reel – the spool of a fixed-spool reel too, for that matter.

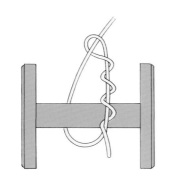

4. Blood loop A very useful knot to know, especially for boat fishing over rough ground. It creates mounting points for traces without the need for swivels, beads and booms and the like, so if you snag up and have to pull for a break, the cost of your losses is kept to a minimum.

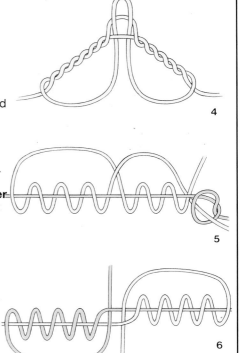

5. Tournament leader The smallest, neatest and, most important of all, the strongest knot for joining two pieces of line of unequal diameters.

6. Blood knot This is a good knot to use when tying together two lines of roughly the same diameter.

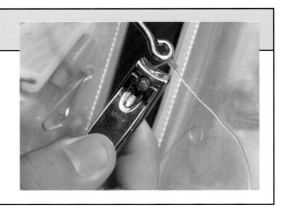

trouble-free casting.

Blood loop When fishing over rough ground, where tackle losses can be high, this knot is an effective way of creating mounting points for hook traces and does away with the need for expensive swivels and booms.

If you tie the loops in very long they are ideal for presenting muppets and artificial eels above a pirk when wrecking; simply thread the loop through the eye of the hook, pass it over the point, then draw tight. You can stiffen the loops beforehand with short lengths of thin plastic tubing so the hooks hang clear of the main line.

Tournament leader knot A shock leader knot needs to be small and neat so that it passes smoothly through the rod rings when you cast. Also, the smaller the knot, the less weed it collects.

The tournament leader knot is the smallest, strongest knot there is for joining two pieces of line of uneven diameter. It is so-called because it is used by many top tournament casters.

If you use a multiplier reel, always lay the knot to one side of the spool before casting, otherwise it can cut your thumb badly as it leaves the spool.

Blood knot This is a good knot for joining two lines of roughly equal diameter and is very strong under a direct pull. It is a little bulky, but not so much that it doesn't pass smoothly enough through the rod rings when you cast. Maximum strength is achieved by making sure that each length of line is wound at least eight times around the other.

Tip Use clippers, not teeth

Use nail clippers not teeth to trim knots unless you enjoy regular visits to the dentist! You don't need to leave a long tag. If you have tied the knot correctly, next to no further tightening occurs. About 2mm of tag proud of the knot is plenty.

◀ *A fine double-figure cod to put a broad grin on any angler's face. Such fish are strong and heavy enough to expose any weakness in your tackle, yet every year many big fish are lost because of inadequately tied knots.*

Tip Tight lines

All knots should be drawn tight slowly after being lubricated with saliva to eliminate friction burns, which weaken line. Don't tug sharply on the line to tighten a knot – it stretches and weakens it. A knot that won't tighten easily is badly tied and should be scrapped.

Beachcasting rods

Walk into a tackle shop and you are likely to be confronted with a wide variety of beachcasting rods. Selection can be tricky unless you think about your fishing and which rod it calls for, says Paul Kerry.

A beachcasting rod is designed to throw a weighted rig out to where the fish are feeding, indicate when a fish has taken the bait, and then to cushion the thumps as the fish tries to get free. However, the conditions under which this is done determine the type of rod you need.

Fishing estuaries or surf beaches for bass does not require a rod with the same power as one needed to blast out 6oz (170g) of lead, plus bait, over 140m (153yd) – or pull big cod out through kelp and rocks.

The budget
Most people have a price range to work to, but you don't need to spend a lot of money to get good performance. In most cases, the more expensive rods are made of top qual-ity materials and offer greater distance casting potential – but only if you have a good enough technique to use it properly.

If you're only going to use the rod occasionally, you won't have time to practise the techniques that help you cast huge distances. A rod capable of up to 110m (120yd) is perfectly adequate and shouldn't cost the earth.

The cheapest rods are made entirely of glass-fibre, or with just a hint of carbon fibre. A rod like this has an all-through action which means even a smallish fish puts a decent bend in it. They are heavy, however, and the action reduces casting potential. If all you need is a budget price rod, this type is ideal, but watch out for cheap reel seats and rod rings.

Tip Rod care

Dropping your rod can set up hairline fractures, eventually causing it to break. Cheaper rods usually have thicker walls and a higher proportion of glass-fibre. This makes them more resilient than light carbon rods with thin walls.

Wipe your rod down with a dry cloth after each session and give the fittings a squirt of WD-40. Before assembly, always wipe both halves of the joint – sand can wear it away very quickly.

▼ *Beachcasting rods are no longer heavy poles with no sensitivity and poor casting ability. It takes a high-tech item to be light, able to cast over 200m (220yd) and still ensure that it's fun to play and land fish.*

There's a rod ring lining...

Ceramic lined rings were a breakthrough when it came to resisting wear and reducing friction, but they are brittle and can crack if you drop the rod. A cracked ring lining shreds the line in no time – causing you to crack off or lose fish. Aluminium oxide, titanium and hard plastics are not prone to this but still have low friction coefficients and therefore resist grooving. They are the standard choice for lining rod rings.

▶ *This angler is using three rods to fish an estuary – two are set up for fixed-spool reels and the other for a multiplier.*

▼ *Casting a heavy weight involves putting a real bend into the rod. Beachcasters have to be very powerful to cope with this.*

Fast action

Most rods in the middle to high price range contain a large proportion of carbon fibre in the blank. Some rods use kevlar to strengthen the stiff but brittle carbon fibre. They are usually stiffer than the cheaper rods and have a faster action. This gives a rod with a rigid butt section for distance casting, a fairly flexible middle section for playing fish, and a light tip giving excellent bite detection.

The more expensive rods generally have the most rigid butt sections – increasing casting potential. Any bending between the hands during the cast absorbs power rather than transmitting it into the blank. However, some bending does make the cast feel smoother, so a compromise is necessary. Either Duralumin or carbon fibre is used to stiffen the butt; carbon is clearly considerably lighter.

Don't confuse action with power – it is possible to have powerful rods with either an all-through or a fast action. Most beachcasters have a casting weight range printed just above the handle. This is a good indication of the power of any particular blank.

Consider the type of fishing you intend to do before buying a rod. If you fish various beaches and shorelines, you'll probably need at least two rods for maximum enjoyment. One of them is for heavy fishing at long range, the other for lighter fishing, often closer in to shore.

Length is important as the longer the rod, the farther the casting potential. Long rods also make it easier to hold line off the water in heavy tides. Since an enormous rod would be impossible to handle, most anglers find 12ft (3.7m) a good compromise. For really long casting, 13ft (4m) or more, used with an off-the-ground technique, or backcasting, can be best. A pendulum cast can also be helped by a long rod, but many anglers cast great distances with this style and a shorter rod. In the end, the choice depends mainly on personal preference.

▲ *If you do a lot of night fishing, make sure your rod is a light colour to show up bites; alternatively, attach a chemical light stick.*

Various positions

Reels can be placed anywhere on a rod butt, though conventionally they are usually placed fairly well up the handle to maximise leverage. It is a mistake, however, to set the reel too far up the butt, as this leads to exaggerated and inefficient casting styles, not extra distance or comfort.

The correct position is between 70-80cm (28-32in) up from the butt end. Find the right place for you by placing the butt cap under your armpit and stretching your arm along the handle. The reel feels natural if you place it just above where the thumb rests.

Some anglers prefer to fit the reel close to the bottom of the handle, especially with a longer rod of around 13ft (4m). The upper hand on the handle is still the stronger one, but the reel is gripped with the weaker one, which some people find more comfortable. The weight of the reel is in the best position for overall balance, and moving the rod through its casting arc is easier. For some casting methods, such as backcasting, a low reel position is vital, though it can be used with any style.

However, this positioning makes reeling in much more difficult (it often requires a butt extension to be added), particularly with heavy weights or in weed. The reel is also more vulnerable to

 Rod overload

When balancing casting weight to rod, many anglers don't take their bait into account – and a hookload of lug is not the same as a whole squid or a mackerel. Overloading a rod during the cast will break it. You can also overload a rod pulling out of a snag, and a large number of rods are broken this way every year. To avoid that sickening crunch, point the rod along the line when you pull, or wrap the line around some wood to take the strain off the reel.

Different set-ups

Beachcasting rods need to be specifically ringed for use with either a multiplier or a fixed-spool reel. The rod on the left has been set up for use with a fixed-spool reel. It has four intermediate rings which are very large to allow for the line coming off the spool in coils. This reduces the friction that cuts down your distance.

The rod on the right has been set up for a multiplier, with seven small intermediate rings. A larger number of rings reduces the angle of the line at each ring when the rod is bent. This in turn reduces the stress and wear on the line when pulling in a fish.

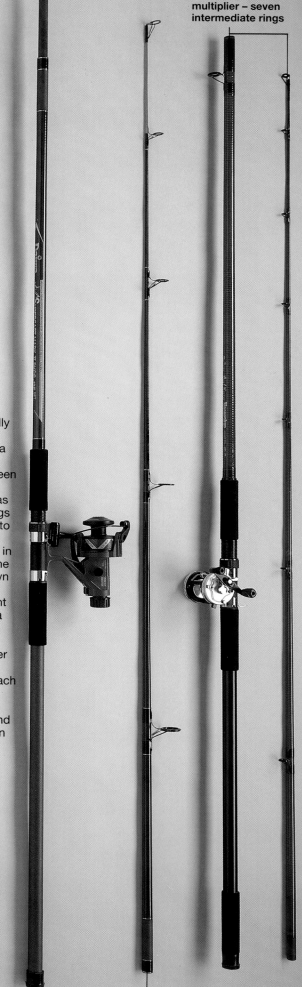

rod set up for multiplier – seven intermediate rings

rod set up for fixed-spool – four intermediate rings

Ringing changes

Whether buying a factory set-up rod or doing it yourself, pay attention to the rings. They need to be lined for minimum friction and maximum resistance to wear.

The number and size of the rings on a rod depends on the reel with which it is supposed to be used. Line is pulled from a multiplier spool during the cast in a fairly straight line. It pulls a cushion of air with it so that it 'hovers' inside each ring. This does not create much friction, so a set of seven or eight fairly small rings is best.

With a fixed-spool reel, line is pulled off the spool in coils during the cast. These coils are present at the first ring (and to a lesser extent all the way up the rod), which causes considerable friction as the line rubs against the inside of the rings. This means it is best to use four or five larger rings. Using these ring arrangements and line of around 0.35mm diameter, the casting performances of both set-ups are very similar.

There are many different rods from which to choose, but most handle a wide range of conditions. Only the most specific location – such as surf beach fishing for bass – requires a specialized rod. A rod that can cast 3-6oz (85-170g) and with which you feel comfortable will serve you very well in most circumstances.

▲ *Rods need to be held so they show bites clearly. Rod rests to do this come in many forms, from tubes like these, to tripods.*

▼ *Fishing in the surf is one of the most exciting forms of sea fishing. You can often fish light, using a 1-3oz (28-85g) weight with lightweight rod to match.*

damage, being closer to the ground when the rod is propped up waiting for a bite.

Rods that have been set up by the manufacturer tend to have reel seats fixed in the conventional position. These are just about in the right place for most people but for fine tuning you can fit your rod with coasters. These are simple screw lock fittings and they are used by many match anglers.

Fixed-spool reels

According to sea angling journalist Bob Gledhill, the idea that fixed-spool reels are somehow second-rate is wrong. Here he explains why these reels should have a place in any sea angler's kit.

The fixed-spool reel still suffers from an image problem in sea angling. It is regarded as somehow being the trademark of a below-average angler. Remarks like these have not been so common in recent years but the idea still exists that real sea anglers don't use 'em.

Pointless comparisons

Fixed-spool reels are easy to use and – ironically enough – it is this that has led to their poor image. It is true that, compared with multipliers, they are very easy to cast with and are usually chosen by beginners for this reason. But an unfair association seems to have grown up between the fixed-spool and the novice.

The issue is further muddied when a multiplier and fixed-spool reel are placed side by side and the advantages and disadvantages of each traded off in a 'which-is-best' competition. This is nonsense. Both are important tools.

A positive picture

Fixed-spool reels differ fundamentally from multipliers. With a multiplier the spool's axis is perpendicular to the rod and line is given out or taken in as the spool rotates. With a fixed-spool reel the spool's axis is parallel to the rod and, unless the drag is slackened – which it rarely is – does not rotate. Instead, line is wound on to the spool over a lip at the front, by means of a bale arm.

The fixed-spool reel's design has several benefits for shore and boat anglers.

Over-runs can be an exasperating problem for the shore angler. (This is where the spool continues to rotate after casting, releasing line and causing horrendous tangles.) With a fixed-spool reel this can't happen. The spool is stationary, so no matter how mistimed the cast or bulky the bait, the line behaves.

▼ *The fixed-spool reel is one of the sea angler's most versatile tools and should have a place in even the most experienced fisherman's tackle box.*

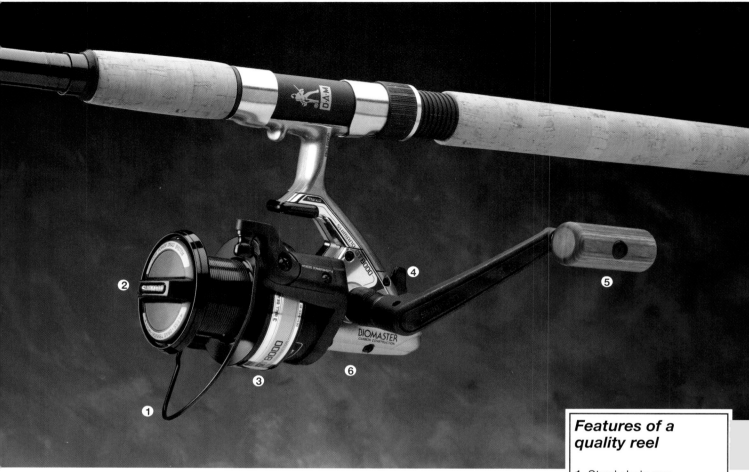

Afraid of the dark? One difficulty when casting from the shore at night is gauging just when the lead is going to land. With a multiplier this means that slowing the spool as the lead approaches the end of its trajectory becomes pure guesswork. Since most anglers are anxious that the reel should not over-run, they tend to err on the early side and shorten their cast quite considerably. With a fixed-spool reel you don't have to worry about over-runs so there is no need to shorten the cast.

The high retrieval rate means that tackle can be dragged up to the surface very quickly. For shore fishing the reel is usually loaded with 15lb (6.8kg) line, but when fishing in weed you can use heavier lines with the fast retrieve to winch the tackle clear.

Light weights cannot be cast with a multiplier because of the spool's inertia – it takes a fair bit of weight to get it rotating in the first place. So for spinning from the shore with light lures for fish such as pollack, bass and mackerel, or for float-fishing, fixed-spool reels are the obvious choice.

Boat casting when the target is moderate-sized cod, ray or smaller fish is a task to which the fixed-spool reel is particularly well suited. Oddly enough, although this technique is popular in Holland, Belgium and Scandinavia it is seldom used in the British Isles.

▼ *Some fixed-spool reels designed for shore fishing have a short stubby pick-up instead of a self-engaging bale arm. (With this type of bale the line has to be engaged by hand after casting.) This is to avoid the problem of the bale arm accidentally snapping shut during the cast. Since this rarely happens – except in the fiercest casting tournaments – it is a feature that the majority of sea anglers needn't bother with.*

Filling the spool

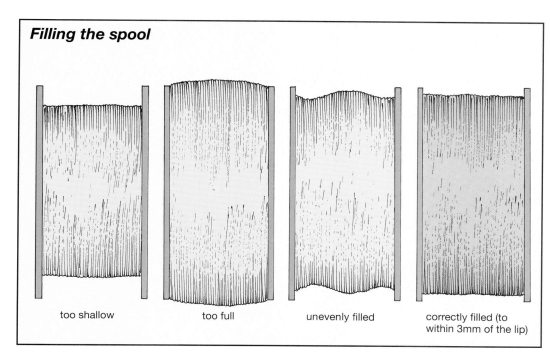

too shallow   too full   unevenly filled   correctly filled (to within 3mm of the lip)

Tip Even line lay

For trouble-free casting it is important that the line should lie evenly on the spool. If your reel doesn't do this automatically you can solve the problem by hand.

Note where the humps and troughs are when the reel is full. Then remove most of the line and wind on compensating humps so that as the reel fills the profile becomes level.

▼ *A hopeful angler punches his bait out into the open waters. Casting moderate distances with a fixed-spool is a relatively simple matter even for the novice.*

A limitation

Although fixed-spool reels are versatile they have a drawback. They are unsuitable for boat fishing with heavy sinkers in deep water. The high retrieve rate, combined with the right angle through which the line is pulled as it comes on to the spool, makes it difficult to pull up heavy weights without a pumping action. Fixed-spool reels are not as strong as heavy duty multipliers and break down under severe stress.

Buying a reel

Of the scores of fixed-spool reels available only a few are suitable for sea fishing. Most are not robust enough to cope with casting heavy weights (and this is true of many freshwater reels which look as though they might do the job). Rather than rushing out

Tip Finger protection

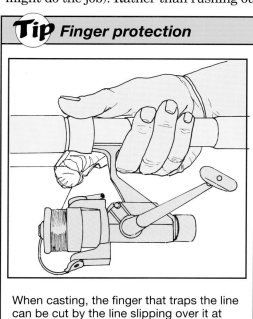

When casting, the finger that traps the line can be cut by the line slipping over it at extreme pressure. You can prevent this by wearing a finger stall.

and buying one on appearances, it is better to read carefully through some manufacturers' catalogues. Robustness and ability to withstand the corrosive action of salt water are the main requirements.

Prices vary widely and in general price is a good indicator of quality – the higher the price the better the reel. Most tackle dealers can be relied on to give a fair assessment of what a particular reel can do without giving you the hard-sell. Top models in the expensive ranges are superior – containing more ball races, machined to closer tolerances and made from better materials than cheaper models. This means that most are stronger and last longer. But some of the budget-priced reels can still cast long distances.

Service and spares Make sure that you can get spare spools for your reel so you can store different breaking strains for all the types of fishing you intend to do.

The largest recognized manufacturers tend to offer the best after-sales service but

▶ *This angler looks suitably pleased with the garfish he caught on a spinner. Fixed-spool reels are the obvious choice for light lure and float fishing simply because multipliers are not capable of casting light weights.*

▼ *Debates over whether fixed-spools or multipliers are better for long distance casting are only relevant to tournament casters. The average angler should concentrate on technique rather than tackle here – since it is largely the angler's skill and not the reel which is responsible for long casts.*

recently there has been an irritating trend among manufacturers towards bringing out new models every couple of years or so and deleting the old models – making it difficult to get spares.

Loading your reel

You need to take care over just how much line you put on the reel and how it is loaded. Incorrect loading is one of the few ways in which the fixed-spool reel can cause problems for the sea angler.

The rule is that the profile of the line on the spool must be level and should come to within about 3mm from the lip of the spool. (If you are a smooth caster then the gap can be reduced to 2mm or even 1mm.) Fill the spool to the brim and the line will simply spring off the front when it is not supposed to, causing tangles. Put too little line on and the friction – caused by the line having to drag over the lip at right angles from deep inside the spool – will seriously shorten your cast.

As well as being about 3mm from the lip, the line should be laid level over the spool. Cheaper reels form humps and troughs in the level while the expensive ones don't or shouldn't. To correct the humping tendency of the reel, hand wind compensating humps and troughs into the level of the spool.

Cleaning and maintenance

Compared with multipliers, the construction of fixed-spool reels is quite simple, making cleaning and maintenance much easier.

Apart from rinsing in fresh water, drying and spraying with water repelling spray such as WD-40, the only regular maintenance required is to run a finger carefully round the lip of the spool to check that no nicks have appeared which might damage the line.

Multiplier reels

Whether you're a confirmed fixed-spool caster who's wary of multipliers, or a regular multiplier user who wants to know how to get the most out of your reel, casting champion Paul Kerry has the answers.

On open beaches, light line of 15-18lb (6.8-8.2kg) b.s. and a well set up narrow-spooled reel can help you cast a long way – putting you among the fish instead of catching nothing.

Multiplier reels are very popular among sea anglers. Indeed, they are the only realistic choice for most heavy boat fishing. On the beach too, many anglers see them as indispensable, but there are still plenty who regard them with suspicion.

This comes mostly from the dreaded backlash or overrun, which is all too possible with a multiplier but which cannot happen with a fixed-spool reel. However, it is easy to avoid once you know what causes it and what steps to take to set up your reel properly.

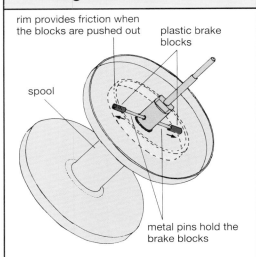
Overruns and backlashes

Because the multiplier is a development of
the original revolving spool centrepin, the
spool must revolve to pay out or recover
line. When you cast with one, the weight
and speed of the sinker as it flies out to sea
pulls line off the spool, making it rotate.

At first the speed of the lead determines
how fast the spool rotates. However, wind
resistance slows the lead, so if the spool
doesn't slow down as much, more line comes
off the spool than the lead needs.

This extra line forms loose coils which
can then catch on the spool as it rotates.
Before you know it the line is winding back
on to the spool but this time it's going on
backwards! Instead of the line coming off
the spool, the excess line is now being
wound back the other way.

With your lead flying in one direction,

With or without?

Baitcasting reels come
with or without a level
wind. The ABU 6500C
(right) has one, the Daiwa
7HT (left) does not. The
level wind mechanism
uses some of the spool's
rotation to drive a line
guide across the face of
the reel. Some casters
reckon to lose 10-15m
(11-16yd) with the extra
friction of a level wind.

For less experienced
casters, the extra braking
effect of a level wind on a
multiplier, coupled with the
evenness of line lay (vital
for smooth casting), may
actually help you get good
distance without endless
overruns.

and the line being wound back in the other,
the least you can expect is an almighty jerk
and a huge tangle. Often your terminal
tackle cracks off as well, which can get
expensive if you make a habit of it.

This can happen with just the plain lead
used in tournament casting. Add to that the
air resistance of a three hook paternoster
and a headwind and you can see how a session of overruns and crack-offs has produced many a committed fixed-spool user.

Braking reels

The solution is to slow the rotation of the
spool in time with the lead – to brake the
spool. That way there's no excess line. With
primitive multipliers, using your thumb to
slow the spool's rotation during the cast was
a good way to do this.

There's no need to thumb the spool of a
modern multiplier if you set it up properly –
the braking is built-in. Overruns are then
more easily avoidable, being due to uneven
line lay or a jerky cast.

Ideally, the spool supplies the sinker with
just enough line so that resistance is almost
zero. This is hard enough to achieve even
under tournament conditions, where your
sinker isn't slowed by bait and traces.

When fishing, you can't expect perfection.
The best you can hope for is that while the
sinker has to pull line from the reel, it
doesn't have to pull too hard, causing you to
lose distance.

The simplest form of braking is using
the end cap or caps. These are the caps on
the side plates of your reel which take up
the side-to-side play of the spool as you

*◄ It doesn't matter how you cast – with a
simple thump to a full blooded pendulum –
if you're not smooth you'll get overruns.*

tighten them. If you take up all this play and then tighten up a touch more, the extra tension acts to slow down the spool. If you rely too heavily on this kind of braking, you can wear holes in your end caps.

Another way to vary the braking of your spool is to lubricate the bearings with oils of different thicknesses. You might be surprised at the difference between reels lubricated with 3 in 1 cycle oil and with SAE 90 gear oil. The thin 3 in 1 is fine for tournament casting, whereas the thicker gear oil provides plenty of braking for a beginner.

This works for all reels, though ball bearings hold the oil longer than plain bush bearings. Indeed, you may find you have to remove the end caps about every ten casts to re-lubricate bush bearings.

The best is built-in

The above two methods work well, but for efficient braking and control they are best used on a reel that features built-in brakes. The most common types are centrifugal and magnetic brakes.

▲ *All distance casting calls for a shock leader. If you use a brightly coloured one, as here, it's easier to see in dim light.*

Tip Watch the wind

The better you cast, the less braking you need, but conditions also have an effect. A tailwind produces less resistance to your bait and lead than a headwind, and so calls for less braking. Magnetic brakes can be a boon here. With them you can easily adjust the braking as conditions change.

◀▼ *Alan Yates uses a pendulum cast to help his rod to lock-up early in the cast. Note that he mounts his reel at the butt end of the handle (below). He says it tends to smooth out the cast and give him greater leverage.*

Centrifugal brakes are very popular and work on a simple principle. Two brake blocks are mounted on a pin which is fixed to the spindle next to the spool. As the spool rotates, the brake blocks are thrown out along the pin and rub against a special drum around the pin – a bit like drum brakes on a car. The friction this causes slows the spool.

Removing one of the blocks reduces the braking, as does decreasing the size of the blocks. However, to change the braking you do need to take the spool out.

Magnetic brakes are a fairly recent idea, but they don't seem to have caught the imagination of many shore anglers. Some systems involve a single magnet which attracts the spool and is moved closer to it for more braking. Others involve banks of magnets which attract each other.

They have a dial which allows you to

change the braking externally. It can be a great help if you want the reel to react to changing conditions such as a headwind getting up, or a change of bait size.

The reel for the job

The heavier the spool, the more momentum it has when it starts rotating, and so the harder it is to slow it. This is why multipliers designed for distance casting have light graphite or alloy spools. Similarly, narrow spools are better than wide ones and since line itself has weight, a fuller spool means more overruns.

Small multipliers with light spools are the easiest to control and give the best distances. For general open beach work with lines of 0.35-0.40mm diameter (15-18lb/6.8-8.2kg b.s.), small baitcasting reels such as the ABU 6500 series or the Daiwa 6HM and 7HT are ideal.

Some situations call for ruggedness and winching power instead of very long casts. For mixed ground fishing, where you're using lines of 0.40-0.45mm (18-25lb/8.2-11.3kg b.s.), the ABU 7000, Daiwa SL20

▲ *The classic birdsnest. Avoid it with a smooth cast, even line lay and a well set up reel. You can also get one if you're late thumbing the spool to a stop when the lead hits the water.*

and the Shimano Speedmaster IICFS are powerful but are still capable casting reels.

For really rough ground fishing where casting potential is unimportant but where robustness is vital, powerful reels like the ABU 9000 and 10000, the Daiwa Sealine and the Shimano Speedmaster III are the best choices. They have the strength to allow you to wind heavy lines on to the spool under enormous pressure without breaking.

Whatever multiplier you use, set the braking to suit your abilities. It's no fun constantly losing terminal tackle and line. A tournament caster may be prepared to risk the odd crack-off for an extra yard or two. But if you are always worrying about cracking-off, you won't be able to concentrate on improving your technique.

Reel set-up by reel type and casting ability

Reel type	Line level	Lubricant setting	Brake	Casting ability and conditions
No built-in braking system eg: Daiwa Sealine, Penn 160, Shimano Speedmaster III	spool ¾ full	SAE 90	–	beginner
		SAE 30	–	average caster most conditions
		SAE 20/50	–	good caster max. range
Medium capacity centrifugal brakes eg: ABU 7000, Daiwa SL20 Shimano Speedmaster IICFS	spool ¾-⅞ full	SAE 20/50	large blocks	beginner
			2 small blocks	average caster most conditions
			1 small block	good caster good conditions
Small capacity centrifugal brakes eg: ABU 6500, Daiwa 6HM or 7HT	spool ⅞ full	SAE 20/50	large blocks	beginner
			2 small blocks	average caster av. conditions
			1 small block	good caster good conditions
		3 in 1	1 small block	tournament
Small capacity magnetic brakes eg: ABU Mag or Ultra Mag, Daiwa PMF55	spool ⅞ full	SAE 20/50	dial setting ¾-max	beginner
			¼-¾	average caster av. conditions
				good caster good conditions/ tournament

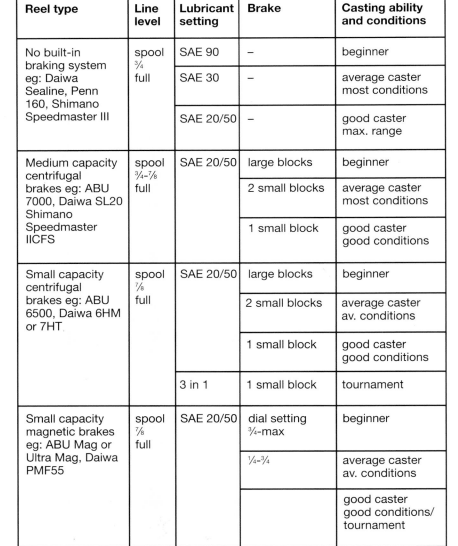

▲ *Cod fishing from steep shingle beaches often calls for big casts – which means a good casting style and a well set up reel.*

Beachcasting

Casting champion, record holder and instructor Paul Kerry discusses the off-the-ground cast. The most easily learned beachcasting technique, with practice it can hurl a bait out over 175yd (160m) or a plain lead over 200yd (180m).

What it's all about

The aim of any cast is to propel a sinker and bait as far as is possible. You do this by giving the weight as much speed as you can. A flexible rod absorbs some of the power of the cast, so a stiff pole is best, and the longer the better for off-the-ground casting. A long rod produces a longer sinker arc.

However, fishing with, say, a 30ft (9.1m) rod would be nigh-on impossible. Also fishing with a totally rigid broom pole makes bite detection difficult, provides no sort of shock absorber for playing fish and would not cushion any jolts within the cast.

What you need therefore is a rod of 12-13ft (3.65-3.95m), with a soft tip for bite detection and shock absorption and stiff lower sections to transmit the power of the cast directly to the sinker.

Early in the cast, much of the power you exert goes into bending the rod. Any good casting style compresses the rod early and fast – locking up the blank. All the power you apply afterwards goes into speeding up the sinker.

Casting techniques have come a long way in the last 20 years. The refinements involved allow serious shore anglers to put a bait an extremely long way out if the need arises. The improvements in technique have been accompanied by significant developments in tackle design so that average anglers with less refined methods can also achieve good distances.

The ultimate

The pendulum cast is probably the ultimate technique for tournament and beachcasting. However, it can be a little too much to go straight on to this from an overhead thump. It's best to work on your casting in three separate stages.

Start with the off-the-ground or South African cast, progress to a simple side-to-side type pendulum and finally, when you are ready, move on to the full-blooded pendulum cast. To get you started, this feature covers only the off-the-ground cast. The more advanced techniques are explained in most books on beachcasting.

The three-stage approach has two main advantages. Firstly, casting off-the-gound teaches important lessons about body rotation and punching the bait out, while the side-to-side pendulum gets you used to the idea of a moving lead before you try to master the intricacies of the pendulum proper.

The second advantage is that each of the stages is itself a good practical casting style. You may find the off-the-ground cast suits you perfectly, letting you blast your baits over the horizon. In that case there's no need to look any further.

Off-the-ground

The off-the-ground cast starts with a static sinker, so you can check that everything is set up correctly before you even move. With a pendulum cast, once the sinker starts to move towards the set up position, it's too late to check.

Also, the final punch and release is very similar for all three casts. For these reasons, off-the-ground is the place to start.

With the rod fully compressed, Ian Golds begins the power stroke, punching his baited rig well over 150yd (137m) to find feeding plaice at Hayling Island.

The set-up – the angles

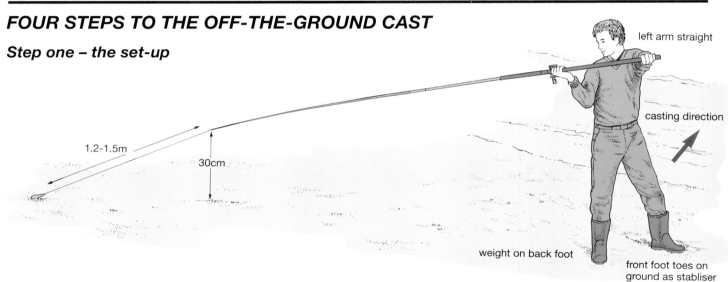

casting direction
12 o'clock

4

feet approximately
shoulder width apart

9 o'clock

3 o'clock

3

sinker thrown out
towards 9 o'clock

1

rod tip at about
8 o'clock

2

6 o'clock

The diagram and numbers refer to the positions of rod and lead in the four stages of the cast (below). To get into the correct starting position, imagine a clock face on the ground, with the casting direction at 12 o'clock. Stand with your feet shoulder width apart. (All instructions are for a right hander – reverse them for a left-handed cast.)

Point your front foot to 3 o'clock, and the back one towards about 4 o'clock. Twist at the waist so your chest faces about 5 or 6 o'clock (or whatever is comfortable), with the rod at about 8 o'clock. The rod arc increases the more you twist. Toss the sinker out along the 3-9 o'clock line and you now have the angles for a good cast.

As you bring the rod round in the cast, the sinker flies off to the right. A crack-off often sends a lead on this trajectory, so look out to the right before casting.

The power stroke

Hughie Smith shows that the punch (right) and release (far right) are the same for a fixed-spool as for a multiplier. Here he is just thumping the bait out, without the off-the-ground set-up and pick-up which compress the blank and add distance.

During the pick-up, don't raise your right hand too fast. If you bring the rod and sinker straight up, you lose much of the power. This causes a great loss of distance, especially later on when you come to try the pendulum cast.

FOUR STEPS TO THE OFF-THE-GROUND CAST

Step one – the set-up

left arm straight

casting direction

weight on back foot

front foot toes on
ground as stabliser

1.2-1.5m

30cm

Step three – the punch

left arm straight

45°

right hand just
above eye level

Step one With your feet set and torso twisted (see above), get the rod ready to pick up the lead. Hold the left arm out straight – hand on rod butt, at about eye level. Bend your right arm with the hand at shoulder height. The rod points down with the tip about 30cm (12in) off the ground. Make minor adjustments until comfortable.

To start with your weight is on your back foot, with the toes of your front foot just touching the ground for stability. In a good cast your weight transfers on to the front foot, putting your body weight behind the cast, as in any throwing action, such as shot putting or hitting a golf ball.

Step three Now that the rod is well compressed and the sinker is moving in an arc, you must punch it into the sky. The left hand pulls the butt end back and across into the chest, while the right hand punches upwards and forwards. Put your full weight behind your right hand. It helps the arms complete the punch and accelerates the sinker even more. At this stage the rod should be at about 45° to the horizontal.

The punch

The release

Step two – the pick-up

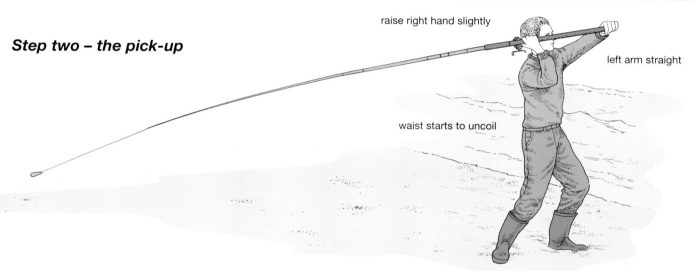

raise right hand slightly

left arm straight

waist starts to uncoil

Step four – the release

aim high

punch right arm forward

pull left arm into chest

transfer weight from back to front foot

Step two Once you are properly set up, you're ready to start. The cast begins when you uncoil at the waist, raising your right hand slightly so that the rod tip comes up. This lifts the sinker a little way off the ground (lifting too quickly is a common fault). By the time your chest faces 3 o'clock your left arm (still straight) is guiding the rod forwards with the right just below eye level. The rod is near the horizontal, the sinker well off the ground.

Step four Release is a little harder than with the overhead thump, but the principles are similar. Aim high – 60° is about right – any lower reduces distance. The rod has a much flatter arc than with an overhead thump, so the effect of an early or late release is exaggerated. Let go too early and the lead goes right, too late sends it left. Take it steadily and get it all right before really turning on the power.

Tip *Experiment with position*

The length of drop, degree to which you twist and angle at which you throw out the lead all depend on you. The longer the drop, and the greater the angles, the greater the potential distance – and problems. Get comfortable when you set up, and don't try too much too soon. You can always increase the angles later.

Steady as a rock

The off-the-ground cast teaches you all you need to know about the power stroke and release. It is also a highly useful cast in its own right. With a long rod, it can cast well over 200yd (180m) on a field.

When you've got everything right you can feel it, and distance comes without effort. Once the cast is flowing sweetly, you can really turn on the power. You might find you're happy with this cast and have no need to try a pendulum, but if you do mean to learn the pendulum, the off-the-ground cast is the best way to start.

► *For decent cod like this from the beach, distance casting can be a real advantage. They are one species for which a good style gives you a definite edge – so get practising in time for the winter!*

▼ *Chris Clark in perfect release position. The rod is aimed high, and all his weight is now on the front foot. The rod tip is flexed slightly to the right, indicating that this is the way the sinker swings round – as it does with all powerful casts.*

Rigs for shore fishing

England International Alan Yates provides a comprehensive range of simple yet effective sea rigs to meet most shore fishing situations.

▼ *At rocky venues such as this in Devon, the weak-link rig (or rotten bottom) in a single paternoster is your all-round best choice, but keep the hooklength short to try and minimize tangles.*

Simplicity is the key to successful terminal rigs for shore fishing. It's easy for novices to become bogged down in the technical aspects of rigs, and terminal tackle is one area where the armchair experts excel.

Complicated combination rigs may look fine on paper or hanging from a rod tip, but they often turn into a tangle of monofilament when they hit the sea bed. That is not to say that they can't catch any fish – they can. However, a more balanced and efficient rig may help you to catch more.

With the exception of a float-fishing rig, terminal tackle should put the bait directly on the sea bed – where most sea fish feed. It should also be streamlined to aid casting, and strong enough to withstand all the rigours of casting and the rough, snaggy underwater features of some venues.

The line of the rig is put under tremendous strain when you cast, so it must be the same breaking strain as the shock leader. An excellent rule of thumb is 10lb (4.5kg) of line for every ounce (28g) of lead. Go under this guide and you risk the line snapping and causing injury – possibly death – to other anglers.

Attach the leads with a link swivel or a clip. Tied directly to a lead's eye, the line can be damaged when the lead is dragged up the beach. Check rigs regularly for damage from sand, rocks and shellfish. For the most part, hook snoods need be no lighter than 20lb (9kg) b.s., with 25lb (11kg) the most suitable. If you are using light lines for flatfish, for example, use booms. The danger of using very light hook snoods is that strong tides can twist and damage them.

The following 10 rigs offer a comprehensive combination to cover most sea angling situations for most species. By placing them in a custom-made rig wallet and labelling them accordingly, you can store them efficiently – and also keep them relatively tangle-free.

swivel trapped between micro beads and Impact Power Gum stop knots

micro beads

Power Gum stop knot

Power Gum stop knot

◄▼ *When attaching your snoods, never make knots in the trace, for this weakens the line.*
Telephone wire (below) and mono or Power Gum stop knots (left) allow you to move the snoods along the trace.

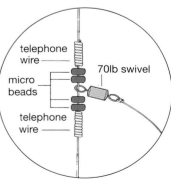

telephone wire

micro beads

70lb swivel

telephone wire

crimp

micro beads

Berkley 40lb swivel

crimp

◄ *To fix the snoods on permanently, you can use crimps (left). Be aware that crimping the line too tightly weakens it, which means that break-offs during casting can be the result.*

1. Basic paternoster This terminal rig provides the overall design and construction for several other rigs. It can be used in one, two or three-hook variations, with a single hook most suitable when you're fishing among snag-strewn ground. It's the most popular shore rig because it is streamlined for casting, and the addition of bait clips aids this even more. Clip the snoods up or down towards the lead.

Hook snoods are positioned along the trace by small swivels which are trapped by micro beads and mono or Impact Power Gum stop knots. Alternatively, you can secure the swivels and beads with wire line crimps or stops made from telephone wire. A proviso is that the hooks mustn't reach the swivel and beads above or below; or they tend to get tangled.

The bait clips hold the hooks and bait close to the main line, making the rig more streamlined. The rig's dimensions, including snood lengths, can be altered to suit the conditions. For example, anglers fishing for dogfish prefer short snoods rather than long ones simply because they reveal bites sooner. But cod anglers prefer long snoods to allow the fish to take the baited hook deeply into their mouths before they move off. Increase the length of snoods to ensure the baited hooks reach the sea bed – this is especially important when you are fishing close in from high pier walls or cliffs.

2. Running leger

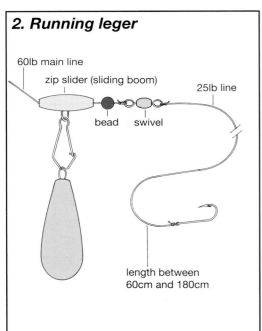

60lb main line
zip slider (sliding boom)
25lb line
bead   swivel
length between 60cm and 180cm

2. Running leger Used by generation after generation of anglers, this rig is popular among novices when using a single hook. The fact that it allows a biting fish to pull the line through the lead, negating the lead's weight, appears attractive to many anglers. But this offers little real advantage. In fact, a fixed lead is more effective because it helps to drive the hook into a feeding fish.

1. Basic paternoster

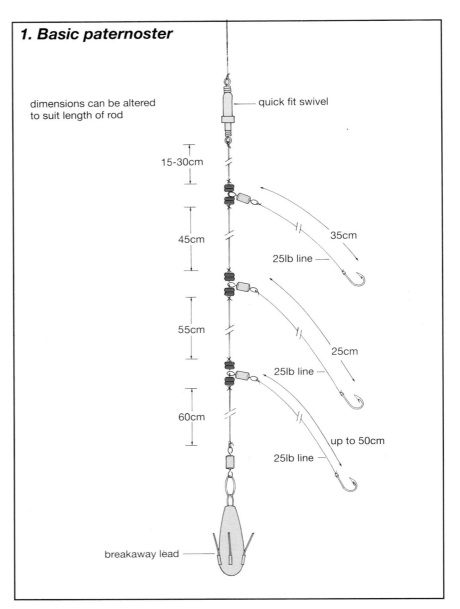

dimensions can be altered to suit length of rod

quick fit swivel

15-30cm

45cm

35cm

25lb line

55cm

25cm

25lb line

60cm

up to 50cm

25lb line

breakaway lead

▶ *A single hook paternoster with bait clip (rig shown) or a wishbone rig cuts through strong wind, getting your bait to the target area and holding it along the bottom – where most of the fish are.*

Tip **Various odds and ends**

● Impact Power Gum is available from most coarse angling tackle dealers. Freshwater anglers use it when they are feeder fishing.
● There are special soft crimps which are more suitable for monofilament line. Look for soft crimps which are slightly larger in diameter than the line you are using. Close the crimp with specially designed crimp pliers.

3. Two-up one-down rig

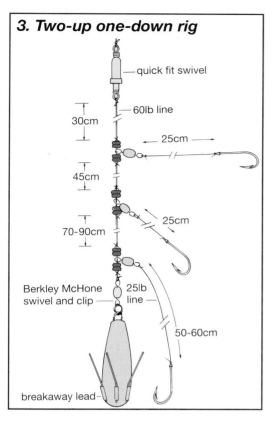

- quick fit swivel
- 60lb line
- 30cm
- 25cm
- 45cm
- 25cm
- 70-90cm
- Berkley McHone swivel and clip
- 25lb line
- 50-60cm
- breakaway lead

▲ **Mackerel and garfish come inshore in the summer and attract young and old anglers alike.**
   Tackle mackerel with a sliding float-fishing rig, and add an extra snood for garfish above the float.

3. Two-up one-down paternoster Two hooks fish above the lead, and another hook, attached to a long trace, fishes below the lead. This rig is popular with anglers fishing from piers or steep shingle beaches.

It is suitable for all bottom-feeding species, and it is ideal in very strong tides. To keep the baits hard along the bottom when the tide is very strong, use short snoods. If you're using a fixed-grip lead, a short twisted-wire boom holds the trace clear of the lead.

Tip Bait clips

If you are going to make your own bait clips from wire, remember that the tubing and wire used must fit tightly on the rig's line. Domestic lighting cable, size 1mm, is compatible with 50lb (23kg) plus breaking strain leader.

4. Swivelling wishbone rig

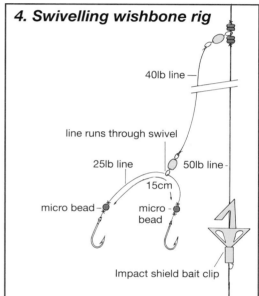

- 40lb line
- line runs through swivel
- 25lb line
- 50lb line
- 15cm
- micro bead
- micro bead
- Impact shield bait clip

4. Wishbone rig The wishbone evolved from the need to cast baits a long distance. It is a streamlined rig using a single bait clip to present either two small baits or one large one. As with most of the rigs shown, it is suitable for all bottom-feeding species – from dabs to cod.

There are two basic designs of the wishbone – the fixed-snood and the swivel versions. Both are prone to tangle if used in slack tidal conditions.

A Breakaway Impact shield bait clip, positioned slightly above the lead, is ideal for clipping down the hooks. The swivelling snood can be 60cm (2ft) long.

5. Pennell rig The name Pennell refers to the inventor and only involves the layout of the hooks on the snood. Popular among bass, conger and cod anglers, the Pennell has two hooks instead of one – this provides an efficient way of hooking fish when large baits such as a whole calamari squid or many lugworms are used. On a simple paternoster the Pennell's snood length can be up to 60cm (2ft).

You can use it either on a paternoster or

5. Pennell rig on single-hook paternoster

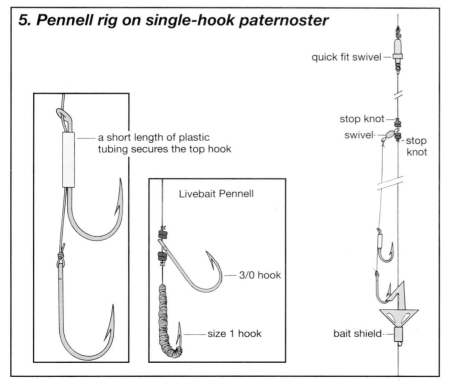

- a short length of plastic tubing secures the top hook
- Livebait Pennell
- 3/0 hook
- size 1 hook
- quick fit swivel
- stop knot
- swivel
- stop knot
- bait shield

running leger. Clipping the baits down at the bottom of the paternoster rig aids casting distance – but this is especially important if you have a large bait.

A type of Pennell rig is excellent when live-baiting for cod. Thread the hooklength through two beads, the eye of a large hook and two more beads. Attach a small hook. Put bait on the small hook, and cast out. You'll soon pick up a small pouting or poor cod which is then left for a big fish to take, the big hook being free to hook the cod.

6. Float rig The sliding-float rig is suitable for float fishing for garfish, mackerel and mullet – and in most situations. By adjusting the stop knot you can fish a variety of depths as long as you add weight to the rig a little way below the float. When fishing in shallow water for surface-swimming garfish, add a fixed hook above the float.

Tip **Clip the bait up or down?**

Casting with a hook clipped down helps to hold it on the bait clip, but if the bait moves far up the snood, away from it, then you are unlikely to hook a fish. To avoid this, place a small bead or stop knot on the snood above the hook to hold the bait firmly.

If you're casting with baits clipped up, the air pressure may force the bait to move around the hook bend; this seems more efficient, but the choice is yours.

9. The slider rig

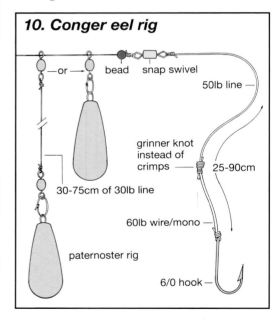

9. The slider rig As its name suggests, this rig slides down the main line to provide a hookbait on the surface or in mid water for species such as pollack, garfish or mackerel. By adding lead to the snood you can fish it on the sea bed away from the main terminal rig for all bottom-feeding species. It's ideal for fishing close-in for flounders or at long range for most other species.

Include a float or a weighted hook on a snood that slides down the main line as far as the leader knot or the rig's top clip. If using the rig in leger form, you need at least a 2oz (60g) lead to ensure that the bait reaches the sea bed. This rig isn't suitable when you're fishing in a strong tide or among weeds.

6. Basic float-fishing rig

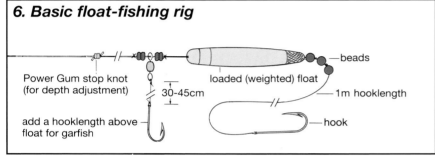

7. Plastic and wire booms

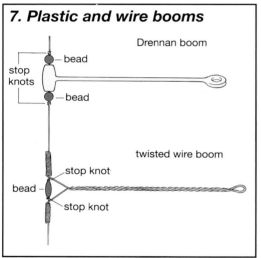

▲ *This excellent shore-caught thornback ray was taken from Co. Clare, Republic of Ireland on a two-up one-down rig.*

7. Booms The main advantages in using booms are that they distance the snood from the main line and that they enable you to use very light snoods which won't wrap around the body of the rig and break off. There are various types of booms; those made of twisted metal and plastic are the ones used most.

8. Weak-link rig (rotten bottom) This rig is good for single hook fishing over very rough ground such as heavy kelp beds or shallow rocky reefs. The lead is attached to a small open wire clip. After the rig hits the water, the lead falls off the clip. If the weight gets snagged on rocks, the light line breaks easily, freeing the rest of the rig.

10. Conger eel rig

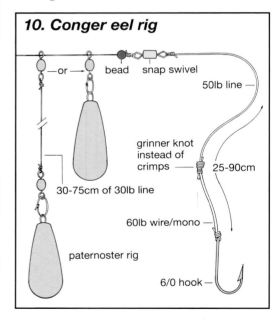

10. Conger rig For conger fishing use a large hook (6/0 minimum). A wire or heavy mono length (100lb/45kg) stops the conger's small but sharp teeth from biting through the hook snood. This is when the single hook sliding trace is suitable, although the sliding paternoster is more popular.

8. The weak-link or rotten bottom rig

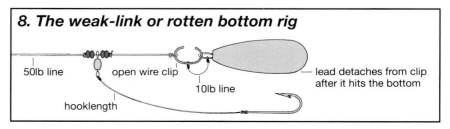

Rock fishing for bass

According to professional angling guide and tackle dealer Ed Schliffke the secret of successful bass fishing is being in the right place at the right time.

Treyarnon is typical of north Cornwall's beaches. Day is less fruitful than night but you can catch if there's a good tumble. The best state of the tide is about 2-2½ hours before low water – when the gullies become accessible.

Bass are warm water fish. The time of their inshore arrival and their departure to deeper, warmer waters varies for different parts of the country. On the north coast of Cornwall they usually arrive around the end of March and leave around October. Farther down the west coast – round Land's End, for example – they stay all year round. Although you can sometimes catch them farther north, East Anglia round to North Wales is about as far as they go in any numbers. Often the specimen-sized fish arrive separately from the other fish. In the Treyarnon area this tends to be the last two weeks in July.

So the first thing you need to do is find out when the bass are in. Ask local anglers, fishing guides and tackle dealers and keep an eye on the angling press. It might sound obvious but you won't catch bass if they aren't there!

The right ground
The type of ground is important for bass. Look for an area of rock stretching maybe 50m (55yd) or more from the high to the low water mark and finally giving way to sand. (Steep rocky headlands dropping severely into very deep water are not suitable.)

The main attraction for bass is food. If the rocks are weed-free and polished smooth there won't be much of that. What you are after is weedy, ideally mussel-covered rock, traversed by crab-infested gullies, and riddled with fissures, nooks and crannies stuffed with natural yum! If the gullies

have sandy bottoms then so much the better. The gullies are really the key elements because bass swim up and down them rather like the way we walk up and down a pavement – except they eat their dinners out of them! The angler aims to 'trap' or ambush the bass in these gullies.

Time and tide
Under the right conditions you can catch during the day, but late evening and night are without doubt best. Fishing the tide down to low water is nearly always more

▼ *To catch a fish like this, you have to go out at the right time of the year and under perfect conditions. Bass never make it into some of our northerly waters and even in the south the season varies. So you must find out when the bass are in – if at all. When it comes to bait, peelers are perhaps the greatest bass all-rounder but lug, rag and sandeel can score.*

successful than fishing up to high tide. (In most places, you can work out when low tide is by looking up the time of the high tide prior to a session and adding about six hours and ten minutes.)

For example, let's say that on a particular day low water is at midnight and that sunset's at around 9:00pm. The theory is that during the day big fish (5lb/2.3kg or more) are out in open water chasing shoals of mackerel and pilchards. Twilight offers them security to swim confidently into gullies and search for crabs, prawns, sandeels and other delicacies.

Often they come in for only an hour – just cruising around. In our example this would be around 9:30-10:30pm. The hour either side of low water can be very poor. The reason is that as the gullies empty the bass feeding area widens out once more, making the bass less likely to come across your bait.

Sometimes as the tide begins to flood back into the gullies they concentrate again. You should know straight away if they've returned. If you don't get an indication pretty soon, don't waste time – move on to another mark or knock it on the head altogether. In any case you never seem to get as many fish as on the backtide.

The right conditions

Unfortunately for the holidaymaker – who often hasn't a choice – fishing in the right conditions is essential. If the weather is wrong there's no point bothering.

Daytime bassing is best during a reasonable tumble – when there's a lively wave action. This helps to churn up the bottom, putting plenty of colour in the water and releasing food. For this reason a storm beach with a prevailing wind blowing on to the rocks is best. A bright, sunny day can be okay if there's a lively sea but an overcast day is generally better.

Night fishing isn't easy. Remember that you are casting into tight spaces and you want the bait to stay there. This is difficult enough without the added aggravation of darkness, strong currents, wind and loose weed washing about.

A still evening with very little wave movement – no more than 60cm (2ft) – is essential. (And don't forget, even on a still evening, an area of low pressure right out to sea can bring up a heavy swell, making it unsuitable for fishing.) If you do want to fish a windy night, a lee beach where the wind is blowing over the top is best. Bright moonlight is convenient.

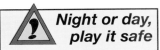
Night or day, play it safe

Some gullies in the Treyarnon area can be 3m (10ft) deep or more and falling into one, irrespective of whether it is full, can be lethal.
● When fishing at night never go alone. At least one of you must know the area intimately.
● Stay close together at all times.
● Unless the moonlight is extremely bright, wear a headlamp. But be careful – outside the beam it is completely dark which can be very disorientating for the wearer.
● If you are fishing when the tide is flooding, beware of getting cut off. Some of the gullies may be 30m (33yd) or more behind you, but they fill eventually!

A typical bass beach – what to look for

Rocky headlands on each side of a surf beach are common features (right). It is around these low-lying rocks that you find bass. Look for fingers of rock jutting out from the main body. Bass must pass these to enter and leave their feeding ground and they make ideal ambush points (1). Gullies into which bass swim in search of food are ideal because you can 'trap' them on the backtide.

Sheltered (lee) beaches are best at night while rougher (storm) beaches are best in the day (2).

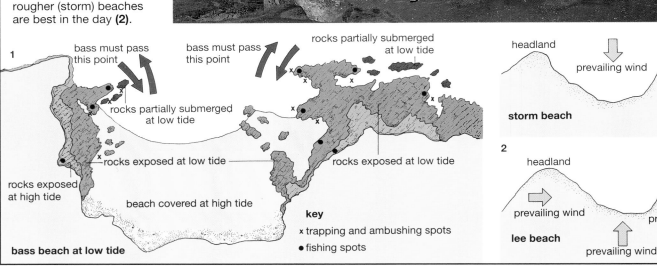

A simple rig and bait for bass

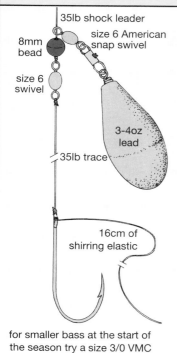

35lb shock leader
size 6 American snap swivel
8mm bead
size 6 swivel
3-4oz lead
35lb trace
16cm of shirring elastic

for smaller bass at the start of the season try a size 3/0 VMC forged hook but be prepared to go up to a 6/0 for big fish

An oval lead is better for rock fishing than a breakaway. When fishing on to sand in rough water you could try a pyramid. Use a heavy trace such as 35lb (16kg) b.s. rather than 10-15lb (4.5-6.8kg) b.s line. Being stiffer it prevents tangles and is unlikely to snap if 'roughed-up' on rocks.

Shirring elastic helps to make a compact bait (above). Ed extracts a pair of edible crabs from a hole in the rocks (right). The peeling hen (upside down) is protected by the hard cock crab. She would make an irresistible bait!

Bass tackle

You rarely need to cast beyond 100m (110yd) and, compared with mullet or mackerel, bass aren't the hardest fighters. A light 12ft (3.6m) carbon beachcaster capable of casting 2-4oz (56-113g) or a heavy spinning rod (or even a coarse carp rod) is adequate. A bit of softness in the top is essential in helping you to feel for bites and useful for fighting fish at close quarters, but the rod should not be sloppy. Some reserve power lower down is necessary for casting and helpful if you snag up.

The right technique

You've put together a balanced rig and chosen a likely looking area. The next considerations are: bait, precisely where to cast and what type of bites to expect.

Bait As an all-rounder you can't beat a fresh peeler cut in half with a pair of scissors. On the first cast use two new halves but after that, on each new cast, remove one old half and replace it with a fresh one. This conserves bait while keeping the hookbait attractive. Shirring elastic keeps it compact and holds it on the hook. Fresh ragworm and lugworm are also good – particularly at night when bass hunt by sense of smell.

Casting area The traditional rule of casting just beyond the third breaker may apply to some beaches but often it's not vital. Indeed, sometimes this might involve a cast of over 400m (440yd)! More often than not you can catch bass closer than 50m (55yd) – sometimes right under your feet.

Start by dropping your bait into a likely looking spot – between two rocks at the

mouth of a gulley perhaps – and then gradually work towards yourself with each cast, searching the gulley as you go. Especially at night, there's no substitute for having a feel for the tackle and knowing the spot you're fishing like the back of your hand. (Even on a still night you can't tell where a lead has landed by listening for the splash.) Keep a tight line to the bait all the time. If the line is blowing in a great bow around the rocks and the lead is dragging along the bottom, you're fishing in the wrong conditions. Keep the bait still and leave it where it is. Bass fishing is about patience and confidence.

If you are fishing straight out in front you may be fishing into 1.8-2.4m (6-8ft) of water, but don't be put off by much shallower water. In a gulley at night, on a back-

⊗ Missed bites

You do miss some bites. When this happens, don't wind in – leave the bait. Fish often return to it – be patient and confident!

▼ *Ed prefers a good fixed-spool reel, such as this one, to a multiplier. A special switch enables him to engage a preset drag when playing a fish, which means it only gives line when he wants it to.*

Tip *A snag in your favour*

If you are fishing in a sandy gulley and your rig becomes lodged in rock or weed, leave it. If it isn't badly snagged and there's a fish about, then the fish should hit your bait and dislodge it.

ing tide, there may be no more than 60cm (2ft) – just be prepared for the fish to surface as soon as you hit it!

A funny feeling Don't expect bass to pull the rod in – they rarely do. You have to learn to read the bites. Hold the rod all the time and use your fingers to feel the line. It's hard to explain but you have to be really 'switched on' for this type of fishing. Bites on crab can be very gentle, perhaps because the bass are wary of them – they expect a crab to fight back. Often all you feel is a gentle bump – almost as if the lead had dropped into a slight indentation in the rock or between the ripples on the sand. Often this can be a big fish.

Really it's only experience that tells you when to strike. When you feel something suspicious, try tightening up to the lead very gently – so as not to disturb it or the bait – feeling all the while for signs of life. If you do feel a knock, rattle or bump worthy of striking, wind down to the fish as you strike to take up any slack or stretch in the line, and to keep the fish out of the rocks.

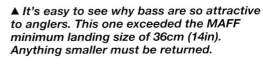

▲ *It's easy to see why bass are so attractive to anglers. This one exceeded the MAFF minimum landing size of 36cm (14in). Anything smaller must be returned.*

▼ ◄ *According to Ed you have to be totally 'switched on' while bass fishing. You must hold the rod (below) and feel for bites with your fingers (left) rather than watch the rod top. Often a bite is no more than a very gentle thud. Ed likens it to the feel of the lead drooping into a slight indentation in the rocks.*

Techniques for thick-lipped mullet

The fight of the thick-lip is acclaimed by many as the best of any fish of its size – but first you must tempt it to take your bait! National Mullet Club secretary David Rigden tells how.

Mullet society

The National Mullet Club has its own magazine, holds meetings and runs outings. For full details, send an s.a.e. to the secretary, David Rigden at 69 Powerscourt Road, North End, Portsmouth PO2 7JG.

▼ *Floatfishing is usually the best way of catching thick-lipped mullet like this beauty which fell to bodied waggler tactics.*

Thick-lipped grey mullet are among the commonest fish in British coastal waters. From spring to autumn you can find them almost anywhere – from rock marks and shallow bays to estuaries and tidal rivers.

While mullet have largely shed their 'uncatchable' label in recent years, they can be frustratingly hard to hook, and as frustratingly easy to lose once hooked! The main problem with hooking them stems from their natural feeding habits. They scrape algae off stonework, filter micro-organisms from mud, and swim open-mouthed along the top of the water, sampling the surface scum. In other words, their natural diet consists of nothing you can put on a hook!

Groundbaiting ploys

Fortunately, thick-lips can usually be weaned away from their natural diet fairly easily by groundbaiting. The most commonly used groundbait is mashed bread, stiffened with dry breadcrumbs where necessary. You can also add minced fish or meat.

Occasional handfuls might be ignored, but few mullet can resist sampling the free offerings when subjected to constant exposure. Possibilities include: treading the groundbait into the estuary mud at low tide; lodging it in rock crevices at rock marks at low tide; suspending it in an onion sack from a harbour wall to be released gradually by wave and tide action; and simply throwing it into the water regularly by hand, spoon or catapult.

Alternatively, fish a mark that is already groundbaited for you. Food dumping from harbourside restaurants, fish waste dumping from trawlers, and pipes discharging raw sewage all attract mullet.

Mullet morsels

Probably 70% of thick-lips are caught on bread, usually fished as simple flake, but

Paternoster rig

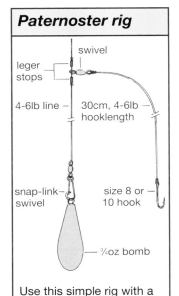

swivel

leger stops

4-6lb line

30cm, 4-6lb hooklength

snap-link swivel

size 8 or 10 hook

¾oz bomb

Use this simple rig with a quivertip when the mullet are feeding too close to a harbour wall or rocky outcrop for you to present a hookbait to them properly with a float.

sometimes as paste or crust.

Small cubes of fish or meat are a good choice if you use these in your groundbait. Earthworms, maggots and harbour ragworms are very effective baits in some places, near useless in others.

Line and hooks

Mullet invariably reject baits presented on the big hooks and strong lines normally associated with sea fishing. You need to use hooks as small as sizes 8 and 10 on line as light as 4-6lb (1.8-2.7kg).

In clear water it pays to use colourless line as mullet often shy away from baits presented on coloured line.

The right reel

A medium sized freshwater fixed-spool reel is first choice. Get the best you can afford, as salt water quickly wrecks cheap ones. And make sure it has a smooth drag, since a big

Feeder rig for thick-lips

6-8lb line   bead   swivel   10-100cm, 4-6lb hooklength

snap-link swivel

cage feeder

size 8 or 10 hook

In strong flows, where groundbait may be washed away quite quickly, use a cage feeder to ensure your hookbait fishes close to at least some of your groundbait. In weaker flows you can use a small bomb instead of a feeder. Whichever, it pays to experiment with the length of the tail according to how the fish are feeding.

mullet takes a lot of line at considerable speed on its first few runs — sometimes faster than you can backwind.

Mullet on the float

Mostly you catch mullet on float tackle, for which you need a rod at least 12ft (3.6m) long – to cast light rigs easily, to hold the line away from marginal rocks and weed, to keep hooked fish away from the same, and to pick line up quickly on the strike. Avoid tippy match rods (which can pull out hooks from light holds) in favour of more through-action, Avon-type rods.

Bodied waggler floats in the larger sizes (from 2½SSG up) are a good choice in most

▼ *Mulleting in the calm, sheltered waters of a south coast harbour in summer.*

Float rigs for thick-lips

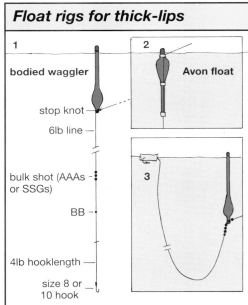

1   bodied waggler

stop knot

6lb line

bulk shot (AAAs or SSGs)

BB

4lb hooklength

size 8 or 10 hook

2   Avon float

3

1. Bodied wagglers ride a swell well yet remain sensitive because of their fine stems.
2. Use Avons in fast or turbulent water. With both types of float, experiment with the distance of the dropper shot from the hook.
3. Rig for floating breadcrust.

circumstances. They ride a swell well yet remain reasonably sensitive because of their fine stems. Fished as sliders, the bulk shot keeps the bait down and you can fish at any depth (float rig diagram 1). In fast or turbulent water, Avon floats are better (float rig diagram 2) – in such swims, wagglers sink when you try to mend the line between rod and float.

Fancy shotting patterns are rarely necessary, but it's worth experimenting with the distance between the dropper (bottom) shot and the hook. On some days the fish want a bait falling slowly through the water and a long tail is needed. At other times, the fish are browsing on the bottom and a short tail results in spectacular lift bites.

There are no hard and fast rules about how deep you should fish. If the water is clear and you can see fish near the surface, it's obviously best to fish shallow. If the water is murky, you just have to experiment. In general, you catch most regularly on or near the bottom – where most of your groundbait ends up. Fish overdepth where the bottom is clean, and slightly underdepth where it is snaggy.

In shallow swims, thick-lips sometimes rise to the surface to take any bits of your groundbait that float. You can also encourage them to rise by scattering pieces of breadcrust. Put all the shot at the base of the float (float rig diagram 3), bait up with breadcrust, cast out and wait for a bite.

Legering for mullet

In some swims the flow is too fast, or the fish too far out, for effective floatfishing. Such swims are best tackled with leger gear, the

Tip Tackle checks

● When bites are very finicky it is tempting to keep stepping down in line strength and hook size. But mullet fight so hard that lines below 3lb (1.4kg) and hooks smaller than size 12 stand little chance of landing them. Try a completely different bait presentation instead.
● Check your hooklength frequently for damage caused by crabs and general abrasion, and replace it if need be.

▶ *Don't forget to take a landing net or drop-net, as appropriate, when you go mullet fishing. These fish don't have the soft mouths that legend would have you believe, but you can't lift them out on only 4lb (1.8kg) line and a size 10 hook!*

most popular rig being a simple running leger.

In strong flows, where groundbait may be washed away quite quickly, this is best made up with a swimfeeder (the cage type holds bottom well) to ensure your hookbait fishes close to your groundbait (see feeder rig diagram). In weaker flows you can be confident of fishing over your groundbait using a small bomb.

It pays to experiment with the length of the tail. Some anglers favour a short tail a

▼ *Outfall pipes such as this are highly attractive to thick-lipped mullet and make handy places to fish from.*
Whether you're fishing from an outfall pipe or from a rocky outcrop, watch out for treacherously slippery patches of seaweed, and be careful not to let yourself be cut off from dry land by a fast-flooding tide.

few centimetres long, so that the fish hook themselves against the weight of the feeder or bomb the moment they pick up the bait. Others like a long tail of around 1m (3ft) so that the fish can get the bait well into their mouths before feeling any resistance. Compromising by using a tail of about 45cm (18in) is rarely successful.

When legering you often get a lot of line bites as the fish mill around the swim. There is no foolproof way to tell these from genuine bites, so strike any indication that lasts longer than a second.

The most commonly used bite indicator for legering is the quivertip, and there are many excellent 10-11ft (3-3.3m) quivertip rods on the market. These are much better than screwing a quivertip into the end of your float rod, which is too long for effective leger fishing and not up to casting heavy feeders. Some quivertip rods come with interchangeable tips to allow for different strengths of flow, which is handy if you fish a variety of venues.

A quivertip rod can also be put to good use when fishing down the side of harbour walls and rock faces. A paternoster can be lowered into the water and suspended at any depth (see paternoster rig diagram).

(see paternoster rig diagram)

Tip Line advice

When you're floatfishing, a floating line aids clean striking. Spray the line on the reel with floatant or smear a bit of line grease on the butt ring.

When it is very windy, however, a floating line drags your float and bait around unnaturally, so a sinking line is better. To make line sink, wind it in through a cloth soaked in washing-up liquid.

▶ *Groundbaiting is often necessary to wean mullet on to your bait. At rock marks, try filling rock crevices with groundbait or samples of hookbait at low tide.*

▼ *Mullet are slow-growing and increasingly threatened by commercial fishing. The National Mullet Club urges all anglers to put them back to maintain the species.*

Rough ground fishing

One of the greatest challenges to the shore angler, rough ground is often the most productive area for a wealth of fish species. Ken Robinson tells you how to tackle our rocky coasts.

▼ *Ken sets up to cast from the rocks on to the fairly clean sea bed of Balcarry, hoping for a monster cod. You must find a secure foothold and be confident of your balance before you cast or you may fall.*

What is rough ground? A rocky shoreline may be only a precarious access point to a fairly clean sea bed. While this is often very productive, it is the really hard ground of reefs, skeers and copious weed that provides the ultimate fishing experience. By its very nature such ground is both a haven and a larder for marauding fish.

With so many places to hang your lead, such ground is daunting to even the most experienced angler, but there are ways to succeed in this tortuous environment. Understanding what lies beneath the surface is the key to consistently good results.

Where to fish

Most species forage around the edges of deeper water. On some rough ground marks this is very close in – you can catch many species almost at your feet.

Generally, fish hunt in the weed on the flood tide but as the tide recedes they move into holes to await the next flood. Fish gather in numbers at these places and you can score heavily if you find one. Once you know the layout of the ground, work out how to get within casting range of various features at the right stage of the tide, (and how to get back again!) and you're made.

Underwater features also provide shelter from rough seas. The fish lie up, feeding on the foodstuffs washed in by the waves. Fish do feed in fairly heavy white water, but they tend to prefer to hang around the edges.

Low water on a big spring tide is the best time to look over areas that uncover with the tide. That's when most is visible. But you can also get clues about the underwater contours from areas that are never uncovered. As the waves pass over ridges and weedbeds they produce broken water, while deep holes show up as dark patches.

Best baits

Bait is a key factor in luring quality fish, so never skimp – always use a big, juicy, well-scented offering.

For cod and bass you can't beat peeler crab, which puts out a superb scent trail. Oily fish baits work well – conger can't resist a big slab or flapper of mackerel lobbed into the right place. Lesser spotted dogfish love sandeel, while their big brothers, bull huss, readily gorge on whole squid.

Retrieving the situation

You need substantial tackle and rigs if you are going to persuade cod and conger from the forests of kelp they prefer, but you can often use lighter gear for bass or wrasse.

TACKLE TO TAKE ON ROUGH GROUND

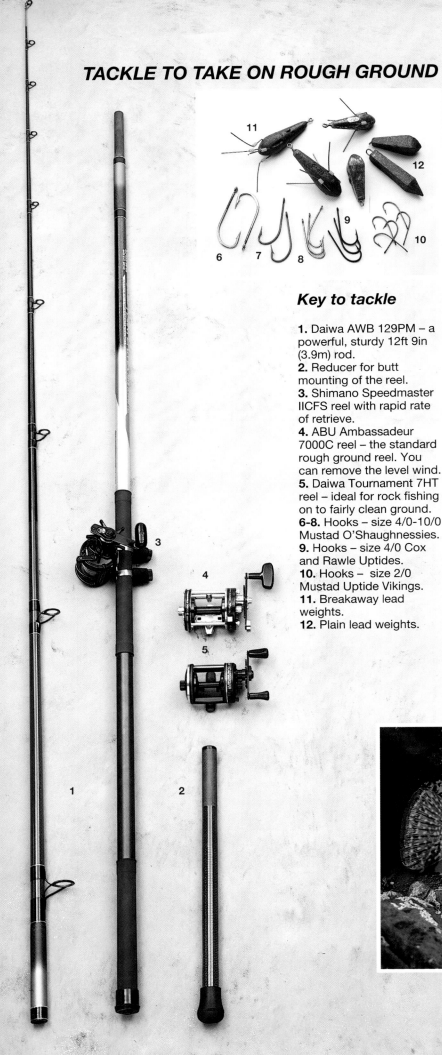

Key to tackle

1. Daiwa AWB 129PM – a powerful, sturdy 12ft 9in (3.9m) rod.
2. Reducer for butt mounting of the reel.
3. Shimano Speedmaster IICFS reel with rapid rate of retrieve.
4. ABU Ambassadeur 7000C reel – the standard rough ground reel. You can remove the level wind.
5. Daiwa Tournament 7HT reel – ideal for rock fishing on to fairly clean ground.
6-8. Hooks – size 4/0-10/0 Mustad O'Shaughnessies.
9. Hooks – size 4/0 Cox and Rawle Uptides.
10. Hooks – size 2/0 Mustad Uptide Vikings.
11. Breakaway lead weights.
12. Plain lead weights.

Occasionally you have to fish over visible surface weed. Using 35-40lb (15.8-18kg) main line straight through to the reel generally allows tackle and fish to be dragged through kelp, and often lets you pull tackle out of snags.

Inevitably at some point you will get hung up with a fish. When this happens, use sufficient pressure to free it without snapping the line. If you're really stuck, try giving the fish plenty of slack line. Frequently the fish swims around until it frees itself and your tackle.

As a last resort, slowly apply pressure to the line by pointing the rod at the snag and walking away from it. Some anglers prefer to wind the line around a piece of wood to take the pressure off the reel, or to bring the line in by hand – you may have to do this in any case if there's no room to walk away with the rod.

Eventually something eases or the line snaps. Keep your face turned away in case the snapped line whips towards you. Don't just yank away with your beachcaster – sharp jerks are much more likely to lose you the fish and all your gear.

Where the bottom is particularly snaggy you can use a weak link to the lead to help you recover your gear (and maybe the fish!) when your lead snags up in rock or weeds. Never use weaker nylon for hook traces or you risk losing your catch.

Great expectations

Although many fish frequent rough ground, several are found only in certain parts of the coast. For example, conger are predominantly found on the south and western coasts of Britain. Find out which species are likely to turn up in your area.

Conger are probably the supreme challenge, reaching gargantuan proportions. Fish weighing more than 60lb (27kg) have been coaxed from the roughest terrain. Conger forage right up to the shoreline and

▲ *Wrasse are very obliging summer inhabitants of rough ground. They feed in calm conditions and take most baits – especially hardback crabs.*

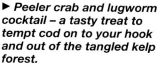

◄ *Bull huss go for whole squid in a big way, as do bass and cod, but make sure the flesh is whitish – that means it's fresh.*

► *Peeler crab and lugworm cocktail – a tasty treat to tempt cod on to your hook and out of the tangled kelp forest.*

Five rough ground rigs

Conger rig

barrel swivel
stop bead
snap link

75cm

Viking hook, sizes 1/0- 4/0

2-4oz lead

20-30lb

Running leger for bass

heavy duty swivel

35lb main line through to reel

stop bead

6/0-10/0 Mustad O'Shaugnessy hook

60-75cm, 50-100lb mono or wire trace

sliding weight on snap swivel or small toggle

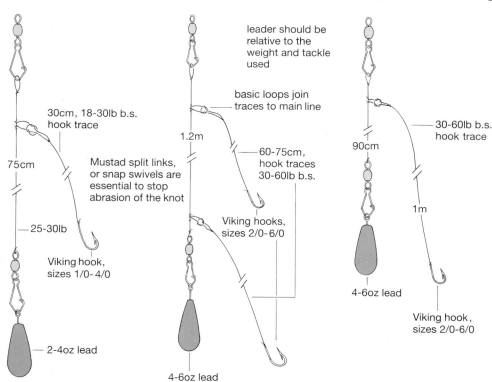

Wrasse rig

30cm, 18-30lb b.s. hook trace

75cm

Mustad split links, or snap swivels are essential to stop abrasion of the knot

25-30lb

Viking hook, sizes 1/0- 4/0

2-4oz lead

Two hook cod rig

leader should be relative to the weight and tackle used

basic loops join traces to main line

1.2m

60-75cm, hook traces 30-60lb b.s.

Viking hooks, sizes 2/0-6/0

4-6oz lead

Single hook cod rig

30-60lb b.s. hook trace

90cm

1m

4-6oz lead

Viking hook, sizes 2/0-6/0

Keep your end rigs as simple as possible. Single hook rigs are often the best configuration.

The advantage of using disposable items like spark plugs for weights is outweighed by their irregular shape which is more prone to snagging. Use a breakaway or fixed-grip lead in heavy seas or strong tides. They help stop the end tackle from rolling around and getting hung up.

Conger rig Conger forage close to shore, especially at night, so distance is not important, making this running leger ideal.

Running leger for bass This is a pleasant way to fish with short, precision casts. You can also use the cod rigs for bass.

Wrasse rig Make sure that the hook trace is high enough so that the hook fishes about 12in (30cm) above the lead.

Two hook cod rig The standard rig for most conditions features long flowing traces with one hook below the lead.

Single hook cod rig In really bad conditions and over very rough ground – or for maximum distance – use one hook for cod.

are particularly active during darkness.

Cod and bass are highly prized and during summer or in calm seas you are far more likely to find them in rocky or weedy ground than anywhere else.

Wrasse live almost exclusively in rocky areas in the south and west of Britain. Large ones set up territories in the weediest, snaggiest places.

Pollack and coalies love snaggy ground which is home to plenty of the small fish and crustaceans they feed on.

Lesser spotted dogfish and bull huss often gather in marauding packs to hunt, and starry smooth hounds join them to forage round the rocks.

Tackle choices

In a snag-ridden environment, you must have absolute confidence in your tackle. Choice of tackle is dictated by the species you're after and the severity of the ground.

Choose a good quality rod with a decent backbone. It needs to be at least 12½ft (3.8m) long to give you the leverage to haul big fish out, and to keep the line away from the weed. The Century 216 and Long E-Zee, the Daiwa Amorphous Whisker Beach and the Zipplex GSi and Bullet rods are all long, powerful and rugged.

The reel also needs to be tough with a rapid rate of retrieve to keep you out of snags. In some cases you also need to cast some way. The ABU 7000C and Shimano Speedmasters are ideal for this. Where you are fishing in less snaggy ground, a Daiwa 7HT is perfect, while for really bad areas, you can't beat the ABU 9000, particularly for the heavyweights – cod and conger.

You can scale down for smaller species such as wrasse or dogfish, but if they have

▲ A sleek 7lb (3.1kg) starry smooth hound. They often explore rough ground looking for crabs.

Tip **Keep on checkin'**

Check your hook point constantly since it can be quickly blunted by constant contact with the rocks. Similarly, scrutinize your hook traces and leader for signs of wear and change them frequently.

to be dragged through kelp or rocks it is essential that the line is strong enough.

Hooks must be very strong – if they snap or lose their points every time they come into contact with rock, change pattern. Vikings up to size 6/0 are ideal for most species, while you need size 8/0-10/0 O'Shaughnessies for conger.

With the right gear and the right approach, you can enjoy some fabulous sport from these fish-rich but hard areas.

Rotten bottom set-ups for fishing on rough ground

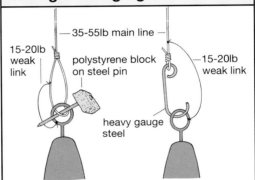

— 35-55lb main line —

15-20lb weak link

polystyrene block on steel pin

15-20lb weak link

heavy gauge steel

If the lead snags, a rotten bottom (weak link) lets you retrieve the rest of your gear (and fish!) since the weaker line snaps first. The systems above give direct contact from lead to shock leader for casting, but when the lead hits the bottom, the hook falls out, or the pin floats away, releasing the weak link.

Tip **Keep on movin'**

Once you've got a fish on the hook, keep it moving and reel in as quickly and consistently as possible at a smooth, even pace. Any slack line allows the fish to dive for cover.

▼ Rock ledges provide some areas of calm water on rough days – and the fish often lie just on the edge of these areas.

In many places you can walk to the end of the ledges at low tide and find deeper water.

Winter shore fishing for cod

Cod are one of the biggest, most widespread species you can catch from the shore in winter, says Alan Yates. So get your kit together, wrap up warm and hit those beaches!

Top cod venues

These marks fish very well but there are many more.
- **Balcarry Point,** Dumfries and Galloway.
- **Chesil Beach,** Dorset.
- **Cullernose Point,** Amble, Northumberland.
- **Dover Breakwater,** Kent.
- **Dungeness Beach,** Kent.
- **Flamborough Head,** Humberside.
- **Hinkley Point,** Somerset.
- **Marine Drive,** Scarboro'.
- **Milford Shingle,** Hants.
- **North Foreland,** Kent.
- **Orford Island,** Essex.

Cod are probably the most popular autumn and winter target for the sea fisherman. Thousands of shore anglers dedicate many hours to them. They grow very big indeed and taste delicious. What more could you ask for in a sea fish?

The British shore-caught record is 44lb 8oz (20.2kg) but any fish over 10lb (4.5kg) is considered a shore specimen. Most shore-caught cod are under 5lb (2.3kg) and are known as codling.

Shoals of cod come within range of the shore fishermen in autumn and stay until spring. The exact timing of this depends on water temperatures. In a mild winter they move in later and move offshore more quickly. In the north of Britain there are inshore cod all year round.

Where and when

Cod are not as common as they used to be due to commercial overfishing. With this in mind, the first task for a novice is finding the fish. Ask about hotspots that are fishing well at your local tackle shop, or join a sea angling club.

No matter where you start, access to deep water close to the shore is of prime importance. Piers, breakwaters, steep storm beaches and rock marks are all popular places to hunt this shovel-mouthed species.

The best times to fish for cod are at night or when the sea is rough and coloured. Cod move close in with greater confidence under cover of darkness or when the sea is stirred up, and plenty of prey animals have been dislodged. Spring tide periods bring the best out of many marks, with the peak time close to high tide.

Baits, big and small

Cod eat almost anything, but while mussels, peeler crabs and ragworm are good baits for codling, lugworm and squid are usually best for bigger specimens.

Small calamari squid fished whole are particularly attractive to big cod. All cod

▼ *Rough weather which stirs up the bottom really seems to suit cod and provides the best chance of a specimen during daylight.*

▲ *If you find a venue that offers easy access to deep water close in, you don't need to be able to cast a long way to reach big specimens like this beauty from Dover Breakwater. Wherever you are fishing, though, fresh bait is essential as cod hunt by smell. A stale bait just won't attract them.*

have big mouths, so a big bait can be the best way to fish selectively for this species and avoid others, such as whiting.

Gear and skills

A 12ft (3.65m) beachcasting rod capable of casting a 6-8oz (170-225g) wired lead over 90m (100yd) is ideal. A sturdy fixed-spool reel filled with 15lb (6.8kg) line is suitable for venues with a snag-free, sandy seabed. For rocky marks and rough ground, you need the power and ruggedness of a multiplier and 30lb (13.6kg) line.

You can cast a long way with this gear, which is important for cod fishing. If you can't cast very far, stick to venues where casting is not essential – piers and some rock marks. Remember that a headwind makes casting more difficult, as does a large bait, so choose your tactics accordingly.

Fishing night sessions in winter calls for thermal clothes – an umbrella or windbreak is very handy too. But whatever you do, don't forget a gaff or landing net. It's sheer folly to find you can't land the cod you've tried so hard to hook. Get it right and it won't be long before your first cod comes rolling in on the waves.

The Pennell rig

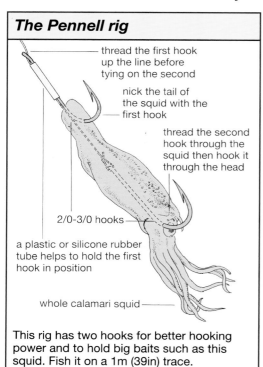

thread the first hook up the line before tying on the second

nick the tail of the squid with the first hook

thread the second hook through the squid then hook it through the head

2/0-3/0 hooks

a plastic or silicone rubber tube helps to hold the first hook in position

whole calamari squid

This rig has two hooks for better hooking power and to hold big baits such as this squid. Fish it on a 1m (39in) trace.

▼ *Cod fishing can be a social activity, and it's safest to fish from rocks in winter in company – they can be extremely slippery.*

CHAPTER TWO

BOAT
FISHING

Day trip charter boat angling

Booking a trip on a charter boat can be a real headache if you don't know where to start or what to watch out for. England International boat angler Mick Toomer offers some advice.

▲ *The journey to the fishing spot is a good time for last-minute preparations. Store your gear neatly – it makes moving about easier.*

Skippers often find single bookings more trouble than they are worth. When a group books the boat, the skipper gets the whole fee no matter how few anglers turn up.

If he takes individual bookings, each angler usually pays a flat rate of about 10% of the whole boat rate. If too few anglers book, or some of them fail to turn up, the skipper could end up out of pocket.

To an outsider trying to book a day out for himself, charter boat angling often appears to be a closed shop. The most productive tides are usually reserved for regular parties, and many skippers are reluctant to take individual bookings.

The reasons for this are straightforward. Any sensible businessman looks after regular customers first – a party which books twenty days a year expects to get some of the best tides. A new customer who might not come back for more usually has to make do with the less productive tides.

As an individual you have even less chance of getting one of the best tides.

▶ *Some of the best fish, like this conger, are found a long way offshore, which means booking a fast boat to get you there quickly.*

▲ *Charter boats are often quite crowded, and even when there aren't too many anglers, it can be hard enough to move around without having to step over boxes of bait and bags of gear. Keep everything as neat and tidy as you can and watch out for crossed lines, especially when you are playing a fish.*

Some answers

One solution to this problem is to leave your phone number with a reputable skipper. Tell him that you are interested in making up the numbers if one of his regular parties needs an extra angler.

Weekend boat places are usually in greater demand than weekday ones. If you can get a midweek day off at short notice you're more likely to get to sea. This can be a shortcut to some top boat fishing.

Many ports offer different opportunities, so choose a venue which provides the sort of fishing you fancy. If you want to use your own tackle, you may find your options are limited.

Most types of boat angling call for specialized equipment. Make sure you know what gear you're going to need for whatever type of fishing you plan to do.

A trip out from the Hampshire coast often requires a wire line kit to cope with

◀ *Inshore boat fishing doesn't always mean smaller fish than those from farther offshore – as this angler is finding out. But with less tide and depth you can often use lighter tackle.*

Tip Real value

Tackle shops at your chosen venue can often recommend a skipper. Make sure that this recommendation is based on the skipper's skill and the quality of his boat and not because he pays the tackle shop a percentage.

Always make sure that you know the skipper's name, the name of the boat and exactly where you are going to meet.

the deep water and strong tides, while fishing off the Essex coast usually means much shallower water and boatcasting equipment. Both of these methods are used at anchor, whereas a trip from Whitby might mean fishing pirks and muppets on the drift.

You may find it useful to join a sea angling club (details from your local tackle shop). Many of them book a series of dates every year for members. Even inland cities and towns have such clubs, some of which exist solely to arrange a few days boat fishing every year. This does save you effort, though it can mean less choice.

The grapevine
Having decided on a venue, the next step is to find a good skipper. The advertisements in the angling press can be a good place to start, though many of the best skippers rarely need to advertise. Word of mouth or reports of big catches in the press are often better pointers.

Under normal circumstances, the best skippers are booked up well in advance, and you are unlikely to get a place on a successful boat at short notice. To get afloat on a specific day you might well have to phone up a number of skippers before you find one with a space available.

At all costs avoid the cowboys who go afloat without licences and insurance. They may be cheaper and easier to get out with than a professional skipper, but there are other considerations. Nobody would get into an unlicenced, uninsured taxi, which had no MOT certificate, and a driver who hadn't passed the test. Treat charter boat skippers in exactly the same way.

If you are unfamiliar with the skipper, it's always worth asking if he has a

Department of Transport (DOT) licence and passenger insurance before making a booking. A good skipper won't be offended – he'll probably be pleased that you are concerned. After all, it's his livelihood, and every angler taken out by an unlicenced boat is one more customer lost to the licenced skippers.

The skipper also knows which species of fish you can expect and what tackle is required. If you need it, remember to ask whether tackle is available and if bait is provided. Sometimes bait is included, but at other times you'll need to pay extra.

Make sure of a good day
You know what fish you're after, where you're going to fish and with whom. Now you need to know whether you'll be charged a flat individual rate, or a share of the whole boat booking price (which depends on the

✖ A wee dram?

Alcohol and boats don't mix – either before or during the trip – you're more likely to blunder about, making yourself unpopular. If the skipper recommends you "bring along a few beers or a dram to keep you warm," look for another skipper.

▼ *On a trip a long way offshore, a life raft like this is a reassuring sight. A skipper with a DOT licence is obliged to carry relevant safety equipment, but you can always ask to see it.*

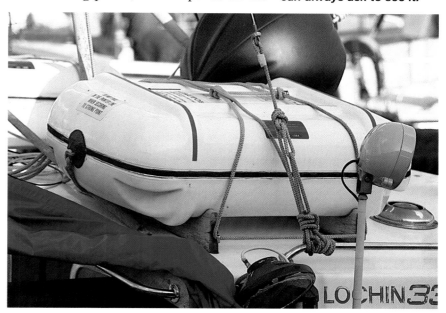

LOCHIN 33

◄ *The cabin of a modern charter boat can be a very high-tech place. Some skippers don't like anglers to use the cabin or other facilities uninvited. It's always better to ask first.*

Be punctual

Try to arrive at least 15 minutes early, but don't board the boat before the skipper invites you to do so. Arriving late annoys both the skipper and the other anglers – they may well leave without you!

The hire tackle on charter boats is rarely top quality – it's mostly to keep holidaymakers happy. It's far better to take your own if you can.

number of people aboard). Once you've agreed the terms of the booking, you should send a brief letter outlining your requirements and the agreed costs.

As an act of good faith you should also send the skipper a deposit of up to half his fee. With a new customer some skippers insist on a deposit before accepting a booking. This deposit is returnable if bad weather forces a cancellation but you are still expected to pay for any perishable bait the skipper has ordered for you.

It's worth remembering that the weather can often be bad enough to make the trip uncomfortable without forcing a cancellation. Be ready for this by bringing suitable clothing. A one-piece waterproof suit made specifically for anglers offers the best all-weather protection. It's better to bring too many clothes than to be cold and wet all day.

Sea sickness – the scourge of the inexperienced boat angler – can turn an enjoyable day into a nightmare. Anti sea sickness tablets work for many anglers but there are other ways to minimize your chances of illness. An excess of alcohol the night before, combined with lack of sleep and little food, is guaranteed to have you doubled-up over the rails all day.

If your chosen venue is a long way from home, think about travelling down the previous evening and staying overnight. This allows you to get plenty of sleep and enjoy a leisurely breakfast before going afloat.

Resist the temptation to have a drink at the bar the night before and make sure you have the right clothing, otherwise you may face a cold and nasty ten hours.

Above all remember that boat angling is meant to be enjoyable. Don't spend lots of money booking a top skipper if you get sea sick on a pedalo. All of these rules are common sense and if you use yours, you are well on your way to some good fishing.

▲ *Once you've found the fish the action can be non-stop. At the end of the day, you might wish you'd brought a spare pair of arms with you.*

▼ *You can catch all sorts of fish from a boat, though you have to feel sorry for the bloke on the left who's posing with the bait.*

Rough ground boat fishing

Rough ground will test you and your tackle to the limit – but if it's sport you're after, take Trevor Housby's advice and your aching arms may never forgive you!

▲ *Rough ground fishing gives you the chance to get to grips with a wide variety of fish and some hefty specimens – as this angler is finding out. The most important thing to remember is to stop a diving fish before it reaches sanctuary.*

Fishing from a boat over rough (rocky) ground offers superb opportunities for catching a wide variety of fish. Conger, tope, bull huss, spurdog, ling, pollack, coalfish, whiting, cod, haddock and sea bream all inhabit rocky areas.

These fish tend to gather in the particularly rich feeding areas associated with steep rock ledges and pinnacles. Fish such as conger and huss usually lurk in holes and crevices while other species are more common in the slacker water downtide of a rock formation.

Tough tackle talk

To succeed at this style of angling, you've got to fish into the really rugged areas of rock. Tackle losses are inevitably high, but that has to be expected and accepted.

For all but the smallest species you need fairly heavy gear. You can't afford to hang around when you hook a big fish over rock – you've got to hold it hard and hustle it into open water as fast as you can.

For most fish a 30lb (13.6kg) class boat rod is ideal but where there are conger of

▲ *A sleek pollack in the peak of condition like this one gives a great account of itself on 20lb (9.1kg) class gear.*

Tip **Holy buckets!**

Take plenty of spare leads and made-up traces for a rough ground trip. Store weights in the bottom of a metal-handled pail and drill holes just below the lip (see below) to hang spare traces.

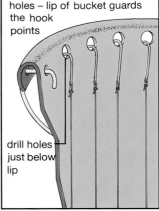

hang traces from holes – lip of bucket guards the hook points

drill holes just below lip

Rotten bottom rig

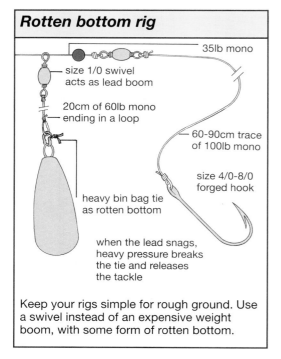

35lb mono

size 1/0 swivel
acts as lead boom

20cm of 60lb mono
ending in a loop

60-90cm trace
of 100lb mono

size 4/0-8/0
forged hook

heavy bin bag tie
as rotten bottom

when the lead snags,
heavy pressure breaks
the tie and releases
the tackle

Keep your rigs simple for rough ground. Use
a swivel instead of an expensive weight
boom, with some form of rotten bottom.

Fishing rocky pinnacles

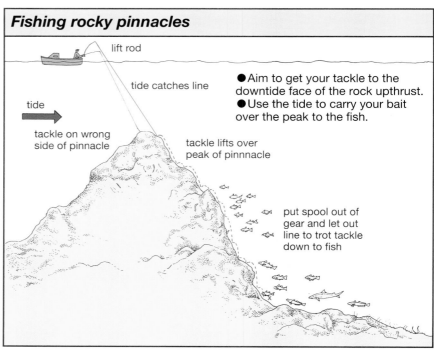

lift rod

tide catches line

tide

tackle on wrong
side of pinnacle

tackle lifts over
peak of pinnnacle

● Aim to get your tackle to the
downtide face of the rock upthrust.
● Use the tide to carry your bait
over the peak to the fish.

put spool out of
gear and let out
line to trot tackle
down to fish

▲ **Tope are one of the
hardest fighting species
commonly taken over
rough ground. They grow
big too – well over 50lb
(22.7kg)!**

around 40-50lb (18.1-22.7kg), a 50lb (22.7kg) rod may be necessary. Buy the best, most rugged reel you can – fishing over rough ground is a great tackle tester.

For smaller fish a 12-20lb (5.4-9.1kg) class rod is fine matched with a smaller (but still rugged) reel.

Pay strict attention to the quality of all the fittings and furnishings. They are a helpful guide to the overall quality of the item of tackle.

Lines and choices

Of the different types of line you can use from a boat, nylon monofilament is usually the best choice for rough ground. Dacron is softer with less stretch and so is nicer to use, but it parts easily when stretched over rock. Heavy mono has a hard surface which resists abrasion.

Wire line is rarely necessary or desirable for this style of fishing: you don't need a full set of roller rings on your rod – a tip roller with ordinary rings lower down is fine.

Match line to rod, but use a breaking strain slightly over that of the class of the rod – 5lb (2.3kg) b.s. over is about right (35lb/15.9kg line with a 30 class rod). Stepping up the line strength like this allows you to apply a little extra pressure when a bigger fish picks up the bait.

Terminal tackle

Keep your rigs as simple as possible. There's no need to get any more complicated than a running leger with a swivel replacing the more normal weight boom.

Most of the bigger species want the baits on or just above the rocks. A rotten bottom enables you to land fish and recover your rig even if the lead snags. In areas with little tide you can use old spark plugs to reduce costs, attached with a thick rubber band. In strong flows, however, you need the greater density of a lead weight to reach bottom.

For whiting, haddock and bream a simple two-hook paternoster or baited feathers work well. They present the baits where these fish want them – slightly off the bottom.

There is a huge choice of baits but for rock fishing fresh mackerel and pouting are hard to beat. For heavyweights a flapper or head-and-guts are ideal while for the smaller species a strip works better.

Finally, if you haven't got your own gear, make sure the skipper has some for hire when you book. However, the quality of hire tackle can vary widely, so unless you know the skipper, try to take your own.

◀ **Big fat cod like this 22½ -pounder (10.2kg)
are one of the main attractions of rocky
areas during the winter months, drawing
anglers from all over the country.**

Deep-water pirking and jigging

Some skippers may look like graduates of a body-building school, but the secret of their physique and fitness is serious pirking. Mike Millman examines the technique.

Pirk fishing in deep water can put a bit of a strain on your muscles. But charter skippers are often successful with a pirk because they are usually fit and capable of pirking over long periods, taking some big fish along the way. So if you are going to do a lot of it, consider a course of exercises to tone up your arm and shoulder muscles.

Pirking is a method of fishing with a weighted lure fitted with a hook (usually a treble). It is a particularly successful technique for deep-water wreck fishing, when the quarry is big, fast, free-swimming species of fish such as pollack, coalfish, cod and ling.

The idea is to tempt these big predators to strike at a lure which looks something like baitfish. Because the competition for food around a wreck is so fierce, predators go for anything that looks like a good meal and an attractive pirk is definitely on the menu.

Bought is best

The basic pirk consists of a single piece of chromed metal fitted with a large treble hook. But there are many different kinds of pirk available – varying tremendously in shape, size and colour. Bright, shiny ones of between 16-26oz (450-740g) have a fine catch record, but others are worth a try. Be flexible and bring along a selection of different types to experiment with on the day.

You can save money by making your own pirks – all you need is a section of chrome tubing (pram handles are best if you can get hold of them). Fill the tube with scrap lead, then flatten and drill it at the ends to fit a hook and swivel by a split ring.

However, there's little doubt that the sophisticated, professionally designed pirks outclass home-made ones for catching ability. The best pirks are attractive to predators because they are shaped to flutter when they are dropped or jigged up and down in imitation of swimming fish.

Jigs are generally smaller lures and often consist of a metal head with a feather or plastic frilled body, instead of the all-metal pirk body. This weighted head gives them an attractive action. They are used in the same way as pirks – relying on the tendency of predatory fish to strike on impulse at the lure bouncing seductively in front of them.

▼ *Where there is a wreck the chances are strong that you'll find conger haunting the nooks and crannies of the hulk. The conger is an opportunist and will attack a pirk if one happens to drop into its territory. If you manage to hook one like this, you will be in for some rod-bending action and a muscle-stretching scrap.*

Fast action

The boat skipper locates the wreck site, and sets up the boat to drift over it with the tide. As it closes in on the hulk, drop your pirks fast at the skipper's signal. (It is important to have discipline and an understanding between the skipper and the anglers in order to avoid high tackle loss in the wreckage. Ideally he will spot changes in the height of the wreckage with his echo sounder, and be able to co-ordinate the lifting and dropping of pirks accordingly.)

When dropping down, put your multiplier into free spool gear, controlling the fast revolving drum with your thumb. Both pollack and coalfish, hunting in open water about 6m (20ft) or more above wrecks, often hit the lure while it is still falling to the wreck, taking the pirk with great savagery.

Mostly the fish are hooked in the jaw but sometimes one makes a sweeping slash at the pirk and becomes foul-hooked outside the jaw area. Speed is vital in pirking and you must be ready to put the reel into gear as soon as you feel the violent snatch.

Killer gear rig

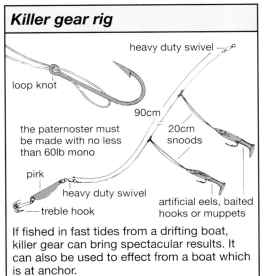

heavy duty swivel

loop knot

90cm

the paternoster must be made with no less than 60lb mono

20cm snoods

pirk

heavy duty swivel

treble hook

artificial eels, baited hooks or muppets

If fished in fast tides from a drifting boat, killer gear can bring spectacular results. It can also be used to effect from a boat which is at anchor.

A second later the rod shows a considerable curve as it takes the weight of the fish and registers the incredible power of its inevitable plunge for the bottom. If you don't set the reel clutch correctly for the weight of line used, you risk a break. It is a good idea to underset the drag slightly, ready for the initial snatch of the fish.

If the pirk is not taken before it reaches the wreck, quickly wind it up above the wreckage line, away from snagging hazards. Again, the skipper should shout out when lines need winding in. When clear of the wreck, jig the pirk up and down by lowering the rod tip to the water then sweeping it upwards in a low arc – continue this action until a fish makes contact or the skipper orders you to retrieve lines. Don't sweep the rod too high or you will have nothing left to strike with. (However, in this type of boat fishing the power dive of the fish after it takes the pirk is usually enough to drive the hook home.)

▲ *Plastic squid or muppet lures are often used on killer gear.*

▼ *Take a selection of pirks and adapt to the conditions on the day. You may need to add more weight to the lure or try pirks with different actions in the water – a particular colour of lure might be effective or a special flavour.*

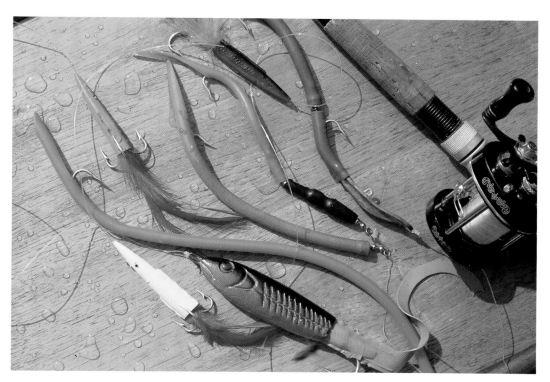

Tip *Reel fast*

You will often get a strike if you let the pirk flutter to the bottom and retrieve it at high speed. To keep up this rapid winding action all day without getting arm ache, use a multiplier reel with a fast rate of line recovery.

◄ *Choose your weapon – an arsenal of brightly coloured artificial eels. When jigged above a wreck site they perform a mesmerizing dance, irresistible to fish.*

▼ *This gaping pollack, taken on an artificial eel, shows how deadly killer gear can be.*
If the fish aren't tempted by the baited pirk, they may well take the lures.

Killer gear

A fairly recent development in pirk fishing is the use of 'killer gear'. This consists of a 3ft (1m) long paternoster trace of nylon monofilament of at least 60lb (25kg) b.s. Two 8in (20cm) snoods formed by a blood-loop dropper knot carry artificial eels with

Finding the fish

Predatory fish tend to occupy different niches in and around a wreck. This pattern of distribution can help you plan your strategy, but there are no hard and fast rules – fish are taken at all levels.

Coalfish	Tend to feed at top levels of wreckage and above, particularly late in day. First to hit pirks on drop – 24-26oz pirk on drift.
Pollack Cod	Usually found just above main body of wreck, but rise higher at last light – pirks baited with squid and plastic streamers.
Ling Cod	Right in and around the wreckage, usually well distributed over the area – use big, baited 24-26oz pirks on drift.
Conger	Close to wreckage in lowest regions. Sometimes big eels move out to hunt over clean ground around hulk – pirk with large bait of mackerel or squid. Late in the day and during the night is the most likely time. A muppet on a wire rig can work well. Always fish on the drift.

6/0-8/0 hooks. A pirk, usually baited with a strip of squid or mackerel, acts as the weight. This rig is fished in exactly the same way as the single pirk, but is often far more effective. It takes fish over a wreck when more conventional tactics have no effect.

Where and when

Generally speaking, spring tides are best for catching with pirks or killer gear. The flow of water carries the boat at speed over the wreck area where the fast run of water tends to stimulate pollack and coalfish to

feed vigorously. Rod-bending action can be constant at this time. Middle range tides are better for cod and ling, which tend to stay much closer to the bottom. They are more likely to be taken on killer gear than on a single pirk, and with baited hooks instead of lures on the snoods. Generous helpings of squid or mackerel – or a cocktail of both – often pay off with these heavy-weight species.

Although smaller pollack do go for pirks, it is mostly large fish that take them at wreck sites and during winter. That's when species like coalfish, pollack and ling group together in considerable numbers. You need strong tackle for these big fish, especially when two or three large specimens hit the lures simultaneously. A couple of big coalies, for example, intent on going in different directions after taking the bait, put a terrible strain on the gear and the angler. Bringing in two or three at a time might take it out of you physically and net a big haul, but you can get better sporting fun from playing a single big fish – perhaps on lighter gear and a flying collar rig.

Occasionally a monster conger takes a pirk – usually if it is baited and happens to drop within reach. A fish of 102lb (46kg) taken on a pirk off Mevagissey, Cornwall, was the first eel to achieve 'ton up' status on rod and line, establishing a British record.

Specialists also fish with a pirk for halibut. Giants of 100lb (45kg) and more have been taken in northern waters on baited pirks, worked near the bottom in very deep water.

Pirking over rough ground gives poor results compared with pirking over a wreck where fish are more numerous. But killer gear can be successful, particularly on a reef where there is a fair depth of water. A minimum of 30m (100ft) is required and the boat must be on the drift. Cod are a favourite in this situation.

Choosing tackle

The right rod for pirk fishing is not less than 6½ft (2m) long and has a firm but good action. Above all, it must have lifting qualities. Carbon, graphite and glass/graphite combination rods in 30lb and 50lb (13.6 and 22.7kg) classes are available from all the top name manufacturers.

A high-geared multiplier is used by specialists, the most popular being a 4/0 which matches up with the 30lb (13.6kg) class rod. A 6/0 complements the 50lb (22.7kg) rod. Load up with monofilament of at least 40lb (18.2kg) test. Use lighter line for fishing reefs. A much heavier leader to the trace or pirk is a safety measure. Avoid braided line as its resistance to the tidal flow spoils the action of the pirk.

◄ *A fine cod nicely hooked in the scissors. A fish can sometimes be foul-hooked if it takes a sweeping slash at a fluttering pirk.*

Fishing the fabulous Flying Collar

Boat fishing over wrecks and reefs with one hook on a long, flowing trace is a deadly and highly sporting way of catching pollack, coalfish and other predators, writes Mike Millman.

Tip Check it!

Always check your trace for signs of wear and your hook points for sharpness each time you wind in. Line fraying and hook blunting are inevitable when fishing over wrecks and reefs.

Also always check the last 30-60cm (1-2ft) or so of your trace after catching a fish – remove it and retie the hook if there is any indication of damage.

◄ *The Flying Collar is THE rig for coalies over wrecks. No wonder this angler is so pleased with his fish – it gave him a great fight after grabbing his artificial eel.*

Pollack and coalfish are the great hunters of wrecks and reefs. They usually harry their prey some way off bottom, so to catch them it's vital to present a moving bait in as lifelike a manner as possible. The best way to do this is with a single hook on a long, flowing trace. Couple this with light tackle and the result is a thrilling take and an exhilarating battle – both fish are extremely ferocious and possess a remarkable turn of speed.

Bass and big red and black bream can also provide exciting sport from a boat over reefs and wrecks using long-trace tackle – the key component of which is the simple but devastating Flying Collar rig.

The Flying Collar

This rig evolved some 50 years ago and to this day no-one has come up with a better one for taking pollack and coalfish from a boat. It comprises one hook on a 3-5m (10-16ft) trace, above which a weight hangs from a sliding boom (see the diagram on the next page).

You can buy various types of booms in tackle shops, but many are far too short. The boom must be at least 20cm (8in) long to allow the trace to flow out in the tide. The best one on the market is also the newest. Amazingly simple but highly effective, it is a 23cm (9in) long PVC tube with a bend near the top from which the weight hangs (see photo on next page). The boom allows you to lower the long trace to the fishing zone swiftly, without tangling, and the bend is angled in such a way that the trace flows out almost horizontally with the tide.

A weight clip allows you to make quick changes of lead size (5-10oz/142-284g) to suit the strength of the tide. Always use conventional, streamlined bomb weights. flat-sided torpedoes and round grip leads offer too much resistance to the tide flow.

Sporting tackle For wrecks, go for a 20lb class boat rod no shorter than 7ft (2.1m). For reefs, a 7-7½ft (2.1-2.3m), 12lb class boat rod is best. Match the rods with appropriate size multipliers loaded with mono –

▲ *You're only using one hook for one fish at a time with a Flying Collar rig, so choose light, balanced tackle for the best sport.*

20lb (9.1kg) for wrecks, 12-20lb (5.4-9.1kg) for reefs. Trace mono should always be about 2lb (0.9kg) lighter, to make it less obvious to the fish and to ensure you don't lose any reel line if you snag up.

Choice baits Natural baits work best over reefs, where the main target is pollack. Live sandeel and the much bigger launce, squid, very fresh mackerel strip and king rag are all good. Mount them on size 2/0-4/0 long shank, black Aberdeens.

Artificial sandeels carrying size 3/0-6/0 hooks usually work better over wrecks for both pollack and coalfish. Experiment to find the best size and colour on the day.

Let it flow

A strong tide run is essential. Without it the trace cannot flow out and the bait or artificial eel is lifeless. When the tide is moving reasonably fast, a 3-3.6m (10-12ft) trace works fine, but in very strong tides you can use one up to 5m (16ft) long.

For pollack over wrecks or reefs, begin a steady retrieve as soon as the rig reaches the bottom, and continue until the bait or artificial eel is taken, or until it reaches a point about 18m (60ft) up.

To establish when you reach 18m (60ft) up, count the reel turns. Continue the procedure until you have discovered the fishes' feeding level. Once you have done this, you can retrieve the trace quickly through

The Flying Collar rig

Simplicity is essential to the design of this rig.

The best boom on the market is the type shown in the photo below – a 23cm (9in), angled length of green PVC tubing. The ends of the tube are fluted to allow it to slide freely without damaging the line.

Artificial sandeels of various sizes and colours work well for coalfish over wrecks. They come with the right size and type of hook ready fitted by the manufacturers.

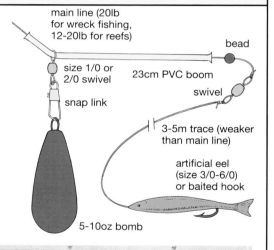

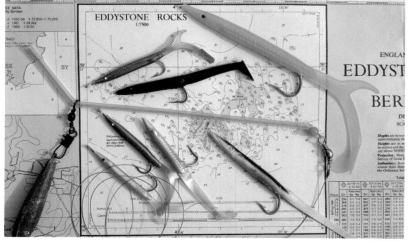

unproductive water.

For coalfish over wrecks it is usually most effective to work an artificial eel much faster and higher in the water.

The instant a pollack or coalie takes, it turns and dives. This is a testing time for your tackle. If you try to hold the fish, you will lose it immediately. You must give line through the reel drag, under pressure. Set the drag precisely to match the breaking strain of your line.

There's no need to strike – the fish's speed is quite sufficient to set the hook. After the first run is over, work the fish steadily to the surface. In deep water a large specimen will make several more strong runs, each a potential line breaker.

In a strong tide, the fish surfaces at least the length of the trace away from the boat and usually a good deal farther. When the boom reaches the rod tip, grab the line and haul the fish in hand over hand towards the waiting landing net.

Wreck tactics

The biggest pollack and coalfish are taken in the English Channel and off Southern Ireland, from wrecks a fair way from land in deep water where, except for short periods of slack about every six hours, there is usu-

▲ Mackerel strip is an excellent natural bait to use with the Flying Collar rig, especially for reef pollack in autumn, but it must be absolutely fresh – ideally caught that day.

▲ Two or three fresh, juicy king rag make a very good natural bait to use with a Flying Collar rig when you are after pollack over reefs in early summer.

Big sea bream bounty

Large black and red bream (below) can be taken over wrecks in summer and autumn with a Flying Collar. Although mainly bottom feeders, they sometimes hunt above wrecks. Use a 15cm (6in) squid or mackerel strip on a 2/0 Aberdeen. Live sandeels can also work well for these colourful fish.

ally a strong tide run. The best time for them is winter, when they gather over wrecks prior to spawning and the big females are full of roe. Smaller fish can be taken over wrecks all year round.

The boat can be at anchor or on the drift. Most long range wreck fishing is from charter boats, and the skipper decides the method of approach.

Drifting has the advantage of allowing a considerable amount of the wreckage to be covered. However, most skippers choose drifting simply because it requires nothing more from them than lining the boat up with the wreck and letting the tide take her across. Drifts are started well ahead of the wreck, and the anglers' lines aren't drawn up until the boat is well beyond the wreck.

Some skippers have the uncanny ability to judge wind and tide with amazing accuracy, and prefer to study the wreck on the fish-finder screen with great care, in the hope of discovering a concentration of pollack or coalfish (both look the same on the screen). Quite often on deep wrecks they congregate over a specific part of the hulk. If so, the skipper then skilfully anchors the boat so the anglers' rigs work exactly the right spot.

Reef pollack

Long-trace reef fishing is mainly for small to medium pollack, and usually from an anchored boat. Spring, summer and autumn are the prime seasons, with winter generally poor.

The top tempter is a live sandeel, mounted on a 2/0 Aberdeen by threading the hook point through its jaw then nicking it into the flesh just behind its head on the underside. King rag is a very good second and is especially deadly in early summer. By the start of autumn, reef pollack also usually take squid and mackerel strip well, having lost the caution they display for

these baits in spring and summer.

Reef pollack can be quite difficult to tempt in spring and at times must be literally coaxed to engulf the bait. They touch it, then drop back. It is said that a good pollack angler is born and not made and there is some truth in this. He has a feel for what's going on below and has the knack of knowing when to slow down and when to speed up the retrieve after getting that first touch.

When live sandeel is the bait, it usually pays to stop or even slow the retrieve as the bait dashes around trying to avoid its attacker. If this fails to produce an immediate strike, wind your line in – the chances are the pollack has stolen the bait or blown it lifeless up the line.

Time not so well spent

The effectiveness of the Flying Collar was demonstrated one day a couple of years ago at a wreck in the south-west English Channel. The wreck was known to hold large coalfish but on this day seven anglers on a top charter boat spent five fishless hours because they ignored the skipper's advice on how the fish could be caught.

With just one hour left the skipper and a photographer (also a very experienced angler) decided enough was enough – and picked up rods. Within five minutes two superb coalfish of 28lb (12.7kg) and 25½lb (11.6kg) were on board after taking artificial eels on 16ft (5m) traces. The others quickly changed over from short traces and bottom-fished baits and in the short time left took six fine coalies. Their main mistake had been not to fish a moving bait – big coalfish rarely go for food that is stationary.

Chasing the silver shadow

You can catch big bass (below) over reefs in spring and summer on a Flying Collar. Drifting usually works best, but not haphazardly – during the day the bass tend to stay in deep gullies. Drop your bait (usually a live sandeel, or better still a big live launce, on a size 4/0 Aberdeen) to the bottom, then work it just above the rocks.

The take is usually savage, the fight always thrilling, and the outcome always in doubt right up until the moment the fish is safely in the net.

Boat fishing for conger

Conger eels often wait inside their lairs for prey to swim nearby, but they may also prowl the ocean depths. Mike Thrussell explains the art of congering.

▲ Small conger, such as this one, are often taken off reefs and rough ground. Weak tides in summer are your best bet to connect with the snakes of the sea.

▶ The skipper marks the wreck with buoys. Get your mackerel flapper or livebait as close to the wreck as possible – even though you may lose a few traces.

Residents of holes and fissures on rocky reefs, conger eels are the legendary snakes of the sea. Immense, muscular fish of littered wrecks, they are at home hundreds of fathoms down. Wreck conger can reach incredible weights – rod-caught fish in Britain up to 110lb (50kg) with 70lb (32kg) conger common. Specimens caught by commercial trawlers are reported to have exceeded 240lb (109kg).

Despite what many anglers think, conger are not scavengers, eating whatever drifts their way. They are adept killers, well practised in the art of ambushing prey as it passes by their lairs.

War-time wrecks

The best conger fishing is over war-time wrecks in the English Channel. It's here that the 100lb (45kg) fish live, taking up residence inside holes and cracks in the wrecks' hulls. Occasionally you find conger under the debris that often lies alongside these metal monuments.

Away from the wrecks, rough ground,

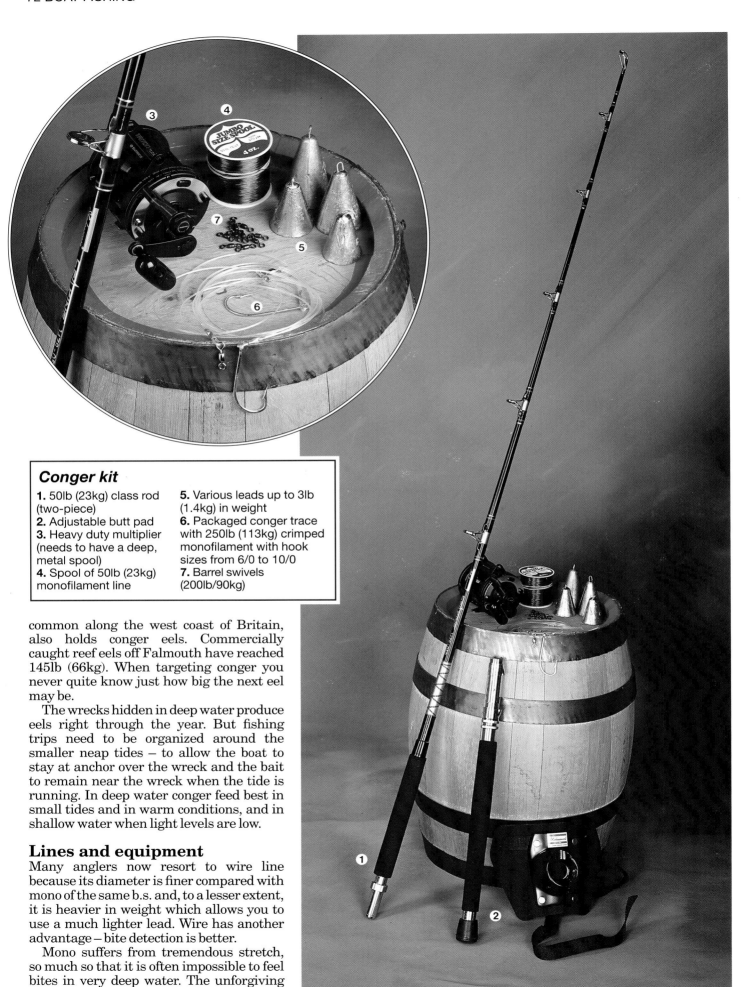

Conger kit

1. 50lb (23kg) class rod
(two-piece)
2. Adjustable butt pad
3. Heavy duty multiplier
(needs to have a deep,
metal spool)
4. Spool of 50lb (23kg)
monofilament line

5. Various leads up to 3lb
(1.4kg) in weight
6. Packaged conger trace
with 250lb (113kg) crimped
monofilament with hook
sizes from 6/0 to 10/0
7. Barrel swivels
(200lb/90kg)

common along the west coast of Britain,
also holds conger eels. Commercially
caught reef eels off Falmouth have reached
145lb (66kg). When targeting conger you
never quite know just how big the next eel
may be.

The wrecks hidden in deep water produce
eels right through the year. But fishing
trips need to be organized around the
smaller neap tides – to allow the boat to
stay at anchor over the wreck and the bait
to remain near the wreck when the tide is
running. In deep water conger feed best in
small tides and in warm conditions, and in
shallow water when light levels are low.

Lines and equipment

Many anglers now resort to wire line
because its diameter is finer compared with
mono of the same b.s. and, to a lesser extent,
it is heavier in weight which allows you to
use a much lighter lead. Wire has another
advantage – bite detection is better.

Mono suffers from tremendous stretch,
so much so that it is often impossible to feel
bites in very deep water. The unforgiving
nature of wire, though, makes the angler

Mackerel baits

With its oily flesh, mackerel is perhaps the most readily available and popular bait for conger fishing. The size of these baits indicates that large conger are the quarry.

▲ *A fine conger eel, pulled up from a wartime wreck, comes to the surface, displaying its brilliant white underside.*

constantly aware of what's happening to his bait. You need a 4.5m (15ft) length of heavy mono at the end of the wire line just to help absorb any sudden stress on the hookhold when striking and playing fish.

Class tackle To begin conger fishing on the wrecks, whether you choose wire line or monofilament, you would be well advised to select a 50lb (23kg) class outfit. If you use wire, you must use a rod equipped with roller rings.

Your tackle comes under heavy stress and needs to be strong to cope with the power of even an average-sized conger. A quality multiplier with a strong spool is essential. Also buy a butt pad to protect yourself from the end of the rod digging into you.

Rigs All conger fishing from a boat is best done with a simple running-leger rig. This means that the lead is static on the sea bed.

▲ *The skipper prepares to unhook the conger at the side of the boat with the trace wrapped around his protected hand.*

The feeding eel can pull line from the reel through the eye of the sinker without feeling undue tension.

Keep the rig set-up as simple as possible. Some anglers recommend wire traces, but commercial monofilament of 250lb (113kg) b.s. is better because it is more supple and less detectable to the feeding eel. The hook trace should be short – no more than 60cm (2ft) to minimize snagging on the wreck. Heavy mono such as this won't knot well; it needs to be crimped to the swivel and the hook.

Hooks shouldn't be too big. Sizes 6/0-8/0 are standard choices, but you may need 10/0s for the very big wreck fish. Carry a sharpening stone and keep the hookpoint ultra sharp at all times.

Bait It's important to realize how conger locate their food – by smell, vibration (through the lateral line) and partially by sight (in the final stages when the eel closes in on its prey). One of the best ways to attract conger is to use a livebait – ideally a pouting or small mackerel. Hook the fish once through its upper lip and lower it gently to the bottom. The conger will sense the

A simple rig

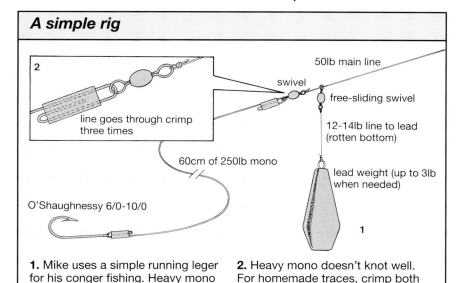

50lb main line

swivel

line goes through crimp three times

free-sliding swivel

12-14lb line to lead (rotten bottom)

60cm of 250lb mono

lead weight (up to 3lb when needed)

O'Shaughnessy 6/0-10/0

1. Mike uses a simple running leger for his conger fishing. Heavy mono is more supple than wire.

2. Heavy mono doesn't knot well. For homemade traces, crimp both the hook and swivel ends.

► *An angler watches as the captain reaches for a small, reef-caught conger. At this point the angler should reduce his clutch, in case the fish decides to make a last-minute bid for freedom.*

Tip Clutch pressure

Set the drag of your reel at 75% of the main line's breaking strain. This may seem a lot, but if you hook a large specimen, you need to use constant, firm pressure to tire and subdue it.

The amount of line surrendered to a wreck conger must be kept to an absolute minimum in order to keep the fish away from its dark, sharp-edged, rusting lair.

▼ *This is the extraordinary British boat-caught record conger; it weighed in at 110lb 11¹/₂oz (50.22kg).*

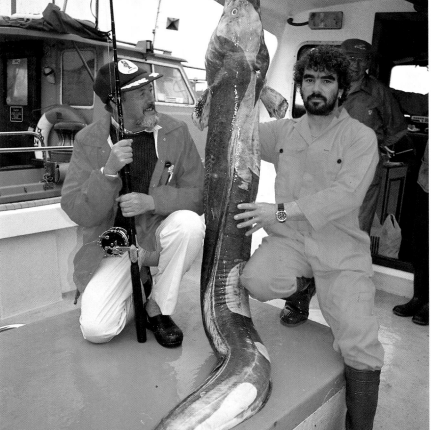

livebait's erratic movements and home in for the kill.

Alternatively, you can use deadbaits. Cut a whole mackerel or pouting through the backbone and tail to leave the flanks of the fish still attached to the head. This is called a flapper bait. It provides movement when the bait is on the sea bed, and smell too.

Hook it through the upper lip, or pass the hook through the mouth, out through the gill and then into the flank with the point left clear to penetrate the conger easily.

The take

Conger feed gently – even the colossal ones. You'll feel a series of light taps on the rod tip. Set your reel with the ratchet on and the spool disengaged.

When an eel demands those initial few metres of line, wind the reel back into gear and strike hard to set the hook. Lift the rod, pulling the fish, and as you bring the rod down, wind in line. Repeat the process, pumping the fish up.

It's important to get the conger into open water quickly, for it often makes a dramatic dive straight back to its lair. If the eel's long tail does find the wreck, your chance of successfully freeing it is very slim. Only constant pressure over several minutes may force it to release its grip. Relieving all pressure often results in the conger finding even safer sanctuary inside the wreck.

Allow the skipper to gaff the fish and haul it aboard. As the eel is brought to the side of the boat and the gaff is readied, reduce the reel's clutch so that, if things go wrong, the eel can take line freely and won't be lost if it dives.

Once aboard, the skipper secures the eel in a purpose-built fish holder or in some other escape-proof container. Small eels under 35lb (16kg) are usually unhooked and released straight away so they can prowl the ocean depths once more.

A boat of your own

John Darling gives a taste of what's involved when you decide to take charge of a small boat. Owning your own brings great fishing flexibility but demands time, effort and money.

Many an angler has succumbed to the allure of owning his own boat. All it takes is a few good fishing days on a friend's boat and you start thinking – "This is the life!"

Pretty soon the glossy brochures drop through the letter box. They're full of gleaming hulls and powerful engines, and you realise the full expense involved.

If you've still got the boat bug after this, consider the easy and cheap way of getting afloat.

First find out what type of boat handles the sea well around your stretch of coast. Then find somebody who is selling a suitable boat second hand. It's important to go for the best choice of boat for your specific purposes. So bear in mind how far offshore you want to go, what sort of sea conditions and depths you want to fish in, and what your budget is.

If you are going to use a trailer and store the boat in your drive, this will restrict the size of boat you can have. Smaller boats are ideal for estuary and close inshore angling but if you want to go further offshore you will have to consider a boat in the 20-30ft (6-9m) class. These larger vessels generally require permanent moorings.

Look for a second hand boat parked outside marinas or in people's driveways. If you see a boat with dirty sun-bleached covers, and weeds and dried leaves around a flat-tyred trailer – it's a good bet. Second hand boats command low prices so you can save thousands of pounds by making a sensible offer to the right person. Get an idea of prices by looking and asking around marinas and boatyards, and checking appropriate publications.

Make it seaworthy

The chances are you'll have to do some reconstruction work on used boats. Any sign of rot in old wooden boats could weaken the structure. Consequently wooden boats demand a lot of care and maintenance.

But with today's glass-fibre construction even the most worn out of hulls can be converted into something as good as new. By careful grinding back (using full protective mask, ear and eye protection) and adding a few layers of resin and glass, anyone with average DIY ability and some guidance can rebuild a glass-fibre boat. Materials can be bought cheaply from factories, and they're easy to use.

▼ *Most anglers enjoy the freedom of being skipper of their own boat. But don't underestimate the amount of work, planning and maintenance required to run a boat for safe and comfortable fishing.*

Basic hull shapes

Displacement hull

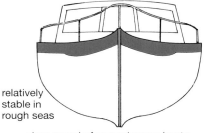

relatively
stable in
rough seas

slow speed of around seven knots

Planing hull

planes over surface of water

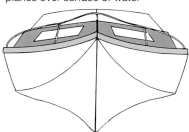

faster speeds can be reached

Ask local skippers for advice about the most suitable hull shapes for the areas you want to fish. You may find that a stable displacement hull design is favoured for sea conditions in some parts. But if speed is of the essence a planing hull is better. Semi-displacement hulls are a hybrid of the two designs which attempts to combine features of speed and stability.

▲ *A flashy speed merchant with a planing hull design rides high in the water.*
   This type of boat is ideal to get you home quickly if the weather starts to turn nasty.

▼ *Low rider – a steady displacement-hulled vessel gives a slower, more comfortable ride. This one features some shelter in front and plenty of room for angling behind.*

It's better to spend time rather than money when buying a boat. Even new ones are not always built as strongly as they should be. Don't be dazzled by a dream boat – always get a second opinion and ideally a test ride. Boats must be capable of handling rough conditions. It's sensible to work out what will be required before embarking on a small boat venture.

By rebuilding an old hull, you become completely familiar with your boat's construction. You can lay the boat out precisely according to your needs and if anything goes wrong you should be able to locate the problem easily.

Tip *Pouch protection*

A good system for secure stowing of equipment on board is to obtain some fine-meshed trawl net and make pouches inside the cabin.

Glue blocks of hardwood to prepared sections of the hull using Sikaflex. Bolt a frame to these and stretch shock-cord along the top edge to keep the pouch shut.

Ship shape

There are two basic hull types to consider when choosing your boat – the displacement and the planing. Take into consideration all the demands you are likely to make on the vessel.

Displacement hull These are often heavy, particularly the wooden ones. They are designed to push water out of the way as they travel forward. Displacement hulls usually ride gently at anchor in an unpleasant sea.

Because they can only travel at a slow speed of around seven knots, a low powered outboard or a small inboard diesel takes you fishing all day on a whiff of fuel.

Planing hull This type of hull comes in two designs. The tri-hull design, such as the blunt-ended dory, tends to slam in short seas and provides an uncomfortable ride.

The deep vee design has a longer V-shaped snout which slices through the

waves, and a flat section behind to lift the hull on to the plane. Sometimes this section has ledges or keels running along it to provide a better grip between hull and sea. Some boats combine both designs.

Planing hulls are fast and require high revving inboard motors or powerful, thirsty outboards. The rewards on the water can be spectacular, but boats in this league also require expensive navigational computers and powerful fishfinders to make them effective.

Whatever boat you use it must be safe,

▲ *Self skippering gives you independence. With a small boat and a trailer it's easy to move between fishing spots and reap rewards such as this fine flush of rays.*

▼ *At sea you rely heavily on your engine, so give it a regular maintenance. Grease as necessary, check for loose bolts, and clean or replace spark plugs.*

▲ *This is what it's all about – getting out to sea when you feel like it. Don't rush when choosing a boat, it's better to make sure you buy something that suits your purposes and pocket.*

with non-slip flooring and high sides to prevent anybody falling overboard.

Engine choosing

Inboard engines take up quite a lot of space on the sort of boats that most people take offshore – namely 15-20 footers (4.5-6m).

Modern outboards are lighter, don't get in the way and provide more power. It is relatively easy to match the propeller and the degree of engine tilt according to the weight of the boat. As a guide to horsepower, the maximum is 5hp per foot of boat.

It's important to have complete familiarity with your engine – you may depend on it in dangerous conditions.

Some outboards are available with separate oil tanks and injection systems rather than using old-fashioned premixed fuel. Some of these engines have been known to seize up when the oil system has failed. Most old hands stick to the tried and tested methods and are suspicious of devices that might fail in the middle of a tide race, at the precise moment when it's time to clear off to safety.

Buoyancy tanks are essential in fast boats because the risk of hitting something hard is greater. Position them in special sealed locations around the boat, or sandwich them in the hull.

Store all loose equipment securely so that it doesn't get thrown into a jumbled pile when the boat starts bouncing over the waves.

Safety is of prime importance at sea – a wrong move can cost lives. However, as you gain experience, it gets easier to read the sea's moods, and to find the fish. That's when you start to experience the real pleasure of having your own boat. It's just that you must realise beforehand that it is going to involve a lot of hard work.

Tip Double up – for safety's sake

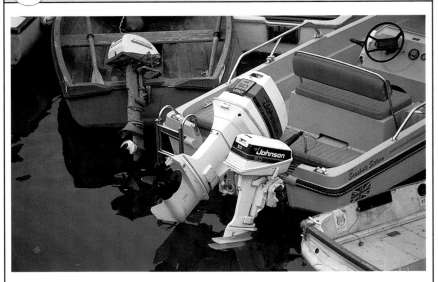

Two engines give added safety at sea. To cut down on the expense of buying two large engines, some anglers buy a large main engine and a smaller reserve one to get back to dry land in emergencies.

Boat fishing for bass

Commercial fishermen are occasionally lucky enough to take huge bass weighing up to 30lb (13.6kg). Fish of only half that weight are also fairly rare, but are prized catches for sport anglers, says Mike Millman.

During the warm months between April and October, when they are most abundant, bass become a treasured target for a swarm of determined, some would say obsessed, boat anglers. If you're thinking of joining the ranks of dedicated bass anglers in pursuit of a dream double-figure fish, you need to know where to go, what tackle to use and the best way to fish for your prey.

Specimen bass tend to occupy prime feeding areas – where sandeel and its larger relative the launce head up the menu. Kent waters are very productive and account for both British Boat and Shore records. Heavy bass are regularly taken by boat anglers near Reculver Sands off Kent, The Needles and other places round the Isle of Wight, Alderney Race in the Channel Islands, Beachy Head, Portland Bill, Lannacombe Bay, Eddystone Reef and the Manacles.

You can also expect bass in estuaries, particularly those with a sand bar. The fish are often willing to penetrate deep into tidal river systems. Salcombe in Devon and Barmouth in North Wales are noted bass fishing areas for the small boat angler.

Rough and ready to feed

A fast tide run is essential for successful bass fishing. The harder it runs the better the end result often is. Most of the famous bass marks feature a hard-running tide and the marks given here are popular with both charter boat parties and private boats for

▲ *The dream bow wave of a rascally bass kicking up a final fuss before submitting to the landing net. The scrapping antics of bass are renowned and respected by many sea anglers, who prize this attractive silver fish above all other targets.*

▼ *One bass, safe and sound in a wide mouthed net. Trying to gaff a bass is asking for trouble. You'll probably damage the fish – if not lose it altogether.*

▲ *A box of bass bits. Fishing for bass with plugs can be exciting sport. There are loads of different plugs available that are suitable to the method. Big S and Yo-Zuri models may just have the edge over the rest.*

Hooking a prawn

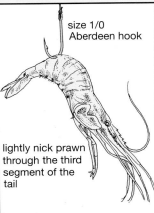

size 1/0
Aberdeen hook

lightly nick prawn through the third segment of the tail

Hook live prawns through the tough part near the tail so they can still operate their moving bits. Make sure you don't hook right through the creature's body or it won't stay fresh and lively for long.

▼ *Prawns in the basket alive, alive-O. These shell-on specimens make a tempting float-fished bait for bass.*

Line For bass fishing on the drift you need a long monofilament trace – up to 6m (20ft) of no more than 15lb (6.8kg) test – which is set up to come off a plastic lead boom. Connect the trace to a swivel with a bead cushioning it where it meets the boom.

Leads and booms Weight the boom with enough lead to keep it tight to the bottom. A square-sided torpedo of about 4oz (113g) is usually enough. It is vital to keep the trace on the bottom and to achieve this you pull line steadily from the multiplier or allow it to go off under thumb pressure. Set the multiplier clutch precisely to suit the strength of monofilament used.

The baits In many cases, nothing beats a live launce or sandeel, though dead eel and even mackerel strip can also work. Prawns and shrimps are a fine alternative, while artificials such as plugs take many fish. For really big bass over wrecks, some anglers use only live joey mackerel.

Hooks and hooking Match the hook to the bait. You need a fine wire hook for a live eel. A Mustad Black Nordic Bend size 3/0 no. 4447B is ideal, but a blued Aberdeen is almost as good. Mount a live eel by passing the hook point in under the jaw and pulling through. Then nick it through the under-belly just behind the head. A gentle pull back seats the hook neatly against the bait fish's head. Be sure you only nick the belly skin or the eel quickly dies.

that reason – the big tides mean big bass.

Many of the best areas don't just have a fast tide run. There is also some sort of sea bed feature – usually a bank or reef – which channels the tide and provides shelter for predators and prey. In the tidal maelstrom around the feature, bass attack the launce, mackerel and other prey fish. This also occurs round some wrecks in big tide areas.

It can be important to fish at the right state of the tide. In Lannacombe Bay, knowledgeable anglers prefer the first two hours and the last hour of the flood to fish for bass on the drift, though you can catch at other times. Bass around offshore reefs such as Eddystone and the Manacles are most active at dawn. Specialists like to be on the grounds before first light.

Set-up and method
If you're fishing from a charter boat your skipper will know the hotspots and steer you to the best zones. You don't need specialized gear but make sure your rod, line and other bits are equal to the job.

Rods and reels A 10ft (3m) uptiding rod with a medium action, or a two-handed spinning rod matched with a small multiplier carrying monofilament up to 20lb (9kg) test, suits the tackle demands perfectly. But the average 7½ft (2.3m), 20lb (9kg) test boat rod is quite acceptable – although this gear is somewhat less sporting and less fun to use.

The method Drift fishing around banks and reefs is a very successful way to take bass from a boat. The trick is to find the productive areas where the tide concentrates the bait fish and the bass (good charter boat skippers know these places) and to work

▲ *Freelined, trolled, float fished or worked along the bottom, live launce, along with sandeel – their smaller cousins, are irresistible to bass of all sizes.*

Sandeel rig

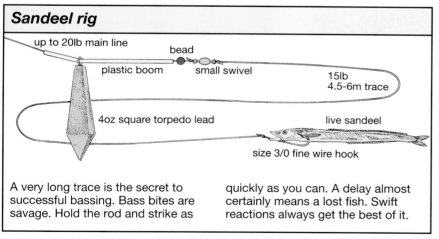

up to 20lb main line
bead
plastic boom · small swivel
15lb 4.5-6m trace
4oz square torpedo lead
live sandeel
size 3/0 fine wire hook

A very long trace is the secret to successful bassing. Bass bites are savage. Hold the rod and strike as quickly as you can. A delay almost certainly means a lost fish. Swift reactions always get the best of it.

Eel condition

Keep your live sandeels in good condition in a 'courge' (livebait carrier). The one shown is made of untreated wood but you can use other materials such as wicker. Put the courge over the side of the boat so a natural and fresh flow of water passes through the holes, maintaining the proper temperature and oxygen level.

your bait along the bottom contours.

Bass can attack baits with great ferocity. If line cannot peel off the reel under pressure, the first rush of a hooked fish either snaps it or pulls the hook free. Every bass puts up the fiercest possible struggle and the power of a double-figure specimen is remarkable, especially in the fast tide. Bass are very cunning and often switch from diving away to heading back up towards the boat. If you're not familiar with bass antics it's easy to believe the fish has broken away. If it happens, retrieve the slack line as fast as you can to restore direct contact.

There is a great danger of losing the fish when it nears the surface. Bass don't like

Trolling rig for bass

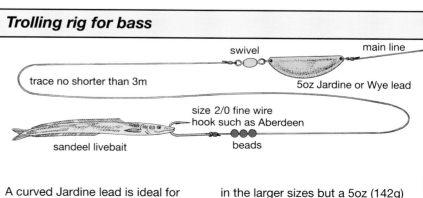

swivel · main line
trace no shorter than 3m
5oz Jardine or Wye lead
size 2/0 fine wire hook such as Aberdeen
sandeel livebait
beads

A curved Jardine lead is ideal for trolling baits above the bottom. It's difficult to get hold of these weights in the larger sizes but a 5oz (142g) lead is generally sufficient for a boat trolling at two knots.

the light and a glimpse of sky invokes an even fiercer struggle to escape. Keep a tight line to the fish and gently but firmly play it, and then you can draw it safely to a wide-mouthed net.

Plugging away

Small boat and dinghy anglers can do well slow trolling in estuaries. Mount a sandeel on an Aberdeen hook with a long trace, and work it well astern of the craft – away from engine noise and prop wash.

If you're looking for bass aboard a small boat, keep an eye open for working birds. A flock repeatedly diving or displaying a high level of activity near the surface often indicates that a shoal of small fish has been driven towards the surface by hunting bass.

Manoeuvre the boat around the disturbance and then turn it at an angle, allowing the bait to pass through the area where the bass are feeding. Small artificial eels and plugs (notably Rapalas) can be particularly effective for this.

Plug fishing for predatory species such as bass is becoming very popular. If you locate bass feeding on small fish you could be in for some exciting sport. Carefully and quietly motor close to the spot, kill the engine and let the boat drift. Cast plugs beyond the disturbance and allow them to sink under the influence of a small Wye or barrel lead, positioned above a swivel set 1.2m (4ft) from the plug. When the plug is 3m (10ft) or so below the surface, retrieve it with a series of jerks.

Tip   Drift slider and prawns

For a change of tactic, try fishing for bass from a small anchored boat. Rig a float as a slider and let it drift back from the stern with the run of water then work it back towards you steadily. Live sandeel and live prawn are two of the best baits for this type of fishing. It can be a very effective method indeed, particularly if there is a fast tide run.

▲ This 7lb (3.2kg) bass was taken on live sandeel. You can gather fresh sandeels by netting them in the shallows at low tide or feathering for them from a boat in summer.

▼ Dawn fishing in the Menai Straits, North Wales. It's a traditional time for bass action. Bass are also very active at last light.

Boatcasting tactics

Boatcasting is a fairly new method, but one that has had an enormous impact on shallow water boat fishing since its development in the 1970s. Mick Toomer explains its uses.

As its name suggests, boatcasting (also called uptiding) involves casting the baits away from the boat. It is most effective in less than 30m (100ft) of water, though it does still have its uses in deeper water.

The best time to boatcast is in a tide run when you're after bigger species. Smaller fish such as pouting can usually be taken more efficiently on conventional downtide tackle.

The advantages
In shallow water, the disturbance caused by the boat's hull and anchor rope tends to scare cautious fish away from the boat. The size of the scare area depends on both the depth of water and the size and type of boat. For an average size charter boat in 12m (40ft) of water, the scare area seems to stretch to some 15m (50ft) on either side of the boat.

As fish move out of the scare area, they tend to concentrate around the edges of the zone. Anglers who find this concentration of fish catch more.

Conventional downtide tactics usually leave the baits in a line downtide of the boat. Fish passing 20m (65ft) or so on either side of the boat may therefore miss the scent trail put out by the baits. Casting the baits away from the boat ensures they are fanned out, so creating a wider scent trail.

Casting into the tide usually requires the use of a wired lead to hold bottom. This means that you can keep your bait on the sea bed with a 5-6oz (140-170g) wired lead where you might need more than 1½lb (0.7kg) of plain lead fishing downtide. A lighter weight is more sporting – allowing both the fish and the angler more freedom – which would make it an attractive technique even if catches were no better than with conventional tactics.

Bait presentation is also different with a wired lead – the bait remains stationary rather than bumping around in the tide as it does when fishing downtide. This point is not yet fully understood, but it is one of the reasons why this technique is successful.

Tackling up
Tackle is perhaps more like beachcasting or pier fishing equipment than conventional boat tackle.

The ideal rod is about 10ft (4.5m) long with a flexible tip and moderately powerful middle and lower sections. Early boatcast-ers had to use cut-down beachcasting rods but these days there are plenty of purpose-built boatcasting rods on the market. One designed to cast 5-8oz (140-225g) is the best all-round choice.

A multiplier is best for boatcasting but it needn't be hugely powerful. However, it must have a good rate of retrieve and a capacity of around 300yd (275m) of 15-20lb (6.8kg-9.1kg) line. Make sure it has a light alloy spool as heavier metal spools make casting difficult and plastic spools can break under extreme pressure.

With 15-20lb (6.8-9.1kg) line you should use a shock leader of at least 30lb (13.6kg). It makes casting safer and, with a heavy hooklength, gives you a bit of confidence

▼ *The author, Mick Toomer, with a couple of purpose-made boatcasting rods. The reels are powerful without being cumbersome and are capable of smooth casting.*

Boatcasting gear

A purpose-built rod with a flexible tip and a quality reel are required.

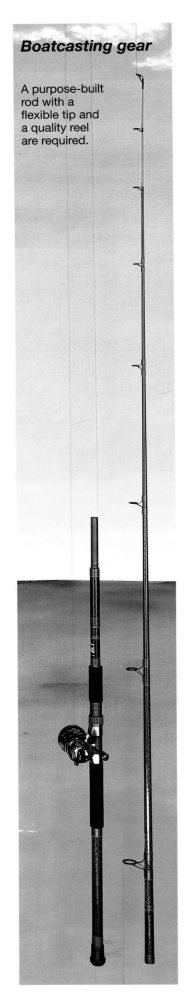

Boatcasting terminal tackle

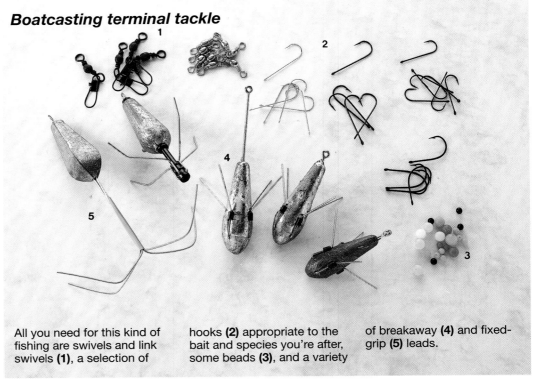

All you need for this kind of fishing are swivels and link swivels (1), a selection of hooks (2) appropriate to the bait and species you're after, some beads (3), and a variety of breakaway (4) and fixed-grip (5) leads.

when a big fish is close to the boat – you don't have to worry so much about losing it. **End gear** usually consists of a single hook rig, with either a fixed or a running trace of 1.2-1.8m (4-6ft). You need a selection of both breakaway and fixed-grip leads of 5-8oz (140-225g) to cope with variations in the tidal flow.

Uptide tactics

The direction you should cast out from the boat depends on the strength of the tide. As the tide increases you need to cast farther uptide and closer to the line of the anchor rope.

To start with, cast about 50m (55yd) uptide at an angle of 45° to the anchor rope.

Fishing outside the scare area

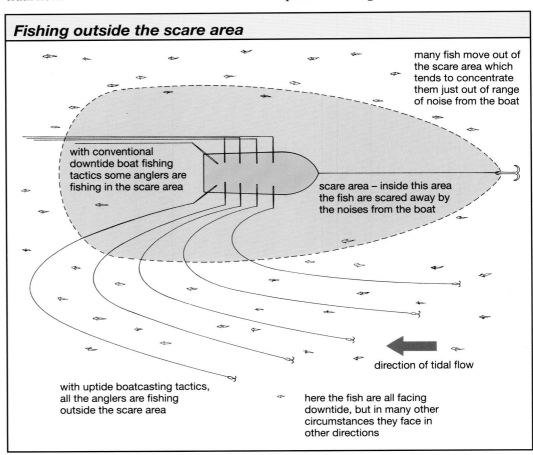

many fish move out of the scare area which tends to concentrate them just out of range of noise from the boat

with conventional downtide boat fishing tactics some anglers are fishing in the scare area

scare area – inside this area the fish are scared away by the noises from the boat

direction of tidal flow

with uptide boatcasting tactics, all the anglers are fishing outside the scare area

here the fish are all facing downtide, but in many other circumstances they face in other directions

Boatcasting end-gear

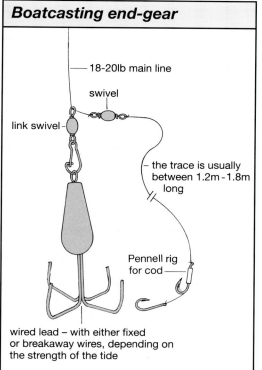

18-20lb main line

swivel

link swivel

the trace is usually between 1.2m - 1.8m long

Pennell rig for cod

wired lead – with either fixed or breakaway wires, depending on the strength of the tide

Find the fish

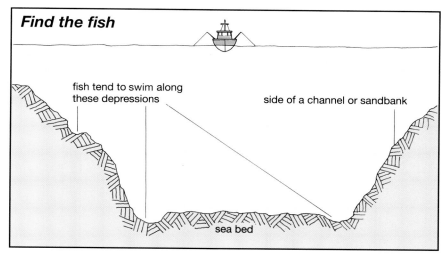

fish tend to swim along these depressions

side of a channel or sandbank

sea bed

Tip Bait stop

If your trace is too long to cast easily, hang the hook over a wire on the lead. A leger stop on the trace stops the bait sliding down the line.

pulling the lead out of the sea bed. This helps to set the hook.

Up on the boat, a typical bite is a two stage event. The rod tip pulls round, and then the line slackens as the lead comes out and the fish drops back downtide. As soon as the line begins to slacken, pick up the rod and reel in as fast as you can.

The fish is usually only lightly hooked at this stage, and is shaking its head in an effort to dislodge the hook. The sooner you tighten the line, the less time it has to get free. Rays are an exception to this – give them plenty of time to get the bait in their mouth – they rarely drop a bait once they are interested.

Do not stop reeling once you have started. It may be tempting to strike when you start

⚠ Cast away!

A boat is quite a cramped casting platform, and safety must always be your first consideration. Make sure you tell the other anglers on board every time you're about to cast away from the boat.

The best way to avoid injuring a fellow angler is to start with your end gear outside the boat and avoid casting over other anglers' heads. This may mean walking to the back of the boat before you cast, but that's vastly preferable to an accident.

Let the line run off the spool even after the lead has hit the bottom. In this way the line forms a bow which tightens in the tide, pulling the grip wires of the lead firmly into the sea bed. The boat's anchor chain and rope works on a similar principle.

The amount of line you need to let out depends on the strength of the tide. Initially you should let the line out until it enters the water downtide at about 15° to the side of the boat. If the lead doesn't hold, use a heavier grip lead, or cast farther uptide and let out a little more line.

Once the lead is fixed in the bottom and the tide has pulled the line taut, put the rod down. The semi-flexible rod tip absorbs the movement of the boat without pulling the wires out of the sea bed. When a fish picks up the bait and moves away, it pricks itself with the hookpoint. The fish then bolts

Tip Concentration

It pays to find any concentrations of fish on the sea bed. These may be due to a feature such as a patch of rough ground or a depression at the base of a sandbank, or to the fish leaving the scare area. Vary your casting distance until you catch a fish and then keep casting to the same area until you stop getting bites.

Smooth casting from a boat

1. Make sure you start with the lead outside the boat and that no-one is in your line of fire.

2. Power the rod smoothly around in a standard overhead thump – just as you might do from a beach.

3. After casting, don't put the reel in gear straight away – leave time for the line to form a bow.

Tip Hook-up

If you are having problems converting takes into hooked fish, check that your hook is sharp and try to reel into the fish at a faster rate. If this doesn't work, a heavier weight can sometimes give you a better hook hold as the fish has to pull harder to get it out of the sea bed.

to feel the weight of the fish, but resist the temptation! An early strike allows the bow of line to slacken, giving the fish another chance to shed the hook. Keep winding into the fish until you can feel its full weight downtide of you. Only then should you lean into the fish.

It is very important that you remember to wind the hook home and don't try to strike it there. Set the clutch fairly tight so that you can really wind down into a fish without giving it any line. Once the hook is properly set, you can slacken off the drag a little if the fish is very heavy and likely to take a lot of line.

▶ *Mick Toomer returns a small thornback taken on peeler crab while boatcasting. Many sea species can be taken with this method as long as conditions are right.*

▼ *This fine 64lb (29kg) tope was taken off the coast of Essex. The water is quite shallow in that area, and so it is an ideal place for boatcasting tactics.*

Fishing sand, rock and gravel banks

Large numbers of fish are attracted to the sand, rock and gravel banks around our shores. Mike Millman suggests how to tackle the many different species found there.

◀ *A specimen blonde ray taken on the famous Skerries Banks off Dartmouth in Devon. They extend for almost seven miles and contain many deep pits and holes, which have a great attraction for blondies.*

▼ *This tide race off Start Point marks the western end of the Skerries Banks. Although the sea is quite calm, the strong tide is pushed towards the surface by the banks rising from the sea bed, causing turbulence.*

Banks of different types are found all around the British coastline. Made from sand, shale, gravel, or a mix of these materials, they are created by the action of the wind and tide. Whatever their make-up and distance from the shore, they have one thing in common – they all attract fish.

Bank deposits

There are banks off most parts of the coast and in all depths of water. They are formed by a complex combination of factors such as wind, tide, river deposits and the shape of the local shoreline.

Constantly shifting, banks act as natural bottlenecks, forcing the tidal flow to accelerate as it moves up and over the obstruction. This funnelling effect helps to concentrate the water-borne food into a much smaller area, making banks attractive hunting grounds for many species of fish.

Tackling up for banks

There are three basic methods for fishing banks; uptiding, downtiding and drifting. **Uptiding** is best suited to fishing over shallow banks, when the disturbance caused by the boat's hull in the tide flow can frighten fish away. It presents the bait in a different way to more conventional downtide methods (see Boatcasting tactics, pages 83-86).

Bouncing back along the bottom

boat at anchor

tide

lead on bottom

lead lifted off bottom

sand or gravel bank

lead dropped back on bottom

lead bounced with tide

To cover as much ground as possible use a lead that will just hold bottom. After a few minutes lift the rod tip, let out a bit of line and lower the rod until you feel the lead touch bottom again. Repeat until the lead is up to 60m (65yd) from the boat. Retrieve slowly.

▲ The tide race is deflected up to the surface by an underwater bank, causing the sea to 'boil'. This turbulence is some way downtide from the bank itself, so anchor uptide and 'trot' your bait back.

Launce flapper

The launce flapper is a superb bait for many fish, especially blonde rays. Insert a sharp, thin-bladed knife behind the head and cut back, following the backbone. Repeat on the other side; discard spine.

Use a 9-10ft (2.7-3m) uptiding rod capable of casting 2-10oz (56-300g), coupled with a multiplier reel holding 250-300m (270-330yd) of 25lb (11.3kg) line.

Downtiding is the method used when fishing from a boat at anchor in deeper water . A 20-30lb (9-13.6kg) class boat rod about 7ft (2.1m) long is ideal. For preference, this should be matched to a medium sized multiplier reel. Choose the 30lb (13.6kg) class tackle if you are fishing well offshore to handle the heavier weights needed to hold bottom in the deeper water.

Fishing on the drift allows you to use a lighter lead than with downtiding, as you aren't fighting the tide to hold bottom. This makes it ideal for fishing in a very strong tide when holding bottom, even with a large lead, is difficult. The same type of equipment is used as when fishing at anchor – it's common to use both methods, depending on the state of the tide.

When faced with fast tide races over banks, some anglers use wire line. This is very effective at cutting through the flow, allowing you to get away with less lead. However, because of its natural springiness wire is not as 'user-friendly' as nylon and does require a rod fitted with a roller tip ring or full rollers throughout.

End of the line

You can't beat a simple running leger with a long trace for bank fishing. For boatcasting uptide you will find it difficult to use a trace more than about 1.8m (6ft) long. Always use a breakaway or fixed-grip lead to hold the bait firmly on the bottom and to give a positive indication of drop-back bites.

For drifting and downtiding it is best to use a much longer flowing trace. To help prevent tangles when lowering your bait to the bottom, use a lead boom to keep the trace away from the reel line. It is similar to the Flying Collar (see Fishing the fabulous Flying Collar, pages 67-70), especially when fishing up in the water for bass.

The longer the boom the better. While Clements and Eddystone booms are effective, the new bent plastic tube type are best of all as they rarely tangle. A swivel joins trace to reel line, and acts as the lead boom stop. A bead between boom and swivel helps prevent damage to the knot. Forged 2/0-4/0 hooks are ideal for bank fishing with most baits and for most species.

Holding bottom

The type of lead you choose is important. Bombs and conical leads tend to roll around too much in the strong currents over banks.

The best sort of lead is the 'watch-grip'

Bank hotspots

● **Adamant Bank, off Weymouth, Dorset** Good for turbot, brill, thornback, blonde and small-eyed rays. Cod and spurdog in winter.
● **Atherfield Banks, off the Isle of Wight** Deep water sandbank with strong tides. Good mark for blonde and undulate rays in the summer and big cod in the winter.
● **Castlemaine Harbour, Co. Kerry, Eire** Series of sandbanks at the harbour entrance are excellent for tope and bass. Anchor in deep water and cast to the disturbed area.
● **Freshwater Reef, off the Isle of Wight** Series of banks across the tide. Fish on the drift for bass; anchor-up for other species. Noted mark for small-eyed rays.
● **The Kentish Knock, off the Kent coast** Very shallow offshore banks, once supreme bass area off S. E. England. Still some good bass to be had – lug and rag best.
● **Lanacombe Banks, off Salcombe, Devon** Inshore sand and gravel banks. Bass, turbot, plaice and some rays. Cod in winter. Drifting with sandeels best method.
● **Severn Estuary, off S. Wales and Somerset** Many mud and sand banks. Bass, tope, turbot, smooth hounds and rays. Huge run of codling and cod to 40lb (18kg) in winter months.
● **The Shambles Banks, off Portland Bill** A large area of sandbanks and rock gullies. Good turbot, plaice, bass, some big brill and a few blonde rays. Sandeels best bait.
● **The Skerries, off Dartmouth, Devon** Large sand and gravel banks with deep pits. Big plaice, turbot, bass and blonde rays. Drifting with king rag or sandeel baits the best method.
● **The Thames and Blackwater estuaries, off Essex** Numerous sand and mud banks. Very large size tope, good bass, smooth hounds and thornbacks. Some cod in the winter months.

type which, being flat, allows the tide to flow over it, pushing the small projections into the sand or gravel. The amount of lead you need depends on the tide and whether you want a firmly anchored bait, or one that you can 'trot' back with the tide.

Bank baits

Many baits work on banks, but there are some that seem to outfish the rest. Sandeels are probably the best. They are prolific over banks, particularly sandbanks, and fish can become preoccupied with them. Bounce them back in the tide on a long trace, alive or dead. Retrieve them slowly at the end of each 'trot' – bass and turbot in particular hit them as they move towards the surface.

Mackerel and other fish baits are also effective, especially for rays. Use flappers, fillets or thin sandeel-size strips. Crabs are also proven fish catchers, with the under-used hermit crab being notably successful. The other killer bait is king rag. All bank dwellers seem to find a big worm fluttering in the tide quite irresistible.

▲ *The tasty turbot, like this fine 18lb (8.1kg) fish, is one of the most highly prized species found on banks. An active predator, it lies in wait on the downtide side of banks for sandeels and other small fish washed into this calmer water.*

Tip Going live

A good bait to use on banks is a small live pouting. Don't catch them on a different rig, which means you have to tackle up again. Tie a small hook, baited with worm, on a short link and tie the link to your big hook. When you get a distinctive pout rattle, strike to set the hook – and your livebait is tethered.

What, when, where?

The different species of fish tend to favour different parts of the bank.

Thornbacks like to sit and wait for prey on top of inshore banks, or lie on the sloping sides when the tide is flowing strongly. Fish baits on a long trace are best. Uptiding in shallow water is very effective.

Small-eyed rays sit in shallow gutters around banks, or wait at the base. Fish baits trundled back with the tide are best.

Blonde rays like deep pits and hollows around off-shore banks. Use a fish bait on a very long trace and keep the bait moving. At the first sign of a bite, give the fish some line and it will take with confidence.

Turbot and brill wait for food in the slacker water just downtide of banks. They love sandeels, so bounce one back with the tide. Use a long trace and remember to retrieve your bait slowly – turbot often follow a bait as it heads for the surface.

Bass are normally found in front of the bank or on top of it when the tide is running hard. King rag and sandeels, both natural and artificial, are favourites. Bass often feed quite high up in the water, so it is not vital to keep the bait on the bottom. Retrieve your bait in a jerky sink-and-draw fashion to tempt them to strike.

Cod scour the pits and gullies behind the bank. Almost any bait will do, as long as it is large and fished close to the bottom.

Plaice are very fond of the top of gravelly banks. Worm baits used with beads and attractor spoons are good for this species.

Tope and dogfish hunt around the base of banks and the tail-end of the tide races. Fish baits on a flowing trace work well.

▼ *Uptiding tactics accounted for this thornback. In strong tide races over banks, try to bring rays towards you underneath the surface. The water's buoyancy reduces their weight and you lose less fish.*

Rig for banks

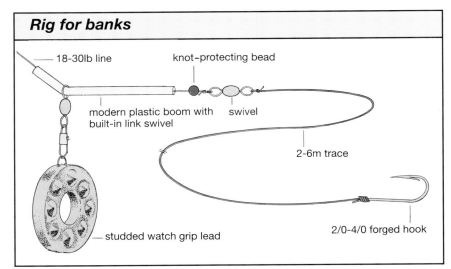

- 18-30lb line
- knot–protecting bead
- modern plastic boom with built-in link swivel
- swivel
- 2-6m trace
- studded watch grip lead
- 2/0-4/0 forged hook

Deposits make banks bigger

The majority of rivers around Britain's coast have sand or mud banks where they meet the sea. Mud and soil deposits are carried downstream with the current and dropped in the estuary. Wind and tide then form it into banks.

CHAPTER THREE

BAITS
AND LURES

Common and yellowtail lugs

**Each worm is a mini reservoir of potent blood and juices – a bait which sea fish find irresistible.
Successful shore angler Alan Yates tells how you find, keep and present them.**

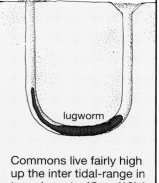

U-shaped tunnel

cast   blow hole

lugworm

Commons live fairly high up the inter tidal-range in tunnels up to 45cm (18in) deep. At one end of the tunnel is an irregular sand cast created by the worm as it expels inedible particles. At the other end is a depression with a small blowhole.

The lug is a natural marine bait but its habitat is so secure that fish rarely encounter it. Sometimes, though, a heavy storm knocks out a sandbank and washes the worms into the surf: then, the fish go on a feeding frenzy.

Lugs take all types of sea fish except for mullet, shark and conger. Digging your own lugs can be a back-breaking business but the rewards of catching plenty of fish using an excellent free and natural bait are certainly worth all the effort.

Worm types

There are two distinct types of lugworm that you can find. They are the common lug and the yellowtail lug.

Common lugworm Commons (other names include blowlug, softlug and redlug) are found in sand and mud fairly high up the inter-tidal range. They have a soft skin and are usually less than 15cm (6in) long but they can grow up to 25cm (10in).

Large commons tend to consist mostly of sand, so the smaller worms are preferable. These have a high water content which causes a fresh worm to explode on the hook,

▼ *A fork is better than a garden spade, there's less chance of breaking the worms. Take a pair of wellies too – bait digging can be a messy business.*

◄ *Where casts are close to one another digging a trench allows you to gather worms with less effort and back-fill more easily.*

releasing an irresistible scent trail to a hungry predatory fish.

Yellowtail lugworm The yellowtail varies in appearance from one coastal area to another and is known by different names including: gullie, black, runnydown and sewie. It grows to between 10cm (4in) and 30cm (12in) in length but a worm of about 20cm (8in) is a good sized bait.

The yellowtail's tunnel is vertical and goes down as far as 60cm (24in). Because the tunnel goes into mud, its cast is blacker than the common's – the blacker the cast, the deeper the tunnel. The shape of the cast is also distinctive – unlike the common's untidy heap, the yellowtail's cast is almost always a perfect conical heap of spiral coils.

Digging

Dig for lugs when the tide is right out. For best results choose the longest spring tides rather than neap tides which expose the least low tide sand.

Digging commons You can either dig worms individually by following the line of the tunnel from the cast towards the blow hole or, where casts are plentiful, by digging trench-fashion.

If the worm's habitat is fairly dry, use a flat-pronged potato fork. A fork lessens the chance of the worm getting damaged and the flat prongs support the sand so that it doesn't break up, making the sand easier to remove. (If the sand is wetter dig with a lug spade.)

When you've dug down to the worm, don't

⚠ Tide watch

A word of warning: when digging, always keep an eye on an incoming tide. Some beaches (Weston-super-Mare, for example) have a shallow slope and the tide can come rushing in and catch you unawares.

▲ Handling yellowtails leaves the fingers covered in a bright yellow iodine stain – but this is a small price to pay for such an effective bait.

▶ Worms stored in a tray of sea water in the fridge can be kept for up to 2 or 3 months but remove any dead ones straight away.

Backfilling

You can often tell where anglers have been digging for bait: the beach looks like a lunar landscape. Apart from looking ugly, holes are a danger to other beach users. Don't be thoughtless, make sure you backfill – fill in the holes – as you go along.

Storage and preparation

In general, fresh, live lugworm is superior to frozen bait but frozen yellowtails can be an effective alternative when fresh bait is not available. Avoid preserved lugworm sold in tackle shops; as a bait it's next to useless.

Commons Because of their high water content, commons are unsuitable for freezing. However, they can be kept alive for up to a week if stored in dry newspaper in the fridge.

It is also possible to keep worms for 2 or 3 months or more by 'tanking' them. Some anglers do this by keeping the worms as they would fish: in an aquarium, with an aeration pump and filter system.

A simpler method of tanking is to put the worms in a shallow bait tray, cover with about 4cm (1½in) of sea water, and keep them at the bottom of the fridge. It is not necessary to use a pump. The important thing is not to put too many worms into one container.

Check the worms daily and remove any dead ones. If you keep a bottle of sea water in the fridge it will be at the right temperature to add to your worms when they need it, but once the tray is set up disturb it as little as possible.

Yellowtails Fresh yellowtails can be stored in the same way as commons. They make an excellent fresh bait because, like the common, they explode on the hook but the tough leathery skin makes them more resistant to attack from crabs and also makes them suitable for freezing.

To freeze, first gut the worm by squeezing out its innards. Next, blanch it by pouring boiling water over it. Then wrap each worm in newspaper and freeze.

Gutted yellowtails stored in the fridge in newspaper are also a useful bait. Check them every so often to see if they've gone off or they'll stink the fridge out.

Tip Keep cool

In hot weather, put a chemical ice pack of the kind used for picnics in the worm bucket to keep them cool, otherwise they will die and go off.

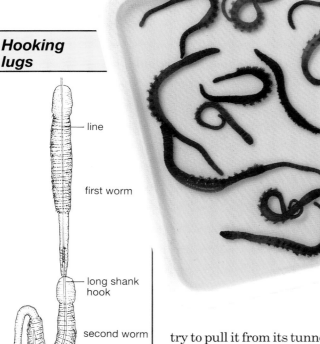

Hooking lugs

line

first worm

long shank hook

second worm

Thread the hook so it enters through the head and comes out at the tail. This lets juices escape, makes the bait look natural and keeps it in one piece when casting.

try to pull it from its tunnel. Instead lift out the lump of sand that the worm is in and break it open to release it.

Digging yellowtails Because of the yellowtail's wetter habitat it is best to use a small lug spade. These can be bought from good tackle shops. Using a lug spade makes the job a lot easier. Follow the worm's tunnel down from the cast, quickly taking out small spits of sand so that the hole doesn't fill with water.

Presenting the bait

Lugs need a long shank hook so that they stay on the hook. An Aberdeen pattern from size 4 up to 2/0 or 3/0 is ideal.

Worms can be threaded on to the hook-shank and snood in twos, threes or fours, depending on the fish you're after. Use fresh worms each cast as the natural juices are quickly sucked out in the sea, making the worms much less attractive to the fish you are after.

Ragworm

Second in popularity only to lugworm as a sea bait, the four main types of ragworm between them appeal to a wide range of fish.

Unlike the lugworm, which filter-feeds peacefully in the shelter of its burrow, the ragworm is a voracious carnivore and scavenger that forages relentlessly through sand and mud. Looking somewhat like a cross between an earthworm and a giant centipede, it propels itself along on a mass of bristly 'legs' and seizes its food – small invertebrates, alive or dead – with a pair of extendible, claw-like pincers.

Red rag are the most common type. They grow to about 20cm (8in) long and are usually found in gritty mud. Red rag catch most species but are particularly good in summer for flatfish and bass.

King rag are like red rag but grow to 50cm (20in) or more and prefer sand to mud. They are excellent for big bass, cod, smoothhounds, pollack, coalfish and rays.

White rag are nearly as big as red rag but are much less common. They are found in clean sand and are one of the shore matchman's favourite baits, being deadly for small fish, especially flatties.

Harbour rag, or maddies, are red in colour and grow to only 10cm (4in) at most. They live in soft estuarine mud and are a superb bait for flounders and mullet.

▲ *King rag can grow up to 50cm (20in) or more in length and be as thick as your finger. Use them whole for big bass and cod.*

◄ *Red rag in shallow aerated trays of fresh seawater. Kept cool – preferably in a fridge – they will stay alive for a few weeks.*

◄ *Harbour rag, or maddies, are as soft as the mud in which they live. Fished on a small hook they are excellent for mullet.*

▼ *White rag are relatively scarce, but no self-respecting shore matchman would dream of turning up for a major contest without them.*

How to hook a ragworm

1 Insert the point of the hook into the head of the worm and thread the whole of the worm lengthways up the shank.

2 Leave the point of the hook inside the worm just before the end of the tail, so that the whole hook is hidden (right).

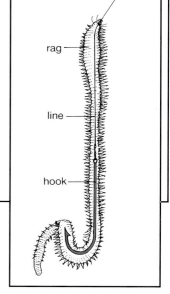

rag

line

hook

▼ *Flounders are the shore angler's bread and butter fish in many areas. Ragworm is one of the deadliest baits for these popular fish – especially harbour rag.*

Digging rag

To dig rag you need a flat-pronged potato fork, gum boots or waders and a pair of old gloves. Always wear gloves because mud and sand beds often contain hidden pieces of broken glass, rusty tin cans and the like.

To find red, king or white rag, walk slowly across the mud or sand looking down at your feet for tiny spurts of water from small holes in the sand. Trench-dig a patch where the spurts and holes are densest. Break open the clods of sand or mud carefully because rag are soft and damage easily.

To help future stocks, take only large, mature worms and only as many as you really need. And always backfill trenches so there are no nasty potholes for unsuspecting swimmers when the tide comes in.

Maddies are much easier to find and dig. Patches of soft mud pitted with tiny holes yield dozens in a matter of a few forkfuls.

Storing rag

Rag require careful handling and storing to keep them in tip-top condition. Unlike lug, they are only useable live. Frozen, they become too mushy.

Ideally you should use rag within a day of digging them, but it is possible to keep them alive and well for a few weeks. Take only whole, undamaged worms. Any broken ones soon die and contaminate the rest.

Red, king and white rag can be kept in shallow tanks or trays of clean, aerated seawater. Store in a cool, dark place – a fridge, ideally – and check twice a day for dead or dying worms.

The day before fishing, spread the rag out on a tray lined with newspaper or moisture-absorbing particle chips, and put them back in the fridge. If you can get some fresh seaweed to cover them with, all the better. In hot weather or when faced with a long drive, it is best to transport them in a cool box.

Maddies are even more delicate, so need even more careful handling. Rinse them clean of mud in fresh seawater then lay them in a tray lined with newspaper. Maddies keep for up to a week in a fridge.

Hooking rag

Always match size of bait and hook. For flatfish and other small species, thread a single red or white rag on a small, fine-wire Aberdeen. For bigger fish, thread two or three on and above a larger Kamasan B940 (a thicker-wire Aberdeen).

King rag can be used in sections for small fish, or whole for big fish.

Maddies need a very small, fine-wire hook and can be fished singly or in bunches, threaded on or hooked through the middle.

Harbour rag

England shore International Alan Yates tells you how to collect, keep and use one of his favourite 'scratching' baits.

Very few big fish give harbour rag (or maddies as they're called) a second look. These small but juicy squirming worms are primarily a bait for hard shore venues where small fish are the target. High on the list of takers are flounders and thin-lipped mullet, but they also attract small pollack, wrasse, garfish, scad, pouting and herring. The only big fish they may tempt are bass and thick-lipped mullet.

Mud-loving maddies
Harbour rag are orange-red and very soft. They live in the thick mud of harbours, estuaries and tidal rivers.

Collecting them when the tide is out is fairly easy in spring, summer and autumn. Dig where the surface of the mud is pitted with hundreds of tiny holes. The worms live just below the surface in big colonies. You *can* simply turn over clods of mud with your bare hands before picking out the worms. However, there's always the danger of cutting yourself on broken glass or a rusty tin can, so it's better to use a garden fork – one with narrow tines is best.

Keep the worms shaded as they quickly die if left exposed to the sun. If you are going to use them the same day, just keep them in a bucket with a little mud. If you are going to use them a few days later, rinse them as best you can in sea water and put them in shredded newspaper or some of the fine

▲ *Harbours, estuaries and tidal rivers all play host to harbour rag, provided there's plenty of mud.*
   Take care when walking across mud flats – it's all too easy to get stuck in unexpectedly deep mud.
   If you don't know the area, check where it's safe to dig with local anglers or tackle shops .

▼ *Once out on the mud, look for areas where the surface is most densely pitted with tiny holes – these show where the colonies of worms are.*

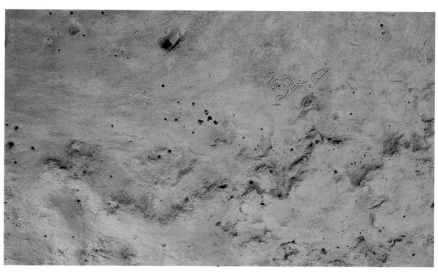

◄ *These anglers have found a colony of maddies in the exposed mud of a tidal river. Though they are combing the mud with their bare hands, it's safer to turn it over with a fork.*

▲ *It doesn't take long to collect enough harbour rag for a day's fishing. If you are going to use them that day, leave them as they are here in a little of the mud they live in.*

► *Harbour rag are found in networks of tunnels just below the surface of the mud. Find a good colony and every clod you fork out can contain dozens of the juicy little worms.*

Tip On the hook

Baiting harbour rag can be tedious and most matchmen use a fine baiting needle. Some favour whipped hooks, to avoid splitting the worms when they are baited in big bunches – but if you use an ordinary fine-wire Aberdeen the eye shoudn't burst too many.

▼ *A bunch of maddies threaded on a small, fine-wire Aberdeen makes a mouth-watering morsel for flounders. Leave the tails free to wriggle enticingly in the tide.*

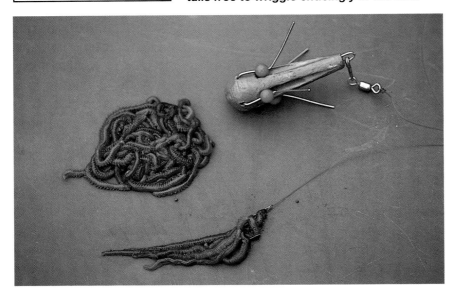

green weed you find around boat moorings and pier pilings. For longer periods – up to a week or so – fridge them in shallow trays of sea water.

In winter, harbour rag are usually scarce in harbours, and those you can find are often thin and green. Look instead in the deepest, blackest mud you can find in estuaries and tidal rivers – here the worms remain fat and bright orange-red.

Whatever the season, wherever you dig, beware of deep mud, don't dig around moorings, boats or pier supports, and always back-fill all holes. Also, when you are digging in tidal rivers, take great care not to undermine the banks.

Maddie power

You can fish harbour rag singly or in bunches, or you can use them to give a bit of wriggle to a large but lifeless scent-trail bait like lugworm. They are so effective that many match anglers wouldn't dare fish a team event without them; they often help to tempt a small, points-scoring fish from apparently barren beaches.

A major problem with harbour rag is that, being so soft, they all too easily fly off the hook in mid-cast. Bait clips can help for smooth, short casts, as can dunking the worms in the sea just before casting (this makes them contract, and so harden). Another dodge is to dry them with tissue paper – this toughens them up a bit (and incidentally makes them turn blood red). For distance casting, though, there is only one answer – a Baitsafe bait capsule. This cleverly designed device encases the bait and doubles as a streamlined casting weight. It opens on impact with the sea, releasing the bait intact.

Collecting and using peeler crabs

For many types of sea angling the best bait is undoubtedly peeler crab. Unfortunately it is also one of the least understood. Alan Yates explains how to treat his favourite bait.

▼ *Collect peelers from around muddy groynes, under rocks or weed, planks of wood, old tyres or anything else which might be a makeshift crab shelter.*

Peelers are an angling enigma – their versatility in catching anything that swims, along with an ability to be species and specimen selective, has delighted and confused sea anglers for years. If you understand the intricacies of their collection and use, the rewards are great, but many trying peelers for the first time, frozen, from the tackle shop, abandon them as an expensive and useless black mush.

Without doubt, one of the peeler crab's main assets as a bait is its tremendous scent – it simply oozes bright yellow, pungent juices that fish can't resist. It has a seemingly magical power to attract fish to your rod while anglers using other baits around you are fishless – the ultimate angling experience!

Spotting peelers

Crabs which are ready have a hairline crack at the back of the shell, and removing the last leg segment reveals a new soft leg, not the white flesh of a hard crab.

You can lift the shell easily. With experience, peelers are easy to spot, as their colour has mellowed slightly.

The darker colour of the peeler's soft new shell is clearly visible.

It's a crab's life

All hard-skinned animals – insects, lice, shrimps and crabs, among others – must shed their skins in order to grow. With crabs, the old skin gradually splits over a couple of weeks and the soft creature eventually crawls out to wait for its new armour to harden. After the appearance of the first split in the old skin, and before the new one is fully toughened, the animal is extremely vulnerable and must hide. Once the crab has emerged from its old shell, it quickly hardens and is useless as bait for most species, except wrasse and smooth hound which are not particularly fussy.

This process of peeling begins when water temperatures rise in spring and early summer, though it varies around Britain. In the south west, the Gulf Stream keeps water temperatures fairly high and peeling occurs all year round in some estu-aries. In other areas, a warm spell can have the crabs rushing to peel in one hectic period.

Cock crabs are bigger and juicier than hens and therefore more popular with anglers. In most areas they peel first. The hens follow and cling to the underside of the newly hardened male – back to belly – while they wait to peel. Mating takes place imme-

▲ Some anglers lay traps for the crabs (tiles, pipework, tyres and so on) along the shoreline, which they search each low tide. Do not steal from crab traps – some trap owners use glass and thorns to discourage thieves.

◄ Pull back some seaweed at the base of a groyne, and there is a perfect pair of peelers.
Remember, the more sheltered and protected a spot appears, the more likely it is to hold peeler.

Hooking peelers without elastic

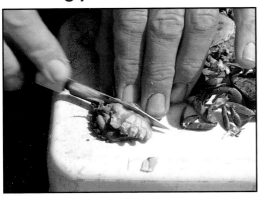

◄ Peelers cut in half release their juices more quickly. A size 2, short shank, wide gape hook is ideal for half a peeler, using the tough leg sockets to hold it in place.

► With half a crab, pass the hook through the shoulder (main shell) twice. Pull the hook and about 3cm of line through, taking care not to tear the soft skin.

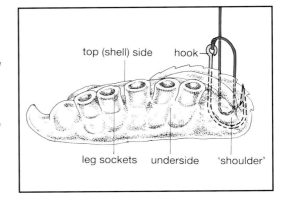

top (shell) side   hook

leg sockets   underside   'shoulder'

diately after peeling, while the female is soft. Two crabs belly to belly have usually mated, with the hen hard once more.

Getting your peeler

Peeler crabs can be bought directly from bait dealers or tackle shops. Many dealers send them by train or post all over the UK, and a few tackle shops stock them on a weekly basis. In some areas, crabs peel in deeper water. They are caught in trawl nets and can be bought from the skipper.

The alternative is to collect peeler crabs yourself, though this can be a tedious and messy business. To avoid predators the crabs hide in weed, mud and rocks, travelling well up the shore, sometimes reaching the neap tide, high water mark. Deep, thick estuary mud is a favourite hiding place as it is warm and supports the soft crab's body.

Once collected, you can keep peelers alive under damp newspaper or weed for up to three weeks, providing a constant supply of bait when you need it. Wet hessian sacking is also ideal for retaining moisture – essential for keeping crabs in peak condition.

If you inspect your peelers you can see that they are in various stages of peeling.

Tip Getting rid of gills

The gills, which Alan is pointing to, are poisonous and you must remove them if the bait is intended for any smallish species.

Some have already shed their shell and are completely soft – use these at once. Others are just about to peel, and some have only started to take on the peeling characteristics. Each stage needs to be treated differently to promote or delay the peeling process enough to produce plenty of baits when you need them. This requires the use of an ordinary fridge.

▲ *Peeler crab catches bass, eels, cod, flounders, congers, dogfish, pout, whiting and many, many more species, including all the flatfish, which are partial to peeled leg of peeler.*

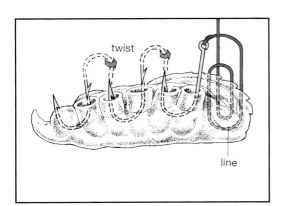

◄ *Pass the hook through the first leg socket, and bring the point out of the next. Twist the hook round to face the third socket, but don't pull it out of the second. Repeat this until you have used all the sockets.*

▶ *Gently pull the line tight so there are no loops, and make sure the hook point is not masked. Use another half crab if you need a big bait.*

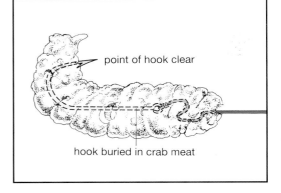

Crabs about to moult are ready for use – they have a hairline crack at the back of the shell. Store them nearest the ice box to slow the shedding process. Cover the crabs with wet sack or weed but do not immerse them in water. Crabs showing signs of peeling can be farther away from the ice box, depending on their peeling condition. Those just starting to show can be encouraged to peel by storing them outside the fridge. For rapid promotion of the peeling process, completely immerse your crabs in fresh seawater, but remember to aerate it if you are keeping lots of crabs in little water.

The big freeze

Many anglers freeze crabs for winter use. This is only effective if the crabs are frozen fresh and in the perfect state. Peelers are often frozen when dead, or not ready to peel. These are useless as bait.

Put a metal tray in your freezer before you start. This helps freeze the peeler quickly, which prevents deterioration. Kill each crab by stabbing it in the head. Remove the legs, shell (including all small segments) and gills, wash the crab under the tap and then wrap it in tin foil or cling film. Freezing crabs singly like this allows small numbers to be removed for use. Take your frozen crabs to the beach in a food vacuum flask. Frozen peelers tend to be softer than fresh ones and are particularly effective for shoaling species like coalfish which are attracted as the frozen crab juices melt.

Using your peeler

With fresh peeler, kill the crab and remove all the shell before putting it on the hook.

Remember to kill it only minutes before you need it – warm sunshine soon renders the flesh useless.

To get the best out of your crabs, use them just before they peel – when at their softest and juiciest. A cycle of collection, storage and use of crab baits maintains a steady supply for the hook. Crabs that are not in this state are internally hard and less juicy, and therefore not so attractive to the fish.

A large crab provides up to three small baits or one large one. For the best results change it after every cast. Baits can be secured with the addition of a peeled leg or claw. Peeler crab is often an ideal scent medium to attract fish to another bait and, in cocktail form, can work as a scent addition to other baits.

▲ *Almost any sort of coast suits peeler and fish take them by preference, even out of season.*

Tip Long distance casting

If you hook peeler through the leg sockets, elastic is not necessary for most purposes. If fishing at extreme range with a big bait, however, elastic helps secure your peeler through the most powerful of casts.

◄ *For bass, large red edible crabs are an excellent bait used whole as peelers, or softback. Both edible and velvet swimming crab peelers are excellent for eel fishing. For smooth hounds and rays from a boat you can use peelers whole, without removing the shell, but for most shore fishing a peeled crab is much better.*

Hermit crabs

Extremely common, rarely seen and little used just about sums up hermit crabs for most anglers. But for those who care to collect them, hermits can be a top bait for smooth hound, stingray and other fish, says Trevor Housby.

Life for the hermit is tricky to say the least. It doesn't grow a hard shell all over its body. Instead it settles for an armoured front end but relies on old whelk shells to provide most of its posterior protection. Once installed in a suitably vacant shell the hermit sticks its pincers and two pairs of legs out of the front. It uses these forelegs to drag its cocooned soft abdomen along the sea bed.

As it outgrows one shell, it looks for larger vacant accommodation. Once out of its home it is extremely vulnerable to predator attack and it has to make a dash for its new residence. A mistake at this stage can be fatal. Even when it finds a new shell it may be forced to share. Parasitic barnacles and small worms are regular lodgers inside shells occupied by hermits and sponges and

▶ *Collect hermits in a weighted pot baited with a fish carcass. Lower it to the sea bed, tie to a buoy and leave for a couple of days. The submarine café attracts plenty of hermits and the odd genuine whelk too.*

anemones often attach themselves to the outside of the shell.

British hermits rarely grow longer than 13cm (5in). Out in the Atlantic, however, closely related species of hermit grow to three times the size. Very much a shallow sea creature, they can thrive in 3-30m (10-100ft) of water. They like to live over mud, sand or shingle bottoms but don't seem to be common over rocky ground.

▼ *The business end of a hermit crab. If threatened the reclusive hermit does a disappearing act. It withdraws into its shell and blocks the entrance with its enlarged right pincer. You don't need to smash the shell to get at the crab, just prise it out carefully.*

Collecting hermits

Gathering hermits is easy. If you're short of time it can pay to strike a deal with offshore fishermen. These men often work the sort of depths that hermit crabs like. For a pound or two, or the odd bottle of whisky, you can guarantee a constant supply of prime hermit. Alternatively, use a large baited drop net to pick up supplies yourself. Hermit crabs are great scavengers and are drawn to anything that resembles a meal – an old mackerel carcass is enough to do the trick.

Keep them in top condition in a bucket of sea water. They keep for a fairly long time if you change the water regularly.

To extract the crab from the shell, use a gentle but constant pulling action. To make things even easier drop them in a container of fresh water. This makes them very lethargic and easy to extract.

► *Bereft of its whelky shelter, the vulnerable hermit is exposed for what it really is – all up-front and not much behind. The combination of crunchy forequarters and succulent tail end gives a bittersweet bait which appeals to many species of fish.*

▼ *Starry smooth hounds such as this fabulous 16lb (7.3kg) fish really go for a hermit. Stingray, smooth hound, bass and dogfish usually hit this sort of bait hard and fast – engulfing the hermit instantly. So be prepared for some excitement.*

Hooking a hermit

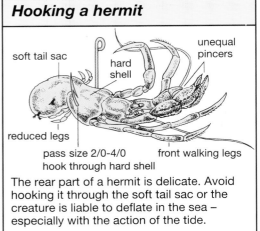

soft tail sac

hard shell

unequal pincers

reduced legs

pass size 2/0-4/0 hook through hard shell

front walking legs

The rear part of a hermit is delicate. Avoid hooking it through the soft tail sac or the creature is liable to deflate in the sea – especially with the action of the tide.

Careful hooking

Hermit crab makes an excellent bait for smooth hound and stingray. They also work well for bass, plaice (especially large ones), codling and dogfish.

For inshore work hermits can be float fished or paternostered for large wrasse. At best, hermit is a very delicate bait. You can cast them but they don't stand up well for long-range work. For this reason they are rarely used by beach anglers. They are considered more of a dinghy or boat angler's bait. But in areas where smooth hound and stingray come close inshore, hermits are well worth a try from the beach.

When hooking one you must take great care not to rupture the jelly-like tail sac. Pass the hook through the harder shell at the top of the body (the thorax). Choose your hook size according to the size of hermit crab and the sort of fish you're after. You can fish two at a time.

For plaice it often helps to pinch off the hermit's head and claws – leaving enough body shell for hooking purposes. Pass a size 1/0 hook through the body remains and bring it out where the soft abdomen starts. This gives a good secure hold without damaging the bait.

For targeting larger species use the whole hermit on a size 2/0-4/0 O'Shaughnessy hook. Pass the hook right through the harder body shell, taking care not to rupture the soft parts.

Shrimps and prawns

Shrimps and prawns are often mistakenly overlooked in favour of other sea baits more easily bought across the tackle shop counter, says Mick Toomer.

Live shrimps and prawns are excellent shore baits in summer for sporting fish such as pollack, bass and wrasse. The higher sea temperatures of summer tempt shrimps and prawns inshore, where they provide fish with rich pickings in the shallow water. With the onset of winter they retreat to the deeper water offshore.

Boiled and peeled, shrimps and prawns are generally much less effective baits – though in the right place at the right time they can be deadly from the shore for such fish as mullet and flounders.

▶ *Shrimps are sandy grey in colour so they blend in with the sandy ground they live over. They grow up to 8cm (3in) long and can be caught by the hundred at low tide in summer.*

▼ *Prawns are much more colourful than shrimps and grow to twice their size. They prefer rocky, weedy pools to open sandy beaches. Many fish like to eat them just as much as we do!*

Tip Whiting bait

Although live shrimps and prawns are not usually much use from a boat, says Mick Toomer, they can have their uses afloat.

Whiting especially are extremely fond of shrimps which on occasion outfish the usual mackerel and lugworm by a big margin.

▲ *The best way to keep shrimps and prawns alive is to put them in a bucket of sea water with an aerator.*

The three most important things to remember are: DO change the water regularly; DON'T overcrowd the bucket; and DO cover the bucket with a cloth or lid.

The American way

The main problem with shrimps and prawns is obtaining them. Very few British tackle shops have live storage facilities. This isn't the case in countries such as the USA, where the value of these baits is much better appreciated and where the majority of coastal tackle shops have their own aerated sea water tanks specially for the keeping of live shrimps and prawns.

Until such facilities become more widespread in Britain the only option is to collect your own. This in itself can be a very interesting task and helps to give you a valuable insight into the life-styles of these crustaceans.

Shrimping and prawning

There are three main ways of gathering shrimps and prawns. Whichever method you use, select only the biggest ones for bait, returning the smaller ones to grow on.

The first way is with a small hand net – the sort sold alongside children's buckets and spades in holiday seaside towns, though you can find them in some coastal tackle shops as well.

As the tide goes out, shrimps and prawns get stranded in rock pools and pools around the bases of breakwaters, harbour walls, pier pilings, jetties and other such structures. Poke the net as far under rock and weed overhangs as it will go then withdraw it quickly to prevent the shrimps and prawns darting out of the mesh.

Larger hand nets can be very effective over open, sandy ground at low tide. Wade out up to your knees and push the net along the sandy bottom at walking pace, working parallel to the shore. Lift the net up every 30m (33yd) or so and among the weed and debris you should find plenty of shrimps

Shrimps and prawns on the hook

When using live shrimps and prawns, the idea is to hook them on in such a way that they can move naturally and attractively in the water. They should therefore be lightly hooked in the tail end, with some anglers preferring to nick the hook under one of the latter segments of the shell (top and bottom right). If you thread the hook through the length of the shrimp or prawn's body (bottom left), the bait won't be able to move at all naturally and soon dies.

Because you want the bait to move in a natural manner, the hook should be as small and as light as possible. When bass are the target it might be necessary to go as big as a size 3/0 with a large prawn, but on most occasions something between a 6 and a 1/0 is more appropriate.

Last but not least, shrimps and prawns are very light, delicate baits, so never try to cast them too hard or too far or they invariably fly off the hook.

and, if you're lucky, a few prawns.

The third method is to lower a baited drop net down the side of a harbour wall or pier. The beauty of this is that you can do it at the same time as you are fishing, to provide a steady supply of fresh bait.

The drop net should have a fine mesh and be baited with a piece of fish. Mackerel and herring are ideal. A kipper can be very effective, although at a push almost any kind of fish or meat will produce results. Leave the net down for about ten minutes then bring it quickly but steadily to the surface. Don't stop lifting even for a second, or the prawns and shrimps will escape. With this method there is always the chance of an edible crab or a lobster as a real bonus!

▶ *As the tide goes out, many shrimps and prawns get stranded in rock pools. You can then scoop them out with a small hand net.*

 Double use drop net

The drop net you use for catching shrimps and prawns need not be very large, but remember that you won't be able to lift big fish out of the water on light tackle. Get yourself a good sized drop net, therefore, so that you can use it both for catching shrimps and prawns and landing big fish.

Alive and well

There are two ways of keeping shrimps and prawns alive. A bucket of sea water is the most commonly used one, but remember to change the water regularly and don't put too many shrimps or prawns in together. A small, battery operated air pump reduces casualties and enables you to keep more shrimps or prawns in the bucket.

Another effective means of storage is keeping them in damp seaweed. Whichever method you use, keep the container as shaded and cool as possible.

Fun float fishing

Floatfishing and freelining are the best ways to fish live prawns and shrimps from piers, breakwaters, harbour walls and rocks, with bass, pollack, scad, coalfish and wrasse the target fish.

Bright days and clear sea conditions are best, as the fish are attracted by the sight and jerky movement of the bait rather than by its smell in the water. Set your hook well clear of the bottom so the fish can see the bait more easily.

Light, sporting tackle is the order of the day, with a carp rod, fixed-spool reel and 6-10lb (2.7-4.5kg) line ideal. Fishing close to the rocks, pilings or harbour wall is usually

◀ *You can catch shrimps and prawns by baiting a drop net with fish and lowering it down the side of the harbour wall. Pull it up swiftly and smoothly or your catch will get away!*

far more effective than casting far out into the open sea, because then your bait is exactly where the fish come looking for shrimps and prawns.

On the menu

Boiled and peeled shrimps and prawns can be good baits off harbour walls where holidaymakers discard food scraps into the sea. Mullet are the main quarry in these circumstances, but in some places other species

eagerly take them.

One that comes immediately to mind is the creek behind the cockle sheds at Leigh-on-Sea in Essex. With a regular supply of shellfish and other seafood regularly deposited into the water, the fish there have become accustomed to such morsels. A shelled prawn or shrimp fished under a float or on a light leger rig produces some excellent mullet and cracking flounders. You might know of a similar place near you.

▲ *The perfect ingredients for success with shrimps and prawns: a blue summer sky and the clear, calm water of a sheltered harbour. These youngsters are fishing close to the weed and nooks and crannies of the jetty for pollack and coalfish. On light float tackle, even a one-pounder (0.45kg) gives you a memorable tussle.*

 Beware weevers!

When you are shrimping and prawning, always check your net for weever fish before picking it over. A sting from a weever is excruciatingly painful.

It's best to wear gloves to be on the safe side. If you do get stung, soak the affected part in as hot water as you can bear and seek immediate medical attention. (For more information about weevers, see pages 187-188.)

▶ *The hard-fighting wrasse is a popular summer fish. Live shrimps and prawns are among the best baits for these colourful characters when fished alongside rocky outcrops and pier pilings.*

Squid and cuttlefish

Overlooked by many anglers, squid and cuttlefish are among the best all-round baits for boat fishing and good standby baits on the beach, writes matchman Tony Kirrage.

▼ *Black bream are great fun on light boat tackle – the best bait for them is often a strip of squid. Left out in the heat of the sun, squid quickly turns mushy then goes off completely, so keep it cool in the shade.*

Strange as it may seem, squid and cuttlefish are molluscs: they have modified shells on the inside. Properly prepared, they are clean, firm-fleshed baits that stay on the hook and catch a variety of fish. They also freeze well, so it's always worth having some in your freezer.

Two types of squid are commonly used as bait: the small Calamari and the much larger common squid.

Calamari squid

Calamari, or Californian squid, can be bought from fishmongers and tackle shops fairly cheaply. A 0.45kg (1lb) box of six to eight 15cm (6in) long Calamaris is ample for one angler for one session.

Calamaris afloat

Calamaris are an excellent bait when boat fishing for predatory fish such as bass, rays, cod, conger, ling, skate, pollack and coalfish. Use them whole, or you can cut off and use just the head and tentacles.

With a whole Calamari, thread the squid up the shank of the hook so that the head is on the bend with the tentacles dangling attractively below. Use fine shirring elastic (buy it from tackle or haberdashery shops) to secure the bait on the line above the eye of the hook. Otherwise the squid slips down the shank. Alternatively, use a Pennell double-hook rig.

▲ *Calamari or Californian squid are a very popular bait with boat anglers, especially for big bass and cod. Try using the head and tentacles in a cocktail with lug for cod.*

Calamaris ashore

Calamaris aren't usually the first choice for beach fishing but they can be useful for cod in winter and bass in summer.

For cod, they are best used in a cocktail with lug. Thread the lug on to the shank of the hook then impale the head and tentacles of a Calamari on the bend below.

For bass, use a whole Calamari, mounted on the hook as described for boat fishing.

Common squid

Common squid are much bigger than Calamaris, averaging 1-1.5kg (2-3lb), and aren't so readily obtainable.

A common squid contains a large ink sac,

Preparing squid for the hook

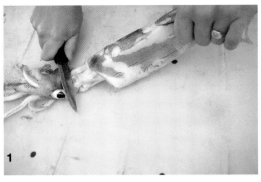

1. Wash the squid well, preferably in seawater, then pin the head to a chopping board with the back of a sharp knife and pull the body away from the head, tentacles, ink sac and guts.

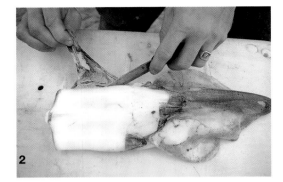

2. Peel off the skin to expose the white flesh.

3. Slit the body open lengthways and remove the transparent bone ('quill') and any remaining guts.

4. You are now left with a flat piece of flesh that you can cut into segments or strips according to the size and species of fish sought.

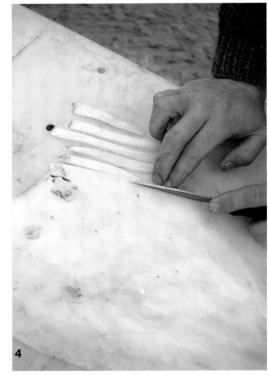

Tip Tenderizer

"When shark-fishing for England in the Indian Ocean off Africa, we used squid and every team member had a small wooden meat-tenderizing hammer – the type with a serrated head. Before mounting the squid on the hook we tapped it all over with the hammer to release the smell of the bait and make it softer. I haven't tried this in the UK, but it could prove a useful tip."

which you must remove intact and discard when preparing the bait. If you burst the sac, the ink discolours the squid and ruins its smell and taste, as well as staining your hands and making a mess. The picture sequence shows you how to prepare a squid.

Using common squid

For boat fishing, small strips of squid are among the best baits for red and black bream. Larger segments and strips and the head and tentacles catch bass, rays, cod,

▼ *Cuttlefish can be a superb bait for conger and large cod from the boat – particularly small cuttlefish, which you can use whole. Larger ones can be used in strips like squid.*

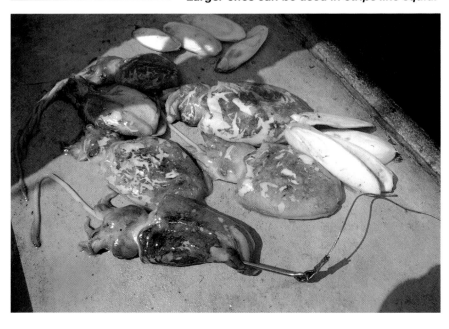

conger, ling, skate, pollack and coalfish.

From the shore, small, thin strips and pieces of tentacle can be good for whiting, especially when used in a cocktail with lug: thread the lug up the shank of the hook and tip the bend with one or more strips or pieces of squid.

Small, thin strips of squid sometimes work well for flatfish, though strangely enough they very rarely catch flounders.

Cuttlefish

Cuttlefish are usually easily obtainable from fishmongers. Commercial fishermen may also sell them to you very cheaply. They aren't usually stocked by tackle shops as they take up too much freezer space.

Cuttlefish make a superb bait for boat fishing, especially for big cod and conger. Use small ones whole for the bigger fish, but first slit them open and remove the bone or shell inside.

Bigger cuttlefish can be cut into strips when boat fishing for smaller fish such as pollack and coalfish. Prepare them in the same way as for common squid.

Razorshells

Razorshells live secure in deep burrows until a storm rips open the inshore sandbars. Then bass and flatties gather for a feast.

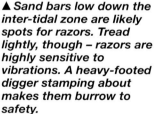

▲ *Sand bars low down the inter-tidal zone are likely spots for razors. Tread lightly, though – razors are highly sensitive to vibrations. A heavy-footed digger stamping about makes them burrow to safety.*

◄ *It is the fleshy interior of the razor that the fish find attractive. You can see the razor's muscular foot just emerging from the closed shells.*

Most species of fish take razors, especially flatties, bass, cod, whiting and pouting. Used in cocktail form they add another dimension to a plain worm bait. Boat anglers in the north-east swear by razors that have been allowed to go 'off' as a bait for cod, whiting and flatfish.

Where to look
Razors are found in the same inter-tidal areas as black lugworm and often appear among tube worms. They live in burrows up to 45cm (18in) deep but you can sometimes see the tip of the shell sticking out of the burrow. Vibrations cause razors to burrow down with great speed, sending up a spurt of water as they go. So if you can't see them, keep a look out for the key-hole shaped entrance to their burrows and spots on the sand where they have spurted water.

Collecting them after a storm is easy. Just pick the dislodged razors off the beach at the high-tide mark where they are eventually cast up by the sea. A winter gale that coincides with a low spring tide is perfect and some large catches of cod and flounder often accompany such storms – especially from venues along the south coast of England.

Pulling them out If you can see a razor sticking up, grip the top of the shell until the fleshy foot of the razor – which grips the

 Razor sharp

Razorshells get their name from their shape – which resembles the old-fashioned cut-throat razor – but they have something else in common as well: they can cut.

Don't grab at a razor that is disappearing down its burrow, and take particular care that they don't splinter when you are splitting them open.

sides of the burrow like a rawlplug – releases its grip.

In darkness, razors come right out of their burrows and you can pick them from the sand in their hundreds.

Salt One method of coaxing them out is to sprinkle household salt at the entrance to the burrow. It doesn't always work but usually the razor emerges and you can pluck it out. The method seems to work best when the sand is dry.

Digging At other times razors need to be dug with a lugworm spade or fork. This is best done at low tide – as the sand dries their burrows become more apparent. Simply follow the line of the burrow until you reach the razor.

Spear In some areas anglers collect razors with a small barbed spear. This is a most efficient way of gathering the bigger specimens.

Presentation

Remove the razor from its shell by prising apart the two halves. Be careful not to splinter the shell in your hand or else the razor

▲ ▶ Salt and spear are two methods by which razors can be extracted. Salt (above) sprinkled around the key-hole shaped entrance to the burrow sometimes succeeds in irritating the razor so that the tip of its shell appears.

If you can't see the shell then try a spear (right), pushed down the burrow and into the shell.

will live up to its name and may cut you.

Small razors of about 3in (8cm) are preferred for shore fishing as they fit a size 1 hook perfectly and can be threaded singly or in twos or threes on to the hook and snood like worms.

Large adult squat razors of 5-6in (13-15cm) – which resemble the old cut-throat razor – live deep in the sand. They are hard to dig up and often too big and yellowy for anything other than bass. However, you can cut them into small pill-shaped pieces and use them to tip lugworms.

▼ Remove the flesh from the shell in one piece. Thread it on to the line and up the snood in the same way that you would put a worm on.

Frozen razors are a fair substitute for fresh bait but need to be blanched in their shells before freezing to prevent them from going mushy. Scald the razors in boiling water, wrap them a dozen a time in cling film or foil and freeze.

Power struggle

look for spurts of water

grip the razorfish firmly until it relaxes its foot

muscular foot

When removing a razor by hand, don't take it on at a tug o' war – your bait will escape. Instead, grip the razor in thumb and forefinger and hold until it relaxes its foot.

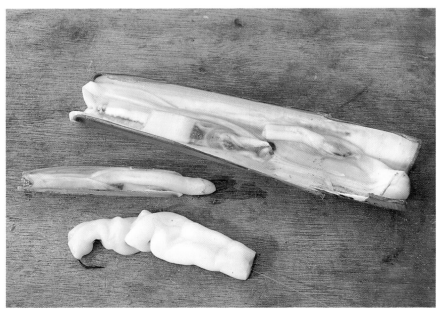

Mussels

Every bait has its day and on the right one mussels can be deadly. Angling journalist Bob Gledhill tells you all about them.

Compared with such baits as peeler crabs, lugworms and ragworms, mussels are extremely easy to find and cheap to buy. Most visitors to the seashore have seen clumps of bluish brown common mussels (*Mytilus edulis*) often forming a dark line along the low water mark. This bivalve mollusc is widespread around the British Isles and large numbers can usually be collected without too much trouble at low tide. If you can't find any along the seashore then try a fishmonger – mussels can usually be bought pretty cheaply.

▼ *At low tide this mussel bed provides a good supply of bait. At high tide it offers a feeding ground for many fish and may be worth a try – especially after a storm.*

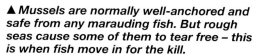

Tip Cool it

Prevent soft mussel flesh from flying off when casting by freezing baits on to hooks (tied to hooklengths) at home.

Carry your baits in a thermos flask and take them out as you need them. They thaw after two or three minutes in the sea.

▲ *Mussels are normally well-anchored and safe from any marauding fish. But rough seas cause some of them to tear free – this is when fish move in for the kill.*

Pick your own

If you want to collect your own, look for them on the coast wherever there is something for them to cling to.

Likely places include rocks, harbour walls, outfall pipes, breakwaters and pier stanchions. Sometimes they form large colonies on estuary mudflats. Hair-like threads (called byssus) grip rocks, stones and weed and intertwine to form a tenacious mat which resists the powerful ripping action of the tide.

Big ones are best – the meat is soft, succulent and more plentiful than in the smaller ones. The biggest are usually found well down the low tide line. Pulling them off can be quite hard on the hands so it is a good idea to wear gloves.

Keeping them alive

Mussels can be kept alive for up to a week if stored at the bottom of the fridge wrapped in a towel dampened with sea water. If you haven't any sea water handy, dampen the towel with fresh water rather than putting them straight into the fridge (which dries them out).

For longer periods it is necessary to immerse them in sea water. Keep a close watch on them, removing dead ones immediately so they don't contaminate and kill the rest. You can tell when a mussel is dead because the normally closed shell opens wide and doesn't shut when the mussel is handled. Change the water once a day or at least top it up from a bottle of clean sea water. Agitating it occasionally helps to keep oxygen levels up but ideally you should use an aerator.

Removing them

Extracting mussels from their shells is not

Taking mussels from a shell

1. Use a fairly sharp knife with a short blade and a rounded end. Clean away the 'beard' from around the edge.

2. Insert the tip of the blade into the middle of the join. Don't let the knife slip and cut your hand.

3. Wiggle the blade all around the join until you can prise it open. Then scoop the flesh out.

▲ *A succulent mussel and worm cocktail makes a tasty mouthful for big shore and boat cod. Wrap shirring elastic around the mussel to keep it on the hook when casting.*

easy. When disturbed, these bivalves use strong muscles to clamp the two halves of their shell firmly together.

Don't smash the mollusc with a hammer or rock – this merely fragments the shell and spoils the bait and you may end up with an eyeful of gunge. Boiling and even blanching them causes the shells to open but unfortunately destroys the bait's appeal (it seems that fish don't appreciate *moules marinières* even if we do).

The trick is to prise them apart with a knife that has been specially ground down for the job. (If you use a normal – long-bladed – knife it may slip off the shell and cut you badly.) Once you have acquired the knack it is possible to shell three or four in a minute.

Storing mussel meat

You can avoid the messy business of having to shell mussels while fishing by preparing them a day before your trip. Keep them in the fridge in a screw-top jar (such as an empty jam jar).

Mussels are a bait that freeze well. Thirty or forty in a freezer bag should be enough – even if sport is more hectic than usual. Finally, a word of warning – don't be tempted to eat mussels you have collected yourself: they are probably not fit for human consumption.

▼ *Many cod like this are taken from the weedy, rocky shores of the north-east on mussel. But the bait also works in other areas for species such as whiting, pouting, dabs and plaice too. Your choice of hook size should depend on the species you are after.*

Cockles

Like many shellfish baits, cockles are not a force on their own but when used in a cocktail they add extra appeal to other baits.

U sed by themselves cockles are good for catching dabs and wrasse, but they mainly attract smaller species such as pouting and rockling which are not the major quarry of the sea angler. They are far more successful as a secondary bait for tipping other baits. The exception to this is during or just after a strong gale, when the cockles in their thousands are dislodged from the shallow sandy burrows in which they live. In these conditions all sorts of fish home in to feed on the cockles – and other shellfish too. At this time they make an excellent codling and whiting bait when fished from the shore. So if you are brave enough to face the elements you could be on for a good catch.

Collecting them

There are several varieties of cockle around the British Isles but the commonest one is the smallest, smooth-shelled variety *Cerastoderma edule*. There is a much larger spiny-shelled cockle (*Acanthocardia echinata*) with a bright red fleshy foot. It is an equally good bait but is mainly found in the

▲ *In some area of Wales cockle beds are so dense that you can use a rake to collect them.*

▼ *To what extent cockles form part of a fish's diet is not clear, but after a storm fish feast on them.*

south and south-west of England.

Habitat Cockles burrow into the sand and live just a few inches beneath the surface. The densest concentrations are found in wide estuaries and sheltered bays where the waves are not fierce enough to scour the cockles out of their burrows. They are distributed all around the British Isles. Local knowledge is the best guide to where to look – so ask in tackle shops.

The simplest way to gather them is to walk along the low water mark. Cockles are sensitive to vibrations and snap shut at the slightest sign of danger. As the shell snaps shut it sends up a little jet of water. So as you stroll along the beach keep a lookout for spurts of water as the cockles feel your footsteps approaching.

The tines of a garden hand-fork are ideal for removing the cockles from their burrows.

If you can't dig them you can buy fresh cockles from a good fishmonger. Do not use any that have been processed in any way, though. They have to be fresh.

Preparation and use

To remove cockles from their shells, place two back-to-back so that the bits which stick out and form the hinge are diagonally opposed. (They should fit together snugly like a key in a lock.) Push and twist one of them while holding the other firmly. One of the shells should open.

Cockles keep for up to a week in a cool damp environment, but check them regularly and discard any that have died and opened so they don't contaminate others.

Tip *Beady-eyed flatties*

Cockles are a particularly good bait when boat fishing for flatties such as plaice and flounders. A few coloured beads on the line above the bait appeals to the flatties' inquisitive nature.

If you are going to use cockles by themselves then you need plenty, because they are small. To make the bait smell strong enough to attract the fish, you may need six or seven cockles on the hook.

Thread the cockles on to the hook and up the shank. If you are going to cast far, lash them on with some fine shirring elastic. It is particularly important to lash them on tightly when fishing for wrasse. These fish tear at a bait savagely and just one or two plucks can strip a soft bait like cockle from the hook before you have time to hit the fish.

▼ *Whiting aren't fussy when it comes to bait – they'll take almost anything – but if the fish are really feeding then why not take advantage of readily available shellfish like cockles?*

For boat fishing it is useful to have a supply already shelled just in case the fishing gets hectic – as it can when a shoal of whiting or codling swims by.

Tip *Cocktails*

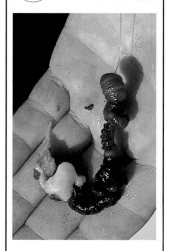

Cockles are often seen as the hook-tip extra to a lugworm. Why lug tipped with a cockle should be more effective than either lug or cockle on its own is a mystery, but it certainly works. One cockle on the point should stay on during the cast.

Limpets and slipper limpets

Don't ignore the baits you can find for free on the shore, says Mick Toomer. Common and slipper limpets are there for the taking.

▲ A colony of common limpets clamped down tight. Because they are easy to collect there is a temptation to gather more than you need.

It's a good idea to use first any damaged limpets you find. They are easier to get into than perfect ones.

Limpets and slipper limpets are often overlooked as a potential bait by serious anglers. But because they are easy to gather, they are a firm favourite with the more casual holiday angler.

Choice of two

The largest of Britain's native species, and the most often used by anglers, is the common limpet. It is 5cm (2in) or more across and found in colonies in rock pools and on rocky shores. A tough bait with a rubbery texture, it stays on the hook well.

The round-backed slipper limpet, more correctly known as the American slipper limpet, is not native to Britain but was accidentally introduced among bargeloads of gravel. Now becoming widespread, it is

▶ If you can't use the limpets you have gathered, roll them in salt and freeze, or cover in wet seaweed while they are still in the shell to keep for several days.

common along the south and east coasts of England and also in south-west Ireland.

Slipper limpets are often found attached to the top of one of their fellows, sometimes forming chains of ten or more. They are considered a serious pest on oyster beds. Reaching a very reasonable size, often more than 4 by 2.5cm (1¾ by 1in), they are an attractive bait.

Movable feast
Sometimes the stones or seaweed the limpets cling to are loosened in gales. They then become dislodged by pounding surf near the shoreline and become part of the natural food supply – so if you use them after a storm they can be a successful bait.

Flounders and other flatfish will already have tapped in and turned on to the fresh feast rolling about near the shore, so if you find any loose slippers try them. But don't cast too far out since the fish may be feeding close in where the limpets have been dislodged.

When using limpets, and especially when fishing over the low water period, there is

▲ *Emerging from the briny like a patterned missile, this ballan wrasse betrays a taste for a limpet and lugworm cocktail.*

often no need to gather a large supply of bait. Another limpet can easily be removed when a bait change becomes necessary. Don't gather more bait than you need.

Lug and limpet
Both types of limpet can be used as bait for small and medium sized fish. For bigger fish such as whiting, bass and cod a clump of limpets is better. Limpet alone provides the most natural and easily obtained bait when rock fishing for wrasse – but they are more usually combined in a cocktail.

Slipper limpets are generally considered a softer, better bait than commons, but both are effective as part of a cocktail. Lugworm is usually the other ingredient – and is accepted by many species of fish.

The tackle for fishing with limpets depends more on the terrain than the bait. As a rule, limpets attract the smaller species, so hooks needn't be too big. Many anglers find a size 2 or 1 covers most situations. One exception is when fishing for cod using limpet to tip a lugworm bait. In this case use a 3/0, 4/0 or 5/0.

Cocktail time

lugworm threaded along shank of hook

soft, fleshy tapered end

size 2 hook

tough foot of limpet

slipper limpet

limpet hooked twice through soft tapered end and again through foot

▲ *Use a blunt knife to take limpets out of the shell. The scooped-out slipper (above) can be coupled with a juicy lugworm to create a delicious cocktail bait (left) for flatfish and codling.*

Mackerel as bait

It's a potent fish attractor and fairly easy to get hold of. When fresh, mackerel is one of the sea angler's most successful baits – oily and enticing to all manner of sea fish.

Sharp reminder

Use a sharp knife and prepare baits on a flat surface – a bait board kept clean so you can see what you're doing. Always cut away from you and stow blades safely on deck.

▼ Feathering for mackerel – the fast-moving fish are drawn to the hooks and feathers which give off air bubbles as they descend – and are instantly caught. Watch out for sharp hooks swinging on board.

To stock up with enough mackerel for a good day's sea fishing, the usual technique in summer is to drop a weighted trace carrying six hooks – each whipped with coloured feathers – over the side of a boat. If you manage to locate the shoals then you're soon hauling in strings of fish – a ready supply of bait full of flavour. Feathering from harbours and shore can also be fruitful.

Fresh fish is definitely best but if you can't get it, mackerel frozen soon after catching can make reasonable bait. Shop-bought or frozen mackerel generally lacks a firm texture and has less juicy fish appeal.

Mackerel on board

Once you have your mackerel there are several effective ways of presenting it.

Flappers Boat anglers after conger rely heavily on a 'flapper' bait to get into contact. Push the point of a knife through the mackerel's body just behind the top of the head. Then, using the backbone as a guide, slice the blade along each side until it emerges at the tail. Cut through and remove the backbone as near to the head as you can. This leaves you with a soft bait consisting of two succulent flaps of flesh, naturally attached to the mackerel's head.

Push the point of a size 9/0 or 10/0 hook through the mouth and upwards through the head, so that you get a secure hold in the toughest part of the bait.

Inverted flapper Alternatively, sever the baitfish's head and tail and remove the backbone, leaving two flapping sides connected by the tail section. Hook it first through the tail and a second time further down the body.

Fillet o' fish A side of mackerel cleanly removed is an excellent bait for specimen pollack and coalfish at wreck sites. Hook through the pointed end of the fillet for a

▲ Small pieces of mackerel cut crosswise from a side are used to catch red and black bream, whiting and pouting. Fresh mackerel flesh stays firm for about six hours and can be cut precisely with a sharp, thin-bladed knife.

Preparing a side of mackerel

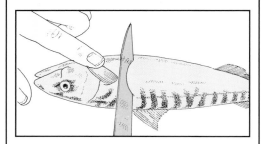

1. Put the fish on a stable surface and hold its head before making a cut with a filleting knife behind the pectoral fin.

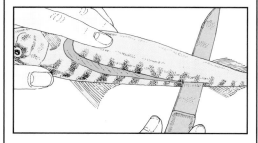

2. Work the sharp knife down the fish with a slicing action. Use the backbone as a guide to run the blade along to the tail.

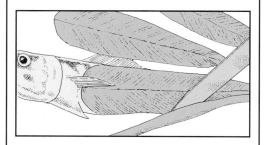

3. Turn the fish over and repeat. A strip of white belly remains which wriggles well on the hook – a perfect turbot bait.

▲ *This pair of anglers are well pleased with their splendid plaice.*
Even bottom fish, which don't feed naturally on mackerel, don't seem to be able to resist the blood and oil-rich flesh of a well presented mackerel bait.

natural swimming action.

Back-to-back baits are particularly successful when you're after turbot, blonde and thornback rays and brill.

Using the tip of a sharp knife, lightly score the inside flesh down the entire length of a side of mackerel. Then fold the fillet shiny side inwards, leaving the fleshy side outwards. A back-to-back bait is very effective when predators are reluctant to feed.

Landlubberly morsels

Shore anglers also make great use of mackerel bait. Flapper style is best for conger as it stays securely on the hook during the rigours of casting.

Long, thin strips can be legered singly or in association with marine worms, squid or crab to make an attractive cocktail. Or fish them on a sliding float rig for bass, pollack, coalfish, garfish, mullet and even other mackerel.

Mullet method Fish for mullet with a flake of mackerel flesh on a small hook, presented in a cloud of pulped mackerel groundbait.

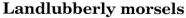

◄ *Head and tail-end mackerel flappers – this light shark rig combines a size 8/0 hook with a long 150lb (68kg) mono trace.*
Whole flappers are also effective baits for conger, skate and tope.

Sandeels

Although some anglers still regard them as a specialist commodity rather than an all-round bait, sandeels have gained popularity in recent years, says top sea matchman Chris Clark.

There are two types of sandeels, the lesser and the greater (launce). The lesser reaches 20cm (8in) in length while the greater can grow to 32cm (13in).

In most boat fishing situations using a live sandeel is often more effective than fishing with its frozen counterpart. When shore fishing, though, you can't cast effectively with a live sandeel.

Few tackle shops have the facilities to keep live sandeels, so blast-frozen ones are a must if you're not in a position to collect your own.

Finding sandeels

Collecting sandeels is quite easy, given the right tidal and weather conditions. Sandbars exposed during spring low tides often have large numbers in the summer.

As the tide ebbs away, the sandeels bury themselves a few inches under the moist sand. Dig them up with a fork or a rake, and put them (no more than 30 or so) in a bucket of sea water with a portable aerator.

▼ A tried and tested bait for pollack and bass, sandeels also tempt specimen brill such as this one.

Though live sandeels are more effective, frozen ones are easier to carry when boat fishing.

Sandeels die quickly if they are not kept in well-oxygenated water.

As you fork over the top few inches of sand, look for flashes of silver: you have to be extremely quick when grabbing sandeels because they try to bury themselves as fast as you uncover them.

Storing live sandeels for any length of time is difficult. Ideally you need a large tank filled with water and an aerator – both placed in a fridge to keep the water as cold as possible. If the water temperature starts to rise, bacteria multiply rapidly, killing the fish.

Storing sandeels

Whether you catch sandeels or buy some from a fishmonger, you can freeze them quite successfully. First kill the eels by hit-

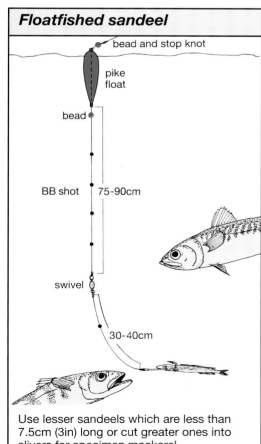

Floatfished sandeel

bead and stop knot

pike float

bead

BB shot   75-90cm

swivel

30-40cm

Use lesser sandeels which are less than 7.5cm (3in) long or cut greater ones into slivers for specimen mackerel.

◄ *Sandeels swim in huge shoals. When threatened by predators such as pollack, coalfish, bass, dabs, brill and plaice, these wriggling, silver-sided creatures burrow into the sandy sea, making a fast, headlong getaway.*

ting them over the head with a small stick (or priest). Rinse them in fresh water and dry them before laying them *individually* on dry newspaper. Place them in the freezer. Once frozen, wrap them in plastic and pack as required.

Using sandeels

Presentation is vital when fishing with dead sandeels. If you're legering on the beach for rays or doggies with lesser sandeels, pass the hook into the mouth and then down the entire length of the eel's body so that the hookpoint emerges about 12mm (½in) from the tail. Wrap the sandeel with shirring elastic to secure it.

Cut greater sandeels into chunks and tie on to the hook with knitting or shirring elastic. Fillet the larger ones.

For float fishing pass the point of a size 2 hook through the eyes and then about 12mm (½in) farther down, just past the gill cover. It's essential to make sure the hookpoint isn't masked. Impale a sandeel not longer than 7.5cm (3in) on a small hook.

▲ ► *This is a popular way of hooking a sandeel for boat fishing (above). It allows the tail to sway enticingly in the current. Catch greater sandeels (right) by using a string of feathers, bounced off the bottom.*

Artificial sandeels

Artificial sandeels are one of the most successful lures of all time. The seductive, waggling tail has been the downfall of countless fish. Mike Thrussell explains.

Artificial sandeels are made of rubber and come in a fantastic range of different colours and sizes.

Colour and class

Both bass and pollack take artificial eels at night, picking up on the vibrations set up by

▲ Live sandeels are hard to beat when boat-fishing (especially drifting) for bass. But artificials are more readily available and are easier to cast from shore or boat.

the waggling tail. But the colour of the eel is an important but often overlooked part of shore and boat angling. Pollack tend to prefer red and sometimes yellow by day — though their peak feeding time is at dusk when, against all logic, a black eel proves most deadly. Bass prefer a white eel during the day with again a black one at dusk.

Mackerel go for the brighter colours — red, yellow and fluorescent green eels fished from beaches, harbours and off rocky areas. Late evening into night and dawn are again the best times to use eels.

The artificial eel comes ready provided with a hook that is well hidden in the body. This can be replaced with a smaller one when shore-fishing for small pollack, for example. But if you're fishing over a wreck,

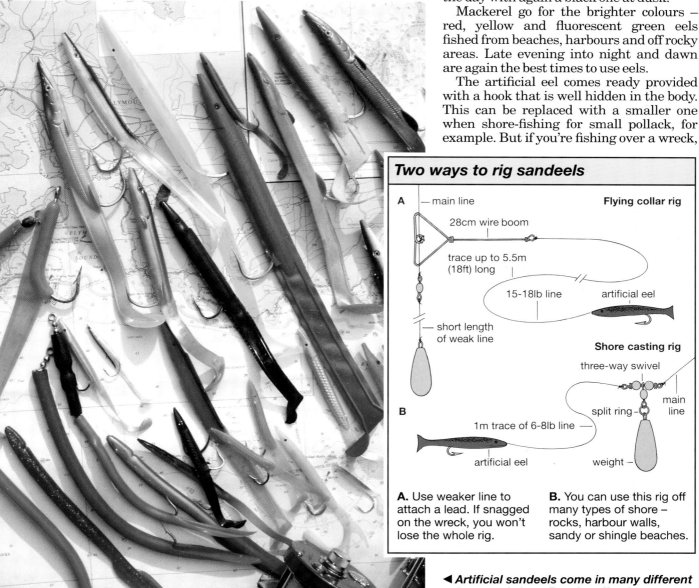

Two ways to rig sandeels

A — main line — **Flying collar rig**
28cm wire boom
trace up to 5.5m (18ft) long
15-18lb line — artificial eel
— short length of weak line

Shore casting rig
three-way swivel
split ring — main line
B 1m trace of 6-8lb line
artificial eel — weight

A. Use weaker line to attach a lead. If snagged on the wreck, you won't lose the whole rig.

B. You can use this rig off many types of shore — rocks, harbour walls, sandy or shingle beaches.

◄ Artificial sandeels come in many different colours and sizes. But the effective waggling tail is the most important feature.

Tip Sizes to suit

Size one artificial eels are 25cm (10in) long.
They represent the offshore launce or
greater sandeel which is common over reefs
and wrecks. Size two, 20cm (8in) long, is
good for bass over inshore rough ground.
The small version (7cm/2¾in long) is ideal for
mackerel, school bass and small pollack
and coalies.

you may want to use a stronger, larger
hook. The rubber body is versatile and can
accommodate different sizes to meet your
needs.

Shore fishing with eels

Artificial eels up to 20cm (8in) or so long can
be used for shore casting for bass and pollack from rock marks facing the open sea,
very rough, boulder-strewn beaches, harbour walls or breakwaters. Try to fish the

▲ This pollack fell for a small, natural-
coloured sandeel fished over a rough,
boulder-strewn mark.

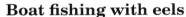

◄ Artificial sandeels fished over old war-
time wrecks often tempt pollack such as
this fine specimen.

eel as close to the sea bed, rocks or weeds as
possible to maximize your catch. Tackle
losses are inevitable, but the fish are there.

If you're after bass, aim to fish near
outflowing freshwater streams, over rough
ground or alongside rocky promontories
where there are small tide races.
Alternatively, simply move a few metres
along the beach with every cast to cover as
much ground as possible.

Boat fishing with eels

Artificial sandeels are also excellent lures
for boat fishing. Trolling a freelined eel 80-
100m (87-110yd) behind a boat to cover
shallow marks usually attracts attention
from bass. The ebb tide is usually the best
time to use this style of fishing, when bass
move back on to the reefs from the beaches.

You can also tempt big pollack and
coalfish by using eels over war-time wrecks.
A flying-collar rig with a long trace is one of
the most popular methods to present the
eel. This long trace is needed to get a proper
action from the lure and, set up this way,
tangles are rare.

Black, red and yellow eels in the longer
sizes (15-25cm/6-10in) are best, but coalfish
in particular are often caught with small,
gaudy fluorescent pink or green eels.

As an alternative you can fish two small
artificial eels above a pirk on very short
hook snoods. This is called killer gear. It is
just jigged up and down close to the bottom
until a fish takes one of the lures.

It is an effective way of taking fish, but is
considered by many to be unsporting.

Making your own pirks

Pirking is a hugely effective way of catching cod, pollack and coalfish, among others, but pirks cost silly money. Mike Millman shows you how to avoid breaking your bank manager's heart by making your own.

▼ *A pollack which found 'killer gear' too much to resist. It was so keen, it missed the pirk in its slashing attack and foul-hooked itself.*

A pirk is a simple lure. All it consists of is a bar of metal with a hook attached, but it has to be heavy enough to get down through the tide to the cod, pollack or other fish. The technique of dropping a pirk to the bottom at speed and jigging it up and down developed in Scandinavia and did not reach Britain until the 1950s.

Pirks make it

By 1970 pirking was established as a superb way to catch cod, particularly at the Gantocks in the Firth of Clyde and several marks in the English Channel. For the first time cod in the 40lb (18kg) class were becoming a feature of boat fishing.

All these fish took professionally made pirks from Norway and Sweden, which were expensive. But dedicated anglers were soon making their own at a fraction of the cost. They used anything bright and heavy enough – such as chrome plated pram or car handles or even just painted bars of metal. Few had the sophisticated shapes of the manufactured lures, but as pirks became more popular in the world of wreck fishing, DIY lures proved just as effective.

Today, the pirk is recognized as a deadly weapon for offshore, deep water wrecking with home-mades outnumbering the shop-bought variety. Perhaps its most successful incarnation is in the form of 'killer gear '– a simple two hook paternoster, with artificial sandeels or muppets on the two snoods, and a pirk (baited or plain) as the weight.

Make a pirk

A DIY pirk can be simply a chromed car door handle with a hole drilled at either end to take split rings – one for the hook, the other for a swivel. However, these tend to be a bit light for deep water work. Perhaps the most common and effective home-made pirks are the lead-filled pram handle type.

The length of handle to use depends on the weight you require. With a bar of 5cm (2in) circumference (it's best to measure round the outside, because wall thickness can vary), an 18cm (7in) length produces a pirk of about 14oz (395g). The same length of 7.5cm (3in) circumference tube produces a 22oz (625g) pirk. The weight of the hook, swivel and split rings is extra.

The cheapness of DIY pirks comes in very handy for fishing over a snaggy, tackle-hungry wreck. And not only that, there's the extra feeling of satisfaction when you catch something on your own creation.

Making a simple but irresistible pirk

Tooled up for a prime pirk

Here's everything you need to make enough pirks for a few wrecking trips. It's essential you have all the gear before you start, especially the protective safety gear – molten lead can be very dangerous if handled carelessly.

1. Eye protector goggles
2. Heavy duty protective gloves
3. Hairdryer to dry the tubing
4. Scrap lead
5. Electric drill
6. Hacksaw
7. Melting jug with pouring lip
8. Camping Gaz stove with stabilizing base
9. Heavy duty vice
10. Lengths of chrome pram handle tubing
11. Heavy-duty split rings, swivels, hooks

1. Clamp the chrome tubing in the vice and cut pirk-size lengths with a hacksaw. About 18cm (7in) is a good attractor size and gives plenty of weight to get through the tide when filled with lead.

2. Squeeze one end of the length of tubing closed in the vice. It is essential you close it completely to stop lead leaking out. Now turn the tubing upright in the vice, ready to pour in the molten lead.

3. Put your scrap lead in the melting jug and heat carefully with a Gaz stove or a blow lamp. You must wear protective goggles and gloves when handling molten lead. Dry the pirk-to-be with the hairdryer – moisture makes the lead spit or even explode from the tube.

4. Pour the molten lead into the dry pirk tubing up to about 2.5cm (1in) from the end and allow to cool. Squeeze the second end closed, drill holes in the ends and add split rings, hook and swivel. You can now decorate the pirk with Flectolite or just leave it plain **(5)**.

Jigging

The jigging of artificial lures to catch predatory fish is a method as old as angling itself. Mike Millman looks at using an old technique with modern lures.

Jigging is a method of catching fish that has been around since man first started using hooks. The word 'jig' simply means jerky motion. In terms of fishing, that refers to any bait or lure that is used in a jerky way – a plain un-baited hook can be a 'jig' if it is made to dance around on the end of the line.

Simple jigs

One of the most basic forms of jig fishing at sea is working a string of feathers. The monofilament trace usually carries three, six or twelve feathered hooks which are lethal for taking mackerel, garfish and small pollack or coalfish.

Although still very effective, the simple team of dyed chicken feathers has now been superseded by the use of man-made materials such as 'Mylar' (braided tinsel) and 'Flectolite' (shiny plastic foil).

The newcomers

The latest variation on this theme has just arrived from the Far East – the oddly named 'shrimp rig'. Odd, because the plastic bodies are in fact shaped like mini-fish, not shrimps. Half the body is luminous, as are the small beads at the head of each lure,

and the tails are made of tinsel.

Another variation of this lure is the 'Hokkai', which also has synthetic feathers in its tail. The effectiveness of this lure has already been established, particularly on large bass, and bigger versions for cod and pollack will doubtless appear soon.

Other newcomers have arrived from America, where lure fishing has always been popular. Most of them are of the lead-head type and have built-in hooks with their points upwards. This makes them much less prone to snagging on weed or on

▲ *These two Jigga lures are being used on short paternosters above a pirk – a set-up similar to 'killer gear'. Jerk them up and down over rough ground and wrecks to provoke cod and pollack into striking them.*

Imported jigs

Recently introduced from the USA are two new lures suitable for jigging.
- **'Ripple Fin'** has two metal barrels mounted on a wire with a spinning blade at one end and a muppet-like rubber frill concealing a treble hook at the other.
- **'Supersquid'** is a muppet type lure with tinsel in the tail. You can add lead to the body.

Key to selection of jigs

1. Two Ripple Fin lures – they can be used as spinners or jigs.
2. Three Supersquid lures – the feathered hooks hang from the tail.
3. Six Porky jigs – leadheaded lures with fluorescent skirts.
4. Three Bonito jigs – more leadheads that fish point-up.

New jigging feathers from the Far East

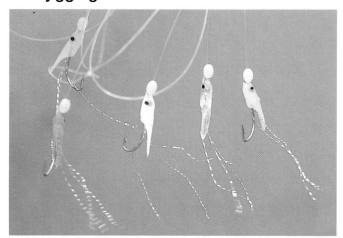

1. Shrimp Rig Strings of five plastic mini-fish with luminous beads and Mylar tinsel tails are mounted on size 4 hooks and 25lb (11.3kg) line. They are absolutely deadly for mackerel and garfish.

2. Hokkai lures Strings of three plastic mini-fish with luminous beads and feather and Mylar tinsel tails are mounted on size 1/0 hooks and 25lb (11.3kg) line. They catch when other types of feathers don't.

rough bottoms and also gives them a very attractive nose-down action.

Leadhead lures

One of the most popular of these self-weighted lures is the Porky jig which features a fluorescent skirt of feathers and Mylar tinsel. The built-in hooks vary in size from 1s to 2/0s according to whether they are 15, 25 or 40 gramme size.

Porky jigs are at their most effective when used on light spinning tackle and retrieved in a jerky sink-and-draw type action, which bass and pollack find irresistible. They can also be used as a team – two or three lures fished on short paternosters above a small pirk.

The Bonito is a similar but less sophisticated lure. Also a leadhead type, this has coloured feathers with a fish shaped white nylon covering and red jewelled eyes.

Another variation on the leadhead concept is the Jigga lure. This is unusual because the line is threaded through the head itself, rather than attached to an eyelet – this means that you can select the size and type of hook used with it. The feathered bodies have a plastic outer layer and the pointed heads are inset with 'Flectolite'.

Tip Spice up your jigs

There are times when even the best jigs won't catch. Try livening them up by baiting with thin strips of fish or squid – this added scent trail often does the trick. Be careful not to overdo it, though – you don't want to ruin the action of the lure, which is the jig's main attraction.

▶ *Jigging one of the sophisticated new lures over rough ground or wrecks is a good way to make contact with big pollack, like this fine 18½lb (8.39kg) specimen.*

Fishing with feathers

Feathers have tickled the fancy of many a fish. Mike Millman reveals how to fish 'holiday feathers' for mackerel.

As long ago as the 17th century, feathers were being used as a means of catching fish in the sea. Today strings of feathers which have either six or twelve hooks – tied to short snoods (hooklengths) – are made by the tens of thousands. They are used principally to catch mackerel. It is likely that the fish are fooled into thinking a string of feathers is a shoal of small prey.

The most commonly used feathers are often called 'holiday feathers' – because of their wide use during short summer fishing trips for mackerel. 'Holiday feathers' consist of a string of six plain or multi-coloured feathers whipped to size 1/0 hooks.

A good trim

There is often too much feather on a commercial hook. A well-used set of mackerel feathers – in which the feather content has been worn down to little more than a wisp – seems to catch a lot more fish. Therefore a good trim with a pair of scissors dramatically improves a string's catching potential.

A string of feathers, with a weight, simply dropped from the side of the boat *will* catch. But your chances of success are much

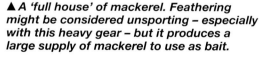

▲ *A 'full house' of mackerel. Feathering might be considered unsporting – especially with this heavy gear – but it produces a large supply of mackerel to use as bait.*

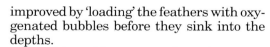

◄ *Feathers also catch cod – try three feathers on a string, fished deep. Mike recommends catching bottom-feeding cod on size 8/0 feathered hooks, with added squid.*

improved by 'loading' the feathers with oxygenated bubbles before they sink into the depths.

To achieve this you cast the string out so that the weight strikes the water hard, creating the necessary disturbance. In calm conditions you can see the value of this as the feathers bubble while they sink. Mackerel, which have an incredible turn of speed, often stop the string as it plummets down.

Suddenly, everything goes light for a second or two, then you feel the weight as you put the reel into gear and the rod takes the burden. Six good mackerel on at the same

'Holiday feathers'

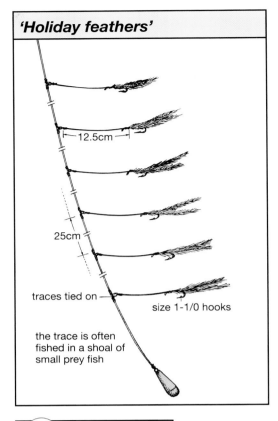

12.5cm

25cm

traces tied on

size 1-1/0 hooks

the trace is often fished in a shoal of small prey fish

▲ *A string of mackerel feathers with size 1/0 hooks. The bold colours readily take the fancy of hungry fish.*

(Tip) Fishy tails

When fishing larger feathers over rough ground try adding king ragworm to the hooks. This ensures that there is plenty of tail to wave attractively as the feathers are worked upwards.

▼ *Larger, multi-coloured feathers appeal to cod and, when fished around wrecks are excellent for pollack and coalfish.*

time – all of them trying to dash about – puts quite a strain on the tackle. A 'full house' – every hook with a taker – can take some bringing up if the mackerel are large.

Experienced boat anglers only use 'holiday feathers' when they are catching large numbers of mackerel for bait – it is considered 'unsporting' in normal angling terms. A string of feathers can also be used to catch mackerel very effectively from the shore, as long as there is a reasonable depth of water. Steep shelving beaches are ideal for this type of fishing.

Big predators

Big, fast predators like pollack and coalfish can be caught on strings of feathers close to the sea bottom. These species are fooled by a size 6/0 hook heavily laden with different coloured feathers which slick down when wet. These are whipped to the shank of the hook with light monofilament and treated to a coating of instant glue. A 5cm (2in) length of bicycle valve tubing worked down over the whipped shank protects the binding and adds to the attractiveness of the offering. This type of feathered hook is usually fished on a long flowing trace called the Flying Collar (see pages 67-70).

Mike once fished a wreck with a three hook rig and 10/0 hooks. At 69m (228ft), three ling hit – a catch of 47kg (105lb)!

'Cornish wreckers'

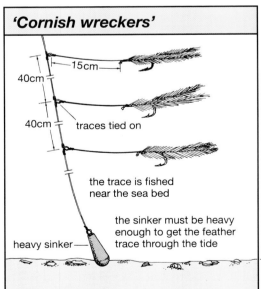

15cm

40cm

40cm

traces tied on

the trace is fished near the sea bed

the sinker must be heavy enough to get the feather trace through the tide

heavy sinker

When fishing for pollack and coalfish a rig with just three feathers and size 6/0 hooks is effective. This is called a 'Cornish wrecker' because the trace is popular for wreck fishing off Cornwall. The trace is carried down by a heavy weight at high speed. If the hooks are not taken on the way down, the trace is jigged back from the bottom.

Flatfish spoons

A baited spoon is probably the most efficient way of catching flatties. Rod Worrall, flatfish spoon expert, explains its deadly effect.

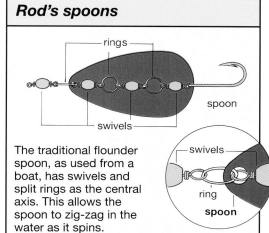

Baited flounder spoons are proven flatfish catchers. You can buy them in a wide variety of shapes, colours and sizes, but the successful ones all have a similar basic design. Use a well designed spoon correctly, and you'll notice such an increase in your flatfish catches, you'll wonder why you haven't used them before.

John Garrad, who wrote under the pen-name *Seangler*, developed the flounder spoon in its current form between the World Wars. His design and techniques remain valid today.

The right stuff

Garrad's design is most useful from a boat as it has little built-in casting weight. The blade is 8-10cm (3-4in) long, usually curved, with a small hole at one end. A split ring through the hole joins the blade to an axis made of swivels and split rings. The blade

Rod's spoons

The traditional flounder spoon, as used from a boat, has swivels and split rings as the central axis. This allows the spoon to zig-zag in the water as it spins.

Rod Worrall makes his own flounder spoons (below) from tablespoons, bits of plastic, wire and beads. These barspoons have plenty of weight incorporated in the central bar for casting from the shore. Note the bend in the hook shank which increases the hooking power of the spoons.

▲ *The sharp end of a baited spoon – the hook. It trails 10cm (4in) behind the spoon, often with attractor beads on the snood, and can be baited with almost anything.*

spins around the axis and the hook is attached to the bottom end swivel.

This produces a sort of barspoon with a flexible central axis. This means that, in addition to the blade rotating about the axis, the whole spoon zig-zags through the water. These spoons are highly effective trolled with the tide behind a slowly moving boat.

From the shore you need a design which incorporates weight to allow you to cast a decent distance. The blade is attached as before, near the top of the axis, but this time the axis is made of wire, on to which you thread a number of pierced bullet or barrel weights. Again the with-the-tide retrieve is essential for success.

This flatfish barspoon is much more rigid than the traditional spoon – which means it doesn't have the attractive zig-zag action. However, if you use light wire as the axis and bend it slightly, you can reproduce this action without sacrificing casting distance. Another solution is to use heavy mono

Tip Colour counts

Rod Worrall takes three different colours of spoon when he goes fishing. He has models with silver, white and red blades.

The white and silver bladed versions are best on dull days when the water is murky. The red version is essential for fishing in clear water on bright days.

▼ *A spoon-caught plaice. This type of baited spoon isn't free to rotate in the same way as the true flounder spoon. However, it is popular for plaice fishing from a boat and can sometimes be useful.*

Attractive attractors

These attractor spoons can entice all kinds of fish to your baited hook but a proper flounder spoon is essential to maximise your flatty catching power.

instead of wire.

A hooklength of about 8cm (3in) tied to the end of the axis improves hooking potential. You can also add attractor beads to the axis and to the hooklength for extra flatfish pulling power. Whatever the design, it is vital that neither the axis nor the bait revolves, as this greatly reduces the effectiveness of the spoon.

There are other types of attractor spoons which anglers use with some success. One common type simply wobbles without rotating, and may help attract a fish's attention to the bait. Other spinning attractors have smaller blades than flatfish spoons, but while these work for other species, they do not tempt flatties.

Why and how

Flatfish spoons are selective for flatfish – the reasons for this can only be answered by the flatties themselves. But it seems to be linked to their bottom-dwelling life-style.

Flatfish always swim and feed moving downtide – with the current or tide – usually in small shoals. This means you must work the spoon with the tide or your catches fall off drastically.

Competition for food within a shoal seems to be quite intense and this may be why spoons work so well. The spoon is supposed to look like a small flatty. As it passes through a shoal, the baited hook makes it look as though it's carrying some food which the other flatties try to steal.

This explains the ferocious bites that you get and may also account for the times a second flatty accompanies the hooked one to the shore or boat. Other anglers believe a spoon simply arouses the fish's interest and when it gets close enough, it sees and smells the bait – and takes it.

Whatever the reason, spoons do work. Just make sure the spoons you make or buy work in the right way. Use them well and you'll add a new dimension to your fishing – and catch a lot more flatfish.

Plug fishing for bass and pollack

Plugs are familiar equipment to pike anglers – but they also make lethal lures for many favourite sea fish.

It's a great moment when some unseen saltwater predator lunges at your plug. On light tackle you face quite a battle – especially when the fish realizes it's been fooled. Bass and pollack are just two of the predatory sea species that fall for the attraction of this type of lure.

Plugs are artificial lures designed to look something like fish. They used to be made from wood, but today moulded plastic is the main type of material used.

Stricken fish
Not only does a plug look like a fish – it also swims like a sick or injured fish. As you retrieve it slowly, it begins to wobble in a stricken way. Small wonder bass just can't resist them.

Plugs were invented in Finland, as a coarse fishing method for pike, and spread to America where they are favourite lures for black bass fishing. They are now a popular lure in Britain. The good thing is that you can use your coarse fishing plugs at sea.

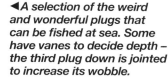

Tip *Losing plugs*

If you are fishing around reefs, remember that there is a fine line between spinning close enough to the rocks to tempt fish such as pollack, and getting snagged and losing your plug. Plugs are expensive.

Plug choices
If you already have a selection of pike plugs you've got a head start in sea plugging. Virtually all of your existing plugs can be used when shore fishing or when boat fishing.

They are generally found in three types: shallow diving floaters, deep diving floaters (that dive steeply when you retrieve them) and sinkers (which sink until you retrieve them). Many are single piece designs but some are jointed to make them wobble more. The most versatile designs are those which have an adjustable vane in the 'mouth' to alter the depth of the dive.

Beating the bass
Bass are a popular fish because they are hard fighters and make good eating. But don't forget that bass are under pressure from over-fishing. Return all small ones.

Shore thing Spinning from rocks with plugs for bass is good sport. When the bass change levels to follow food fish shoals, you can change depth as well by changing your

◄ *A selection of the weird and wonderful plugs that can be fished at sea. Some have vanes to decide depth – the third plug down is jointed to increase its wobble.*

▼ *These two anglers are fishing plugs off the rocks in a Devon estuary. Surf like this brings bass close to the shore.*

the deeper water down below.

Dawn and dusk are good times for bass. Work a standard Rapala or Abu Killer and you may be surprised at how close to the shore you find them.

Plugging pollack

Pollack have a go at virtually every type of lure – plastic eels and plugs seem to be the best when you are fishing close to the shore. Again, light tackle with a 7ft (2.1m) rod and a small multiplier or tough fixed-spool reel makes the fishing very sporting.

Plugs can also be used for wreck fishing from a boat. Cast uptide of the wreck, allowing time for the lures to work at the correct depth. Pollack often move closer to the surface at dusk, and they may even jump right out when hitting a surface-fished plug.

The fish then crash-dives with its 'prey' and fights all the way down. Don't panic when this happens. After that initial dive its subsequent struggles are seldom as determined. Other hard fighting fish such as coalfish also take plugs, while mackerel may snap at smaller lures.

Deep or shallow plugs?

plug

very deep

fairly deep

medium depth

shallow

surface

The position of the vane, or 'lip', of the plug determines the depth it will dive to on retrieval.

▲ *This pollack was caught close to the shore on a small, shallow diving plug. Plugs vary from 2.5cm (1in) long midgets to 30cm (12in).*

plug or by resetting the adjustable vane, if it features one. Simply reset the vane higher or lower.

Plugs are useful in the openings to wide, rocky gullies where the water is choppy. Big bass (and pollack) wait in these waters for baitfish caught in the breaking water. They have to strike quickly at passing fish in such conditions and this means they have little time to discover the plug is not what it seems.

Also try using plugs over rocky sea beds, clear water reefs and around piers. Cast your lure out some way and bring it back as if the lure is slipping from boulder to boulder or pile to pile. Try watching how fish behave in such waters and see if you can get the plug to mimic this.

Boat fishing Bass fishing is partly a question of tide, time and place. Plug fishing from a drifting boat is very effective, provided you know where the fish are. Using plugs with movable vanes means you can find the bass near the surface – preying on schools of sandeel – or in

▶ *This bass has fallen to a jointed plug – one called a sliver. It is a good imitation of a sandeel.*

Muppet fishing

Artificial squid with sci-fi looks, muppets are powerful lures – top boat angler Norman Message explains how to harness their attractive qualities in the water.

There's no accounting for tastes – especially as far as sea fish are concerned. You can understand how a trout might fall for an exquisite Mallard and Claret, Yellow Humpy or aptly named Irresistible. In fact, it's difficult to see how a discerning trout could resist these delicate artificial flies which imitate insect prey with such finesse.

But by comparison it's hard to imagine the fishy appeal of the boldly coloured, flaccid, faintly comical lures known as muppets. Vaguely squidish in appearance, they don't mimic directly any particular baitfish. However, their effectiveness as sea fishing lures is undoubted – guaranteeing the zany muppet a place somewhere in every sea angler's tackle box.

Muppet on a string

Plastic muppets come in several colours and in three sizes – small, medium and large. They are a must as an extra lure and are used in many combinations for shallow and deep-water fishing.

Pollack, coalfish and cod are rather partial to muppets, and bass, mackerel, ling, pout and many other fish go for them if used with sea baits or pirks.

▼ *It looks as though this fish might have a soft spot for pink blancmange – but in fact it has succumbed to a large and brightly coloured muppet.*

Small muppets are used when boat fishing for pollack, coalfish and bass. They are successful fished in a three-hook combination on 50lb (22.7kg) line, with a lead weight or pirk attached at the bottom. The best hook sizes for these rigs are between 2/0 and 4/0. A good colour for the muppets is fluorescent light green when you're after pollack, and dark red, blue or black for bass and coalfish.

Medium and large muppets are ideal for pollack and cod if you drape them over a large treble 8/0 or 10/0 hook fixed to a large pirk. Red and pink lures on a pirk account for many cod and pollack catches from wrecks or rocky ground. In deeper water, where there is not much light, the colour of the muppet is not as important as the action and shape of the lure as you jig it up and down to attract fish.

▲ *The eyes have it – this platoon of beady-eyed muppets is just the sort of colourful selection that seems to tempt fish. Combined with baits and pirks they take a wide variety of species.*

▲ *A recipe for successful fishing at anchor: take one muppet, garnish with fresh mackerel strip, and then present the cocktail on a leger rig with French boom.*

▼ *A big cod taken on a pirk and red muppet. Fishing over wrecks or rocky ground with this combination produces some good catches of pollack and cod.*

Insurance policy

When used at anchor, muppets left to flutter in the tide take a number of species. The best method is to team them with mackerel, lug, rag or even squid baits on a French boom which is fixed on about 1m (3ft) above a leger rig. The trace line can vary from 1-1.8m (3-6ft) depending on the strength of the tide – use longer traces when the tide is strong. This technique is doubly effective because the muppets continue to attract fish even if the baits have

been pinched off the hooks. Pollack, bass, bream, pout and whiting all fall to this particular method.

When fishing three muppets on a three-hook dropper rig, try different colours and find out which one is most effective on the day. Once you know, you can put down all three of the same colour and improve your catch rate. It is handy to make up at least two or three rigs of each colour beforehand, ready for use when needed.

Fit the large muppets to your pirks on the day. To do this make a cut in the top of the muppet's head and push through the treble so the eye protrudes and the hook is covered by the muppet skirt. You can then attach the eye to a split ring on a pirk.

Keep your large muppets in good condition by packing them away in separate compartments or plastic bags in your tackle box until you need them.

Jigging with jellies

A recent American import, 'Mister Twister' and other jelly lures are catching on over here. Top boat angler Mike Millman explains how to get the best from them.

Attach the line to the hook before threading the jelly on. It is important to cover the hook eye completely with the jelly, as shown here. Leave a long tail that will flutter and twist enticingly in the water.

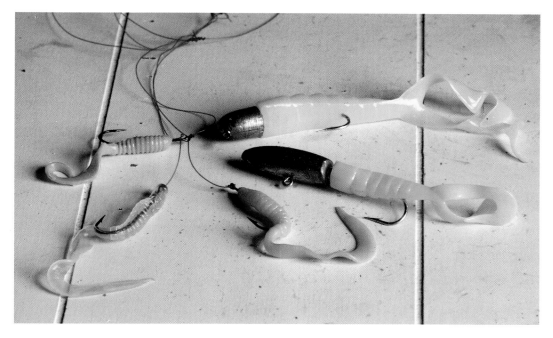

▲ *Three unweighted jellies, with two leadheaded Mister Twister twin tail jelly lures.*

▼ *With such exotic names as Firetail, Hot Volcano, Neon Grape and Bruised Banana, this is a small selection of the thousands of types of jellies available. Many more are to be had in the USA.*

Anglers keen to catch fast predatory species on the lightest tackle are proving that colourful 'jelly lures' offer advantages over more common artificial baits. Mostly innovations from America, they can be just as successful this side of the Atlantic for bass and pollack, as they are for species in sun-drenched blue water.

Soft and squidgy

Jelly lures come in every imaginable colour and a never-ending array of twists and shapes, which glitter and flutter invitingly as they are worked through the water. As the name implies, the body is made of very soft oily plastic, which feels almost alive when handled. Wriggly, twisty, flexible and mobile, it is easy to see why they appeal to fish which expect their meals to move.

Some jelly lures have the sophistication of a weighted head, often with bright eyes painted on – but whether these increase catchability is unproven. They certainly have the kind of look that increases the confidence of the angler casting it out.

Leadheads

Using jelly lures with built-in lead heads has several important advantages over other artificials. There is no need for up-trace leads or booms, so they rarely tangle; because the hook points upwards it is much less prone to snagging; and most fish are hooked in the more secure top jaw.

Mister Twister – perhaps the best known type – is among the top three lures in the world, and has an incredible track record throughout America, Australia and the Caribbean. Indeed, wherever there are hungry fish, in both salt and freshwater, this lure will catch.

Using Mister Twister

Casting and retrieving are key elements when using weighted jelly lures. Medium

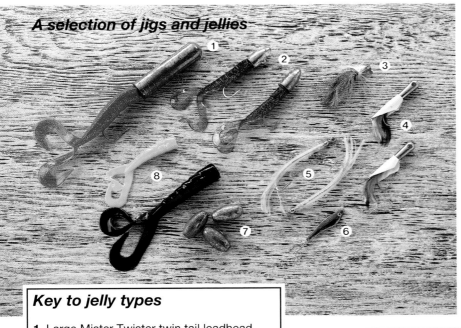

A selection of jigs and jellies

Key to jelly types

1. Large Mister Twister twin tail leadhead
2. Small Mister Twister twin tail leadhead
3. Porky jig with fluoro feathers
4. Bonito jigs with jewel eyes
5. Squeels (squid-eels)
6. Pilk jigging lure
7. Leads for using with unweighted jellies
8. Twin tails for replacing chewed ones

If the fish does not take the lure fully, allow it to drop back, then restart the retrieve, again using the same jerky motion. This usually results in a more determined take.

Using unweighted jellies

Unweighted jellies are threaded on to the hook – usually a long shanked fine wire Aberdeen – in much the same way as a natural worm bait. Although they can be spun or fished on a long trace in a fast tide, they do not seem to be quite as effective in these situations as the conventional 'working tail' artificial bait.

However, unweighted jellies are very successful in deep water wreck fishing, when used on a tough paternoster. Fish them in tandem on short snoods, jigged just above the sea bottom. If you get snagged, they cost much less to replace than most types of artificial sandeels.

spinning gear with lines no heavier than 12lb (5.4kg) test is ideal for working a Mister Twister or similar lure from a small boat. Bass and pollack are the usual quarry. They often hunt for small fish in disturbed water close to a rocky shoreline.

Cast into this disturbance, allow the lure to sink a few feet below the surface and then retrieve with a jerky sink-and-draw action. The predator's instinct to attack is stimulated by this sudden irregular movement. It looks like a small frightened fish trying to escape – an easy meal for the hunter.

▲ *Unweighted jelly lures can be spun by attaching a Wye type lead 50cm (20in) in front of them.*

◄ *A nice pollack caught on a Firetail jelly lure. These are cheaper than 'working tail' artificial sandeels.*

 **Tip** Recycling jellies

Jelly lures that have become well chewed or damaged can be re-used. Cut them into thin strips and whip them in bunches on hooks. They make cheap and effective mini-muppets or mackerel feathers.

CHAPTER FOUR

KNOW
YOUR FISH

Cod

Despite being a commercially important fish and popular with anglers, little is known about the movements of the secretive cod.

Record cod

● The British rod-caught record (shore) is 44lb 8oz (20.2kg), landed at Toms Point, Barry, Glamorgan by B. Jones in 1966.

● The British rod-caught record (boat) is 53lb (24.0kg), landed at Start Point, Lyme Bay in Devon by G. Martin in 1972.

● Specimen weights for cod (shore caught):
North Scotland: 15lb (7kg)
South Coast: 25lb (11kg)
(boat caught): 30lb (14kg).

Like a marine vacuum cleaner, the cod scours the sea bottom for edible morsels – shellfish, marine worms and fish all form part of its diet. This lifestyle is reflected in its appearance; from above the cod appears a mottled, neutral colour, making it very hard to spot against the sea bottom. Its back can vary from reddish brown to grey-green, depending on the type of sea bed and diet, while its belly is a whitish colour.

Follow the feeding

Cod are out and out predators and there is very little they won't eat. When gutted, some have even been found to have munched their way through a plastic cup just before being caught! However, their usual diet consists of fish. Young cod up to two years old feed mainly on crabs and other crustaceans but as they grow they

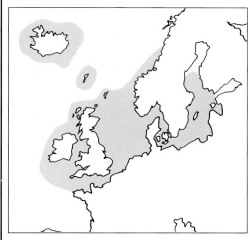

Distribution

There are several almost totally distinct populations of cod separated by deep water. Britain is at the southern end of the cod's geographical range, with only small numbers living around the continent.

eat more fish. The large mouth enables these voracious feeders to swallow quite large prey – cod of 7lb (3.2kg) can swallow whiting of over 1lb (0.45kg) whole!

In most areas of Britain there is a

Vital statistics

Scientific name: *Gadus morhua*
Maximum weight: 100 lb (45kg)
Average weight: 9-11lb (4–5kg)
Maximum length: 5ft (1.5m)
Life-span: 15 years.

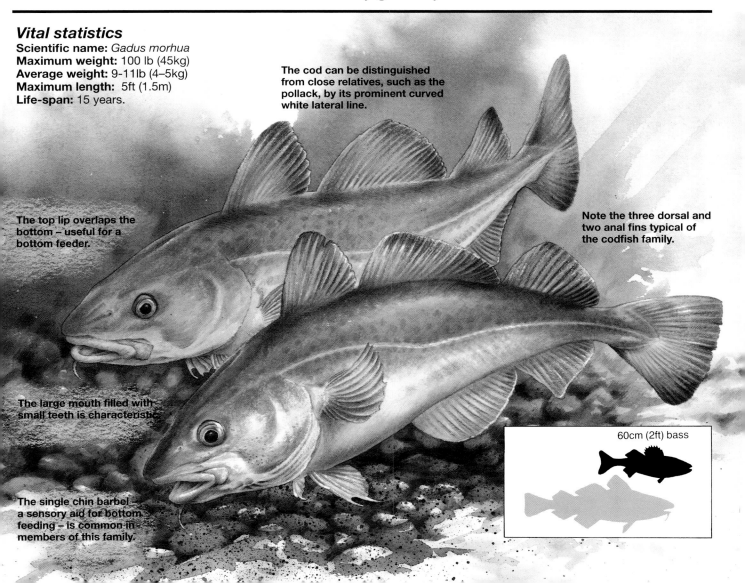

The cod can be distinguished from close relatives, such as the pollack, by its prominent curved white lateral line.

The top lip overlaps the bottom – useful for a bottom feeder.

Note the three dorsal and two anal fins typical of the codfish family.

The large mouth filled with small teeth is characteristic.

The single chin barbel – a sensory aid for bottom feeding – is common in members of this family.

60cm (2ft) bass

Top cod hotspots

Alan Yates, shore fishing expert, recommends . . .

● **Hampshire:** Milford shingle
● **Dorset:** Chesil Beach, Weymouth
● **Devon:** Berry Head, Brixham and Hope's Nose, Torquay
● **Kent:** Dungeness Point and Sandgate
● **Bristol Channel:** Hinkley Point
● **East Anglia:** Aldeburgh and Orford Ness
● **Humberside:** Spurn Head and Withernsea
● **Yorkshire:** Filey Brigg and Flamborough Head
● **County Durham:** Horden
● **Dumfries and Galloway:** Balcary Point, Kirkcudbright

▲ *Large cod such as this fine specimen are becoming scarce. So, while it is not yet a rare fish, cod stocks need to be preserved.*

tendency for mature cod to follow the sprat shoals inshore during winter. Good shore fishing can be had at these times as they often feed right up to the water's edge in pursuit of their prey. They also move to the shore after an onshore gale has stirred up the sea bottom, dislodging many prey species and providing a veritable feast for the hungry cod. Such heavy feeding tends to occur just before spawning, as the cod feed up in preparation, and again afterwards as they recover.

Life-cycle

Cod inhabit the continental shelf. They are most common at 30-90m (100-300ft) and are rarely, if ever, found any deeper than 180m (600ft). They tend not to move very far from their spawning grounds, certainly no more than 100 miles (160km), which means that there are several fairly separate populations of cod around Britain,

though these do overlap. These groups are to be found in the Irish Sea, West of Ireland, around the Hebrides, the North Sea, as well as towards the Kent and Cornwall ends of the English Channel.

Between January and April cod move into the deeper waters of their spawning grounds. Up to nine million eggs are released by the female close to the sea bed where they are fertilised by the male. These eggs then drift slowly to the surface. However, only a small percentage of the larvae survive to become adults.

Codling

After about a year the codling – the name for young cod up to 6lb (2.7kg) – move to nursery areas in shallow waters. This explains the numbers of codling found around British coasts for most of the year. These fish move out to deeper waters once they mature at three to four years old. Being predominantly bottom-living fish, cod are shy of daylight. They mainly forage close inshore at night or at times when the sea is opaque (such as when the water is highly coloured after a storm) so these are good occasions for fishing.

Overfishing

The maximum and average sizes that cod reach have decreased because of overfishing. Fish of up to 100lb (45kg) have only been recorded in trawlers' nets and these have been much less frequent since the Second World War.

The recent resurgence of the North Sea herring after a ban on catches may mean less cod. Herring feed on cod larvae and very small fry so less may survive to breed.

Cod are so prolific, however, that even one good spawning year means that catches will improve in subsequent years.

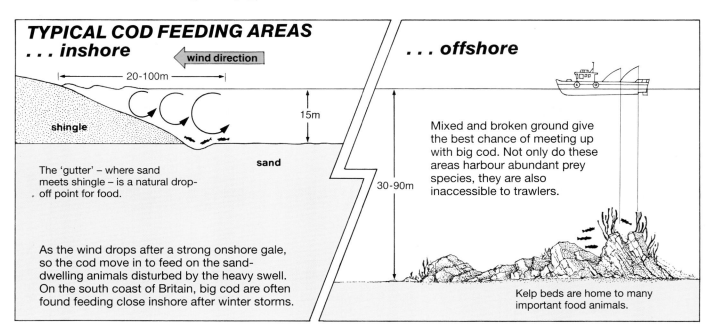

TYPICAL COD FEEDING AREAS
. . . inshore   wind direction   **. . . offshore**

20-100m

shingle

15m

sand

30-90m

The 'gutter' – where sand meets shingle – is a natural drop-off point for food.

As the wind drops after a strong onshore gale, so the cod move in to feed on the sand-dwelling animals disturbed by the heavy swell. On the south coast of Britain, big cod are often found feeding close inshore after winter storms.

Mixed and broken ground give the best chance of meeting up with big cod. Not only do these areas harbour abundant prey species, they are also inaccessible to trawlers.

Kelp beds are home to many important food animals.

Plaice

Plaice have a one-sided view of life with both eyes on the right – camouflaged – side. They are masters of disguise – sea chameleons.

Distribution

Plaice can be found all around the UK. They like sand or muddy sand. Best spots are the central and southern North Sea, and estuaries of the north-eastern Irish Sea.

Plaice marks

● **Beach fishing** Plaice are widespread around the UK coastline. River mouths, such as those in Devon and Cornwall, offer the best chances.

Notable areas include Brighton and The Wash. Try the shallows in summer.

● **Boat fishing** Plaice can be caught in waters of about 14-18m (48-60ft) off many coasts.

● **Scotland** Sea lochs are successful spots.

● **Ireland** Shallow bays host good stocks as yet untouched by commercial fishermen.

Because plaice are widely available in shops and restaurants, it is easy to think that there is an inexhaustible supply. But the plaice is no longer a fish that anglers can catch regularly.

They *are* still fairly common around British shores but – like any other fish species in demand for the table – they are under considerable pressure from fishing fleets.

Chameleon colours

Unlike skates and rays – species which are flattened from top to bottom – the plaice in fact swims on its side. The mottled brown top surface is really the right side while the pure white underneath is the fish's left.

Colouring varies from brown to grey because the plaice is able – chameleon-like – to match the colour of the sea bed. The small red or orange spots on the top side appear on plaice from any habitat. The skin is smooth though there are small ridges on the head

which distinguish it from other flatfish species. The lateral line is slightly arched.

Life-cycle

Life for the young plaice begins with spawning time during January or February in depths of 27-55m (90-180ft). The eggs –

Vital statistics

Scientific name: *Pleuronectes platessa*
Maximum weight: 12lb (5.4kg)
Average weight: 3-4lb (1.3-1.8kg)
Maximum length: Possibly 36in (90cm)
Life-span: 20 years or more. Few fish reach this age because of netting.

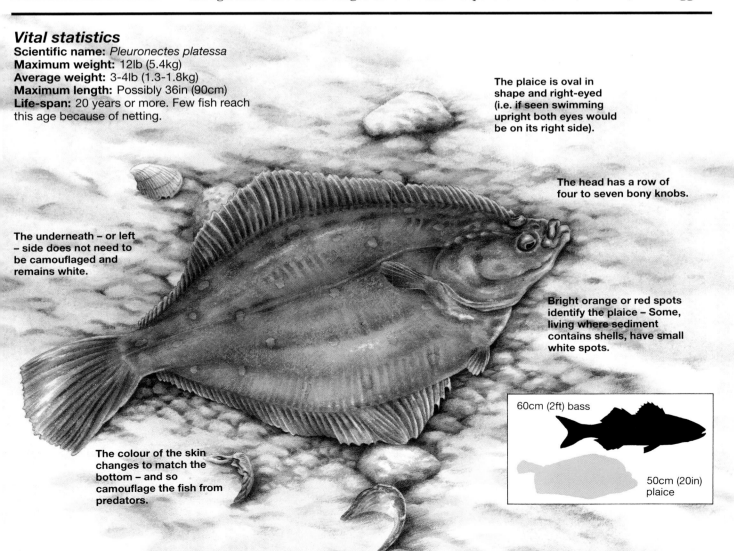

The plaice is oval in shape and right-eyed (i.e. if seen swimming upright both eyes would be on its right side).

The head has a row of four to seven bony knobs.

The underneath – or left – side does not need to be camouflaged and remains white.

Bright orange or red spots identify the plaice – Some, living where sediment contains shells, have small white spots.

The colour of the skin changes to match the bottom – and so camouflage the fish from predators.

60cm (2ft) bass

50cm (20in) plaice

▲ *A pleasing brace of plaice. The British record boat-caught fish is 10lb 3oz (5.35kg), caught at Longa Sound in Scotland.*

about 2.5mm in diameter – float in the sea. Up to a quarter of a million eggs can be produced by one 1.5kg (3¼lb) female. The eggs hatch in 10 to 30 days depending on water temperature. Newly hatched larvae measure around 8-9mm long.

Plaice look like any other fish at this stage – being rounded rather than flat. But when the larval plaice is between one to two months old – and 10mm long – one eye starts moving around to join the other one. The young soon start to swim like adults, with their left side facing the sea bed. Being bottom-feeders, plaice only need to be camouflaged on one side.

Their early life is spent feeding on microscopic plankton, until they can graduate on to small cockles and mussels.

Growth is fairly slow. Plaice take four years to reach 30cm (12in) in length. They are quite long-lived – a number of fish over 20 years old have been caught and it is likely that they could live for as long as 30 if commercial fishing were less intensive.

They reach maturity between their second and seventh year; the males are normally a year behind females in development.

Feeding plaice

Plaice move seasonally from their deeper spawning grounds, reaching the shallows in spring and summer. In shallow waters they feed mainly on bivalves such as mussels, razorfish and cockles. The smaller organisms are swallowed whole, the shells being crushed by powerful throat muscles and pharyngeal teeth.

Their preferred habitat is sandy or pebbly bottoms, but they also inhabit areas where rocky ground is interspersed with sand. Here mussel beds are common – a major attraction for plaice. Camouflage is essential in such beds, where large predators often lie in waiting.

Plaice are particularly active at dusk. Smaller ones can sometimes be found in estuaries where they may be confused with dab and flounder.

The not so common plaice?

In the early 1800s there was such a glut of plaice the Lord Mayor of London ordered that they should be given free to the poor people of London.

In contrast many areas that were once well-known for shore-caught plaice have none today. In the early 1980s, 150,000 tons of plaice were landed every year from the Continental shelf.

Rye Bay, Sussex, despite being a protected area, was trawled so heavily that the mussel-beds were destroyed by trammel nets and the plaice – their food gone – never returned.

It is thought that plaice can reach 90cm (36in) in length and live for around 30 years, but because of intensive fishing large plaice are very rare.

Do your bit to conserve stocks by making sure you return smaller plaice alive and well.

◄ *The plaice has excellent camouflage, making it virtually invisible against some backgrounds.*
The angle of the plaice's mouth shows clearly it is in fact really lying on its side... only the left eye has moved round.

TRACKING DOWN PLAICE

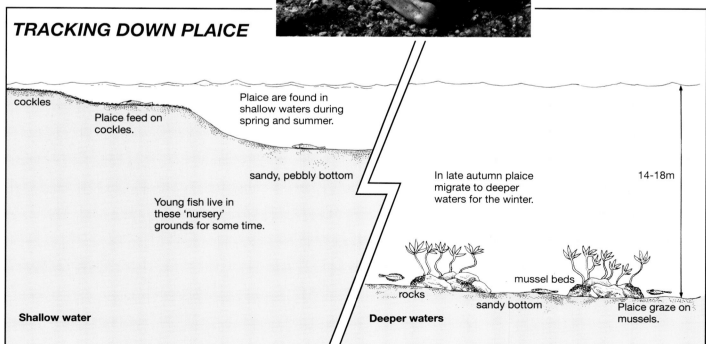

cockles

Plaice feed on cockles.

Plaice are found in shallow waters during spring and summer.

sandy, pebbly bottom

Young fish live in these 'nursery' grounds for some time.

In late autumn plaice migrate to deeper waters for the winter.

14-18m

rocks

mussel beds

sandy bottom

Plaice graze on mussels.

Shallow water

Deeper waters

Pollack

Inhabitants of wreck and rock and capable of powerful, surging dives, pollack can be difficult to winkle out of the kelp.

Distribution

Pollack are found all round the coast of Britain though they are more common in the west, especially off western Ireland. Pollack can be found anywhere where there is deep water over rough ground.

Record pollack

● The British shore-caught record pollack is 18lb 4oz (8.28kg) for a fish caught in February 1986 at Abbotsbury Beach, Dorset by C R A Lowe.
● The boat-caught record is 29lb 4oz (13.28kg) and was taken by William Mayes fishing out of Dungeness in Kent in July 1987.
● The specimen weight for a shore-caught pollack is double figures while for a boat-caught fish it is over 20lb (9.1kg).

Pollack, also called lythe, can easily be confused with another closely related member of the cod family – the coalfish or saithe – but there are a number of ways to tell them apart. Coalfish have a light coloured, straight lateral line – quite different from the darker curved line of pollack. Coalfish jaws are fairly even but with pollack the lower jaw juts out. Coalfish also have a much more obviously forked tail and a tiny barbel on the chin, where pollack have none.

Both have dark green backs, silvery flanks and white bellies, though pollack usually have a more golden sheen to their sides. These colours are variable and young pollack living near kelp beds can even have a brownish-red hue.

Rock-hunting predator

Pollack larvae drift in the top layers of the sea, feeding on plankton. Once they reach the shore they grow to a length of a few inches on a diet of shrimps, crabs and other crustaceans, though these young fish also eat marine worms, shellfish and any other small rockpool creatures.

Mature pollack feed mainly on fish, particularly sandeels and open water species such as herring and small members of the cod family, which they ambush from behind cover. Their preferred method of feeding is to hover, head up, in the lee of a

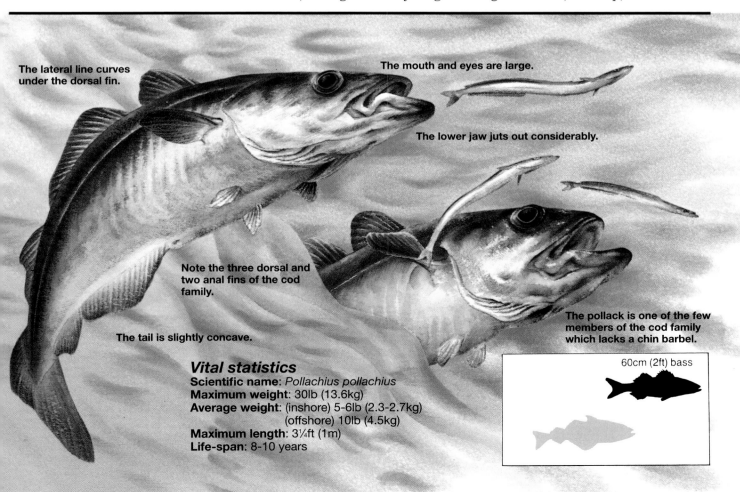

The lateral line curves under the dorsal fin.

The mouth and eyes are large.

The lower jaw juts out considerably.

Note the three dorsal and two anal fins of the cod family.

The pollack is one of the few members of the cod family which lacks a chin barbel.

The tail is slightly concave.

Vital statistics
Scientific name: *Pollachius pollachius*
Maximum weight: 30lb (13.6kg)
Average weight: (inshore) 5-6lb (2.3-2.7kg)
(offshore) 10lb (4.5kg)
Maximum length: 3¼ft (1m)
Life-span: 8-10 years

60cm (2ft) bass

Top pollack marks

The best time for both boat and shore-caught pollack is October – February, when the fish shoal closer inshore and over offshore wrecks, in preparation for spawning. Mike Millman, pollack and coalfish specialist, recommends these ports for fish over 20lb (9.1kg):

● **Devon** Brixham, Dartmouth, Plymouth and Salcombe.

The best rough ground pollack fishing is at:
● **The English Channel** Hands Deep and Eddystone Reef
● **Western Ireland** The west coast of Ireland is excellent for pollack.

The following inshore rock marks provide some of the most exciting sport:
● **Devon** Berry Head and Stoke Point
● **Cornwall** Penzance round to Porthcurno
● **North Cornwall** Trevose Head

The most consistent beach mark is:
● **Dorset** Chesil Beach

◄ *Mick Toomer holds up a 19lb 2oz (8.7kg) pollack taken from a wreck off the coast of Guernsey. Mick was using a red gill and the fish made several powerful surging dives before he could subdue it.*

wreck or reef. They wait in this position for the tide to bring them food.

Life in reef and wreck

Pollack favour habitats with plenty of cover – reefs, wrecks, piers and rocks – anywhere with nooks and crannies and plenty of weed to harbour prey fish. For this reason they are most common on Britain's western coasts, which are exposed to the full force of the Atlantic and have a more rugged rocky coastline than more sheltered parts of the British Isles.

Small pollack live in kelp beds close inshore, but as they grow they move out into deeper water, spending their time over wrecks and rocky marks. Adult pollack spend most of the year at depths of around 100m (330ft), though they can often be caught in shallower water around cliffs and piers.

Spawning takes place between February and May, at depths of 100-200m (330-660ft), though usually at the shallower end of the range. Each female lays up to four million eggs which drift in the top layer of the sea until they hatch. The few larvae which survive in this layer are carried to shore by currents to feed and grow in the kelp.

TRACKING DOWN POLLACK

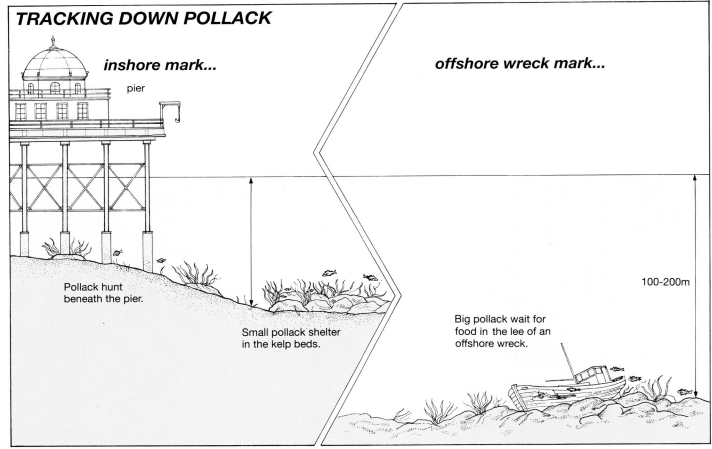

inshore mark...

pier

Pollack hunt beneath the pier.

Small pollack shelter in the kelp beds.

offshore wreck mark...

100-200m

Big pollack wait for food in the lee of an offshore wreck.

Thornback ray

The thornback ray or roker is the member of the skate family most likely to be met in shallow British waters. During its spawning period it can be found in less than a foot of water.

Distribution

Once extremely common fish, thornbacks live in shallow water all round Britain. They are also found further south, as far as Madeira and the Mediterranean, though these stocks, too, are depleted.

Thornback hot spots

Commercial fishing pressure has reduced the population of British thornbacks to the point where comparatively few are being caught on rod and line. Some areas, however, are still recognised as giving the beach and dinghy angler a fair chance of tangling with one:
● The Thames estuary
● Many Welsh bays from Cardiff round to Rhyl
● The Bristol Channel

Thornbacks are rays, as opposed to skates. The main difference is in their appearance – rays have much shorter 'noses' than skates. Though both skates and rays look very like flatfish such as plaice, sole and halibut, there is no relationship between their two families. The resemblance is due to the similarity of their bottom-dwelling lifestyle. In fact, rays are very closely related to sharks. The 'backs' of both flatfish and rays are coloured to suit the type of ground they inhabit, as a means of camouflage.

The dorsal surface of the thornback is mottled and blotchy and varies from brown to grey with many dark spots and yellowish patches. In juveniles these lighter patches tend to be more distinct, with a dark outline. The underside is off-white with darker edges.

Follow the feeding

Thornbacks feed mainly on the sea bed and are not particularly fussy about what they eat. Immature flatfish and other bottom dwelling fish such as gobies and sand eels

Vital statistics
Scientific name: *Raja clavata*
Maximum weight: 40lb (18kg)
Average weight: 10lb (4.5kg)
Maximum length: 38in (97cm)
Width (across wingtips): 24in (61cm)
Life-span: 15 years

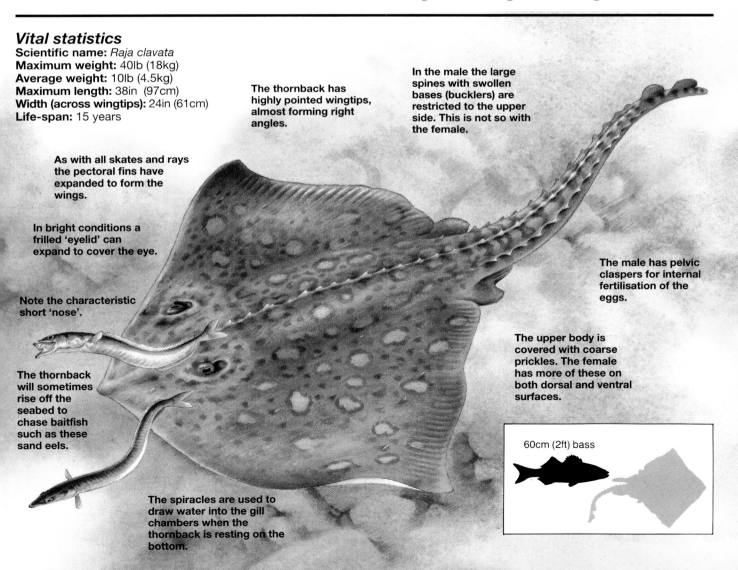

The thornback has highly pointed wingtips, almost forming right angles.

In the male the large spines with swollen bases (bucklers) are restricted to the upper side. This is not so with the female.

As with all skates and rays the pectoral fins have expanded to form the wings.

In bright conditions a frilled 'eyelid' can expand to cover the eye.

Note the characteristic short 'nose'.

The thornback will sometimes rise off the seabed to chase baitfish such as these sand eels.

The male has pelvic claspers for internal fertilisation of the eggs.

The upper body is covered with coarse prickles. The female has more of these on both dorsal and ventral surfaces.

60cm (2ft) bass

The spiracles are used to draw water into the gill chambers when the thornback is resting on the bottom.

▶ *The thornback is one of the larger fish that can be caught in shallow water around Britain and they used to be a regular feature of catches from dinghies. Nowadays they are just a bonus to the day's catch. This fine specimen will make good eating but given the length of time taken to reach spawning age, it is important that all small thornbacks are returned to the sea.*

Commercial fishing

Despite being the most common ray in British inshore waters, or perhaps because of it, the thornback has been extensively overfished and stocks could be nearing critical level. Anglers have noticed catches dropping off alarmingly over a relatively short period. The problem is really the ray's own 'fault' – its preference for clean ground makes it easy prey for trawlers. Indeed most of the 'skate' we eat is thornback.

Record thornbacks

● The British rod-caught record for a thornback taken from the shore is 21lb 12oz (9.866kg). This fish was captured in 1985 by S. Ramsay at The Ross near Kirkcudbright.

● The largest British thornback taken from a boat weighed 38lb (17.237kg) and was caught by J. Patterson in 1935 off Rustington in Sussex.

● The specimen weight for a shore-caught thornback is about 15lb (7kg), though fewer and fewer fish this size are being caught. For boat fishing the specimen weight is about 22lb (10kg).

will be eaten but the preferred diet consists of crabs, shrimps and shellfish. They tend not to pursue prey over long distances; instead they lie in wait, camouflaged against the bottom.

The mouth is on the underside, well suited to bottom feeding. The flattened triangular teeth are useful for grinding up molluscs and crustaceans. Despite this, large thornbacks have been known to chase herrings and sprats in the shallows.

Life at the bottom

Thornbacks are shallow water seafish, rarely, if ever, found in the depths. Juveniles and mating adults can be found in very shallow water of only a couple of metres but most of the year is spent at 9-60m (30-200ft). They prefer to live and feed over mud, sand, shingle and gravel, though they will also forage over mixed and rough ground from time to time.

While not migratory, there is some movement towards shore during the late winter and early spring, probably to breed. The spawning period offers the best chance of catching a thornback from the beach. Mature females are the first to move inshore and do so when almost ready to spawn. A few weeks later, when the eggs have ripened, the adult males also make the journey. This segregation may account for the large catches of one sex that tend to occur from time to time.

Fertilisation takes place internally by means of the claspers. The egg capsules, known as mermaid's purses, are laid in shallow coastal waters between March and August, with each female laying about 140 in all. These 'purses' are dark rectangles about 7cm by 9cm (2¾in by 3½in) with a conical horn at each corner. They can often be seen washed up during the summer months.

After 16 to 20 weeks, the young hatch out, fully formed though still sporting a yolk sac, and soon begin to feed on small crustaceans. They gradually move into deeper water as they mature. Sexual maturity is reached at seven years for males and nine years for females.

A TYPICAL THORNBACK HABITAT

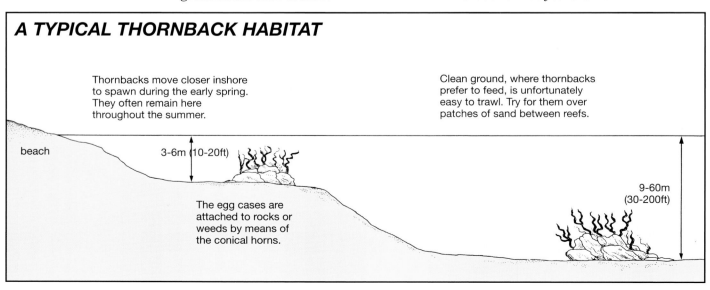

Thornbacks move closer inshore to spawn during the early spring. They often remain here throughout the summer.

Clean ground, where thornbacks prefer to feed, is unfortunately easy to trawl. Try for them over patches of sand between reefs.

beach

3-6m (10-20ft)

The egg cases are attached to rocks or weeds by means of the conical horns.

9-60m (30-200ft)

Mackerel

Although very slow-growing, mackerel are one of the most beautiful fish in the sea. They are migratory, living in shoals and feeding on tiny marine organisms and small fish.

The Atlantic mackerel is a very common sea fish around the coasts of Britain and Ireland. A relative of the much larger tuna, it is beautifully streamlined and built for speed. Its head is pointed, while its body tapers to a forked tail. The eyes and mouth are large. Near the tail on both the dorsal and ventral surface is a series of four or five small fins. There are two dorsal fins, both of which fold flat to produce a sleek, streamlined shape and reduce friction while the fish is swimming at high speed.

The mackerel has distinctive colouring – its back is metallic turquoise overlaid by dark, wavy bars. After the fish dies, the colour fades rapidly to dull grey-blue. The flanks are iridescent silver with rainbow tints of pink, gold, purple and blue. The overall colour provides ideal camouflage in the open sea, helping the fish to avoid the attentions of predators.

Distribution

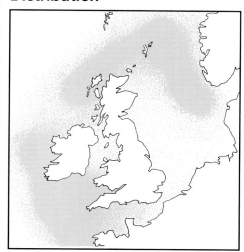

Mackerel move into deep water during winter, usually well off the coast of southern Ireland. When summer approaches, they move to shallow waters to feed.

Swim or sink

Mackerel are active swimmers, and it is said that they never stop swimming. This may help them breathe easier because more water passes through their gills. Another possible reason is that they don't

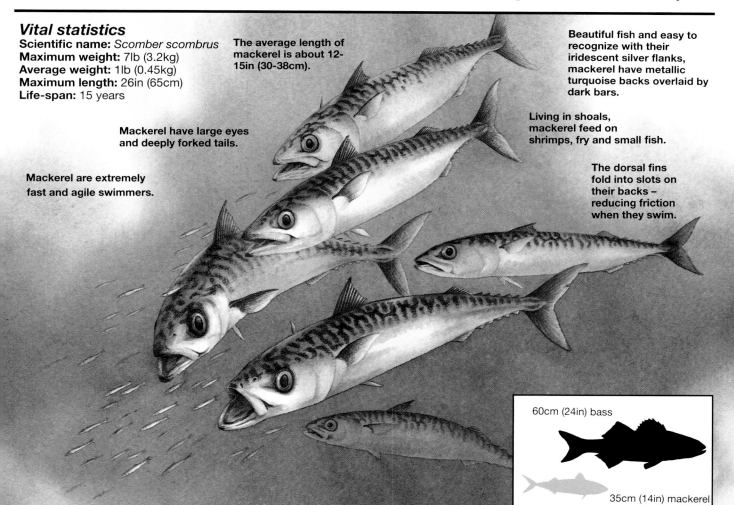

Vital statistics
Scientific name: *Scomber scombrus*
Maximum weight: 7lb (3.2kg)
Average weight: 1lb (0.45kg)
Maximum length: 26in (65cm)
Life-span: 15 years

The average length of mackerel is about 12-15in (30-38cm).

Beautiful fish and easy to recognize with their iridescent silver flanks, mackerel have metallic turquoise backs overlaid by dark bars.

Mackerel have large eyes and deeply forked tails.

Living in shoals, mackerel feed on shrimps, fry and small fish.

Mackerel are extremely fast and agile swimmers.

The dorsal fins fold into slots on their backs – reducing friction when they swim.

60cm (24in) bass

35cm (14in) mackerel

▲ *These four mackerel were caught on light spinning tackle in late spring. At this time of year mackerel can be found off all types of coastlines, preying on small fish.*

have swim bladders (an organ which fills with air to allow fish to stay at a particular depth). If they stopped swimming, they would probably sink to the bottom!

Feeding habits

Mackerel winter in huge shoals in deep water near southern Ireland and along the Continental Shelf. It's here that they are most vulnerable to Eastern European and Russian trawlers which plunder huge stocks. When spring comes, they move inshore to spawn. They are a schooling fish – that is, similar-aged fish swim and feed together. At night they move near the surface. Mackerel hunt mainly by sight, so if you are fishing for them, look for them in the morning and evening. They swim down to deeper waters in the day-time. Occasionally, schools of small fish may tempt them to feed near the surface during the day.

Like most sea fish, mackerel eat anything that swims or is small enough to be swallowed, including plankton, shrimps, worms, squid, fish eggs and fry. They also browse on the sea bed and eat a variety of molluscs and crustaceans. They don't grow large, the average length being about 14in (35cm), but fish up to 7lb (3.2kg) have been recorded off the US coast.

Mackerel are a very popular summer fish. Casting three to five feather baits (on one line) off piers is a popular method of catching them. Other anglers prefer to wade in shallow surf beaches, using light baitcasting rigs with small spinners.

Life-cycle

Mackerel spawn from January to June. Each female sheds up to 500,000 eggs which float at the mercy of the current. Every egg contains an oily globule to help it stay buoyant. Recently-hatched larvae feed on their yolk sacs; when the yolk is used up, they sieve plankton through their gill rakers. In 40 days the fry are about 2in (5cm) long.

They are an extremely slow-growing species, perhaps the very slowest. A 1lb (0.45kg) mackerel is about six to eight years old, and a 2lb (0.9kg) fish is about ten to twelve years old. Larger fish – including sharks – prey on them.

Top mackerel hot-spots

Most types of coastlines around Britain have substantial populations of mackerel. These are some of the most productive areas.
● **Tor Bay, Brixham, Devon** Produces many good-sized fish, including the shore-caught record.
● **Mount's Bay, Penzance to Porthleven, Cornwall** Many fish, caught on feathers.
● **The Eddystone Reef, off Plymouth** Contains many 4-5lb (1.8-2.3kg) fish.
● **Isle of Man coastline** Regularly produces 4lb (1.8kg) mackerel.
● **Flamborough Head, North Yorkshire** Casting small spoons and feathers is effective for 2-4lb (0.9-1.8kg) fish.
● **South Coast, Dover to Eastbourne** High numbers of medium-sized fish.
● **Southern Ireland from Rosslare to Bantry Bay** The coasts of Ireland are exceptional mackerel areas. Fish up to 5lb (2.3kg).

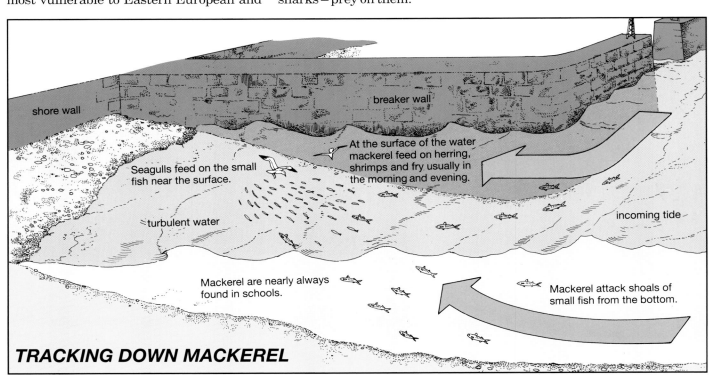

shore wall

breaker wall

Seagulls feed on the small fish near the surface.

At the surface of the water mackerel feed on herring, shrimps and fry usually in the morning and evening.

turbulent water

incoming tide

Mackerel are nearly always found in schools.

Mackerel attack shoals of small fish from the bottom.

TRACKING DOWN MACKEREL

Conger eel

A voracious predator which lurks among offshore wrecks, rocks and coral crevices, the conger eel is perfectly suited for life in the shadowy ocean depths.

Distribution

Conger are mostly found in the English Channel, all round Wales and Ireland and as far north as the western coast of Scotland. The east coast has very few.

Record conger

● N. Ball caught the biggest British boat-caught conger – it weighed 112lb 8oz (51kg). The fish was taken off Dartmouth in 1992.

● M. Larkin holds the shore record with a conger of 68lb 8oz (31.1kg) caught off Devil's Point, Plymouth, in 1991.

● The Irish record is a 72lb (32.7kg) fish caught by J. Green in 1914.

Many people who see a big conger for the first time can't believe that it's a fish. The brown-grey, elongated, scaleless body is a curious sight, impressive in its sheer muscular power. The serpent-like head, large eyes, pointed mouth (lined with rows of small, triangular teeth) and lack of pelvic fins also don't help the conger look like a fish. Doubts aside – despite its deceptive appearance, the conger is a unique migratory fish.

Habitat

Conger were once widespread all round the British Isles coastline. In the 1990s they are found mainly around the south and west coasts, in the Irish Sea and along the west of Ireland. Limestone reefs and rocky bottoms which contain many cracks and crevices offer ideal hideouts for them to set up home. Some wrecks and debris such as pipes also provide excellent shelter. In fact, wrecks attract many other species of fish and supply the conger with food in addition to shelter.

Vital statistics

Scientific name: *Conger conger*
Maximum weight: 250lb (113kg)
Average weight: 30-40lbs (14-18kg)
Maximum length: 9ft (2.7m)
Life-span: 15-20 years

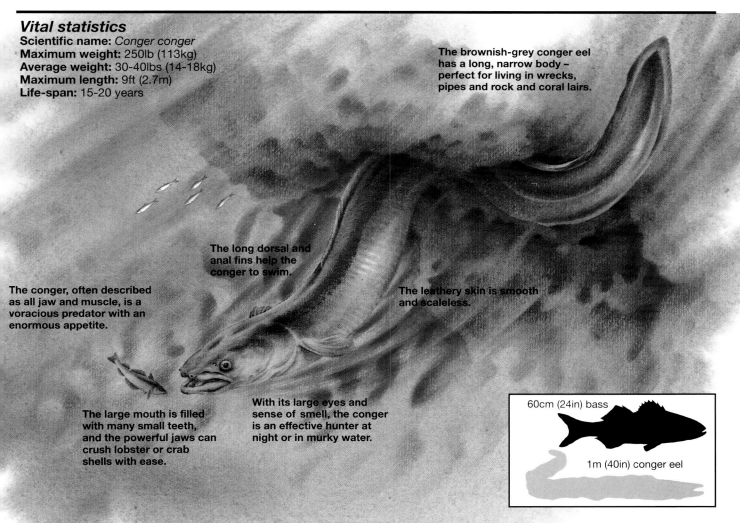

The brownish-grey conger eel has a long, narrow body – perfect for living in wrecks, pipes and rock and coral lairs.

The conger, often described as all jaw and muscle, is a voracious predator with an enormous appetite.

The long dorsal and anal fins help the conger to swim.

The leathery skin is smooth and scaleless.

The large mouth is filled with many small teeth, and the powerful jaws can crush lobster or crab shells with ease.

With its large eyes and sense of smell, the conger is an effective hunter at night or in murky water.

60cm (24in) bass

1m (40in) conger eel

Conger are remarkably adaptable fish; they can survive (and even thrive) in depths from 10ft (3m) to 13,000ft (4000m).

The dream fish

Many anglers dream of catching a large conger from a wreck. Fighting against this muscular giant is a formidable task – the fish undulates and swims backwards as you reel it in. And be careful when handling one because it has been known to bite!

Legering mackerel on heavy tackle is perhaps one of the most popular and effective ways of catching a big conger.

Feeding habits

Octopus, squid, crabs, rockling, pollack and flatfish are the conger's main prey. But it isn't selective about its food – it scavenges, robs lobster pots, lies in wait to ambush unwary prey and chases shoals of fish in the open.

In shallow waters a conger often hides in its lair or crevice during the day. Under the blanket of night it searches for food along the bottom, usually in slack water. The conger tries to avoid strong tides because it's harder for the eel to swim. In deep water where light doesn't penetrate it comes and goes without waiting for the cover of night.

All fish living in shallow water are at risk from sudden temperature changes. Prolonged severely cold weather can kill a conger. Many dead eels have been found along beaches after a bitterly cold spell.

Life-cycle

The conger has a unique and complicated spawning process. The fish migrates to the Sargasso Sea in the Atlantic (between the Azores Islands and the Bahamas). On the way its bones lose their calcium and become very soft; its stomach shrinks; and it stops feeding. A female conger sheds up to eight million eggs in depths up to 13,000ft (4000m).

The eggs develop into leaf-shaped larvae which drift in the surface layer of the sea and feed on plankton. The North Atlantic Drift distributes the larvae randomly. As their bodies continue to lengthen, they begin to resemble their parents and establish lairs until it's their turn to begin the journey to the Sargasso Sea.

◄ *This 100lb (45kg) conger was caught over a wreck off Brixham, Devon. The fish is nearly 7ft (2.1m) long and as thick as a small tree! Notice its large eye and huge mouth.*

Top areas for conger eels

Consult a sea-side tackle shop for more specific information about names and telephone numbers of skippers who fish over wrecks.

The following are proven conger fishing areas.

● **Plymouth, Devon** Many conger taken inshore and over wrecks every year.

● **Torquay-Brixham, Devon** Boat and shore marks are excellent for big conger.

● **Newhaven, East Sussex** Some enormous conger, coming close to the boat-caught record.

● **Anglesey and Lleyn Peninsula, North Wales** Many small conger.

● **Chesil Beach, Dorset** Medium-sized conger caught from shore.

● **Durlston Head (south of Swanage), Dorset** Produces many fish.

● **Portland Bill (west of Pulpit Rock), Dorset** Rocky shores with many fish.

TRACKING DOWN CONGER

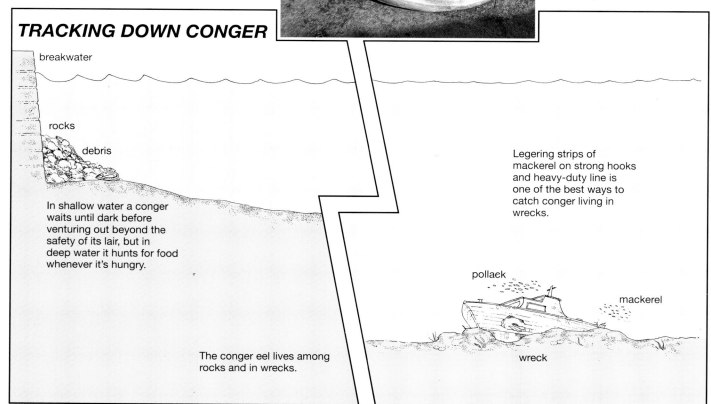

breakwater

rocks

debris

In shallow water a conger waits until dark before venturing out beyond the safety of its lair, but in deep water it hunts for food whenever it's hungry.

The conger eel lives among rocks and in wrecks.

Legering strips of mackerel on strong hooks and heavy-duty line is one of the best ways to catch conger living in wrecks.

pollack

mackerel

wreck

Whiting

Despite commercial overfishing, whiting are still common around the British Isles. They are one of the fish most frequently caught by shore anglers, particularly over a sandy sea bed.

Whiting are common all around the British Isles. They are most abundant in the protected shallow waters of the North and Irish Seas, over sand and shingle.

Record whiting

● The British boat-caught record is held by N.R. Croft for a fish weighing 6lb 12oz (3.061kg) off Manacle Rocks, Falmouth, Cornwall in 1981.
● The shore-caught record is for a 4lb 4dms (1.826kg) whiting caught by T. Dell in 1984 off Abbotsbury, Dorset.

Members of the cod family are abundant in the seas of Northern Europe. Although haddock and cod are more important commercially because of their larger size, whiting are perhaps the most plentiful of them all.

Whiting are slender-bodied fish with narrow, pointed heads. The upper jaw overhangs the lower and, in addition to smaller teeth, the mouth is filled with a staggered row of large, outward-pointing teeth, useful for hanging on to wriggling prey.

Like other members of the cod family, whiting have three dorsal and two anal fins, which are all joined together at the base. You can distinguish whiting by the white edging on the anal fins, and by the black spot at the upper edge of the pectoral fin. Whiting do not have a chin barbel, although a minute one can occasionally be spotted on young fish.

Their colouring is subtle and varies with habitat. On sandy shores whiting have pale brown backs and elsewhere they may be greeny-blue, but they always have light

Vital statistics

Scientific name: *Melangius merlangus*
Maximum weight: 7lb (3.15kg)
Average weight: 1½lb (0.68kg)
Maximum length: 60cm (2ft)
Life-span: 5-8 years

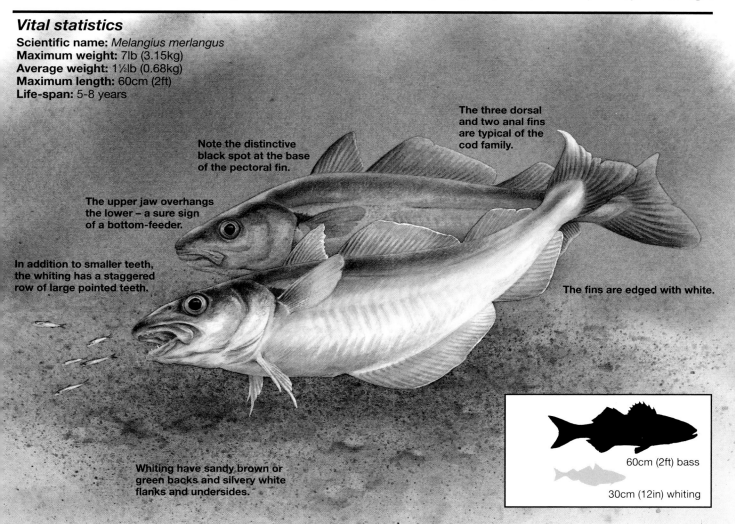

Note the distinctive black spot at the base of the pectoral fin.

The three dorsal and two anal fins are typical of the cod family.

The upper jaw overhangs the lower – a sure sign of a bottom-feeder.

In addition to smaller teeth, the whiting has a staggered row of large pointed teeth.

The fins are edged with white.

Whiting have sandy brown or green backs and silvery white flanks and undersides.

60cm (2ft) bass

30cm (12in) whiting

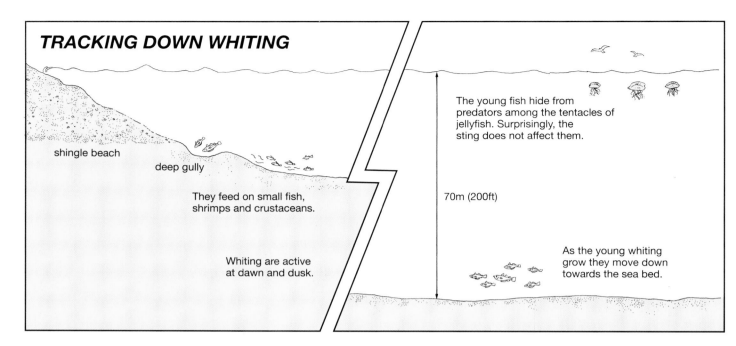

TRACKING DOWN WHITING

shingle beach

deep gully

They feed on small fish, shrimps and crustaceans.

Whiting are active at dawn and dusk.

The young fish hide from predators among the tentacles of jellyfish. Surprisingly, the sting does not affect them.

70m (200ft)

As the young whiting grow they move down towards the sea bed.

silver sides and belly – hence the name whiting.

Shallow waters

Whiting are common in most shallow inshore waters – young fish can be caught in a few feet of water, but larger specimens live at depths of 30-100m (100-330ft). They tend not to be found in estuaries since they prefer very salty water.

The North Sea and the Irish Sea, and both the Bristol and the English Channels are the main commercial fishing grounds. In the North Sea, however, trawlers are not permitted to bag any fish below 23cm (9in) in a bid to counteract over-exploitation.

Feeding time

Whiting appear to be most active at dawn and dusk – they eat large quantities of small fish such as young herring, sprats and various members of the cod family. Sandeels are important in their diet though the present scarcity of sandeels is probably one reason for the whiting's decrease. Young fish feed heavily on crustaceans, particularly sandhoppers and brown shrimps.

Life-cycle

Spawning begins in mid January off Spain and continues to late May off Iceland, so those around Britain and Ireland spawn in March/April. They spawn offshore in mid-water when the temperature is 10-15°C (50-59°F). Once the eggs have hatched the young live out at sea for up to a year before drifting inshore.

Young whiting are often seen in the company of large common jellyfish which float near the surface. They dart between the jellyfish's tentacles, and don't seem to be affected by the venom-filled stings. In this way, whiting gain protection from predatory fish and birds. They may also pick up

food from the jellyfish which have small crustaceans living on them. No-one is sure how, or if, the jellyfish benefits from this association. Whatever the advantages, little is known about this unusual behaviour in one of our most common sea fish.

▼ *This fine bag of whiting was caught off the Cornish coast. Since they have a tendency to swallow the hook, you need a good pair of pliers or forceps.*

Greater and lesser spotted dogfish

Rough hound, bull huss, nurse hound or common dogfish – whatever you call them, there are plenty to be caught.

Distribution

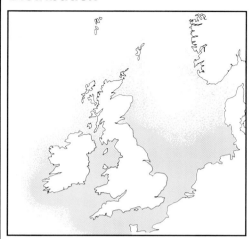

Dogfishes are common around the British Isles, though the nurse hound is only abundant off the south coast. Both species are also widely found in the Mediterranean down to the north-west coast of Africa.

Record dogfishes

- **Sandy dog – boat-caught** 4lb 1oz (1.865kg) off Newquay, Cornwall in 1976 by B.J.Solomon.
- **Sandy dog – shore-caught** 4lb 15oz (2.244kg) at Abbey Burnfoot, Scotland in 1988 by S. Ramsey.
- **Nurse hound – boat-caught** 22lb 4oz (10.092kg) off Minehead, Somerset in 1986 by M.L.Hall.
- **Nurse hound – shore-caught** 17lb 15oz (8.136kg) at Trefusis Point, Cornwall in 1977 by M. Roberts.

Although dogfishes lack the glamour of the fast-moving, hard-fighting big sharks such as the tope, blue and porbeagle, they are important to the British sea angler simply because they are so common. (Curiously, where we call them dogfishes the North Americans know them as cat-sharks!)

They have several features common to all sharks – blunt heads and long, tapering bodies with a skeleton made entirely of cartilage (not bone) to give the body greater flexibility. Although sharks lack a swim bladder, their large, oil-filled liver does a similar job, keeping the fish buoyant in the water. The skin of both species is covered with hundreds of fine, backward-pointing 'teeth'. (In days gone by it was used for polishing wood and copper under the name of 'rubskin'.)

Spot the difference

There is often confusion when trying to tell these two dogfishes apart, since the terms greater and lesser refer to the size of the fish, not to the size of the spots. As a result, the names sandy dog (lesser) and nurse hound (greater) are often used.

Vital statistics

SANDY DOG (LESSER-SPOTTED)
Scientific name: *Scyliorhinus canicula*
Maximum weight: 5lb (2.3kg)
Average weight: 2lb (0.9kg)
Maximum length: 39in (1m)
Life-span: Up to 5 years

NURSE HOUND (GREATER-SPOTTED)
Scientific name: *Scyliorhinus stellaris*
Maximum weight: 23lb (10.4kg)
Average weight: 8lb (3.6kg)
Maximum length: 47in (1.2m)
Life-span: Up to 10 years

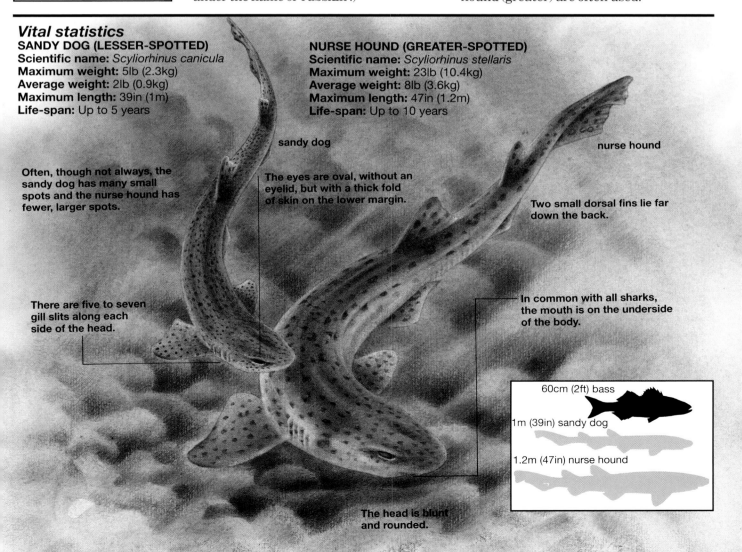

sandy dog

nurse hound

Often, though not always, the sandy dog has many small spots and the nurse hound has fewer, larger spots.

The eyes are oval, without an eyelid, but with a thick fold of skin on the lower margin.

Two small dorsal fins lie far down the back.

There are five to seven gill slits along each side of the head.

In common with all sharks, the mouth is on the underside of the body.

60cm (2ft) bass
1m (39in) sandy dog
1.2m (47in) nurse hound

The head is blunt and rounded.

Both have sandy or grey/brown backs with dark brown spots, and although the nurse hound commonly does have larger spots, these are not an ideal means of identification.

The conclusive way of telling them apart is to look at their nasal flaps. In the sandy dog the nasal flap, which overlaps the upper lip, runs continuously from one nostril to the other. In the nurse hound the two nasal flaps are separate and each is fused with the snout near the midline.

The sandy dog lives in sand or fine gravel, its colouring matching that of the dappled sea bed; it is usually found at a depth of 20-75m (65-245ft). The nurse hound is also a bottom-living shark but is normally found on rockier ground at depths of 20-65m (65-215ft). Both fish stray into much shallower waters at times.

The nurse hound tends to be a bit of a loner, so is not usually caught in large numbers, but the sandy dog frequently forms large schools, often being a nuisance to the bottom-fishing angler. Unfortunately, trawlers fishing over inshore grounds often catch thousands of sandy dogs in a haul, and although they are usually dumped overboard, many are killed in the process.

Case-bound life-style

Most members of the shark family bear their young live, the fertilized eggs staying in the female's body until maturity – but dogfish differ by laying eggs in cases.

Mating takes place in the autumn, after which the female moves into shallow waters for spawning between November and July.

The cases, also known as 'mermaid's purses', are tough and leathery with tendrils at each corner; these anchor the egg case in place by twining around the stems of seaweed, or round wrecks and other solid structures. The pup remains inside the case for up to a year, feeding off its yolk sac

The noses have it

sandy dog

Nostril grooves are connected to the mouth.

nurse hound

Nostril grooves are not connected to the mouth.

before being ready to hatch.

As youngsters the dogfishes feed on sand hoppers and other small crustaceans before graduating to crabs, shrimps, molluscs and bottom-living fish. The nurse hound also eats large crabs (especially hermits), octopuses and even smaller dogfish.

▲ *Here is a fine specimen of a 17lb (7.7kg) nurse hound (greater spotted dogfish) caught on a legered mackerel strip. Sandeels and squid are also ideal baits for catching dogfish, though they will eat almost anything you throw at them.*

◀ *The dogfish lays its eggs in tough, leathery sacs with long tendrils at each corner; these tendrils anchor the case to seaweed, wrecks and piers for up to a year until the pup is ready to hatch.*

TRACKING DOWN DOGFISHES

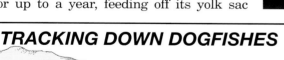

Both types of dogfish prefer weedy, rocky ground with patches of clear sand

Dogfish are popular with match anglers. They take most baits and can be caught in shallow water even in bright sunlight – provided there is some weed cover.

As a general guide, nurse hounds are found over rougher ground among the rocks

In some areas dogfish are scarce because anglers kill them out of sheer contempt. Now, these same anglers are regretting the disappearance of this species.

Sandy dogs tend to prefer sandy patches between the weeds

Bass

Every summer anglers pile into boats and rush to beaches in pursuit of the hard-fighting bass. Its reign as one of the most sought-after sea fish is undisputed.

The bass, a member of the perch family, has an elongated body with two dorsal fins. The front one is spiny, and the fish can raise it at will. Each dark gill cover has a sharp spine. Colour varies little – the fish has a grey back, distinctive silver sides and a white underside. The eyes and mouth are large, and the teeth are small.

Feeding habits

Bass are predatory. Their huge mouths enable them to swallow large food items, but they also go for small minnows and crustaceans such as peeler crabs. They eat whitebait, slipper limpets, razorfish, squid, pilchards, sprats and herring. In the daylight they hunt by sight near the surface, where young sprats or herring gather. Casting an artificial lure (spoons, pirks or squid) in front of, or behind, shoals of smaller fish is a good way to catch bass. Sometimes you can locate them after fierce storms which stir the sea bed, for they come inshore at night or when the water is murky, using their excellent sense of smell to locate ragworms, lugworms and other food.

Distribution

Bass are primarily a warm water species, preferring the southern waters of England, Ireland, and Wales. Few are caught in Scotland and northern England because of the colder conditions there.

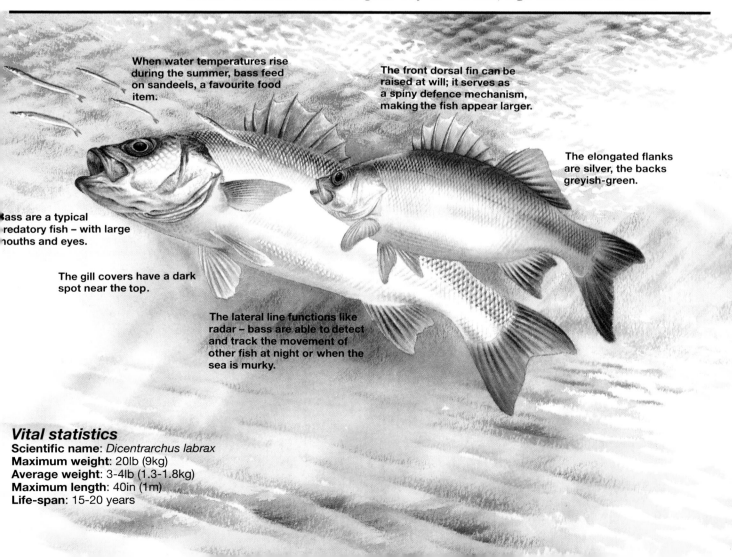

When water temperatures rise during the summer, bass feed on sandeels, a favourite food item.

The front dorsal fin can be raised at will; it serves as a spiny defence mechanism, making the fish appear larger.

The elongated flanks are silver, the backs greyish-green.

Bass are a typical predatory fish – with large mouths and eyes.

The gill covers have a dark spot near the top.

The lateral line functions like radar – bass are able to detect and track the movement of other fish at night or when the sea is murky.

Vital statistics
Scientific name: *Dicentrarchus labrax*
Maximum weight: 20lb (9kg)
Average weight: 3-4lb (1.3-1.8kg)
Maximum length: 40in (1m)
Life-span: 15-20 years

▶ *This 7lb (3.2kg) bass, taken off the coast of Guernsey, is an excellent specimen. Because bass grow slowly, a fish this size may take years to develop. It is important to return slow-maturing fish to the sea to preserve future stocks.*

Top bass areas

● **Eddystone Reef, Plymouth** Many 10-15lb (4.5-6.8kg) fish.
● **Gower Peninsula, South Wales** Many good-sized fish.
● **Dover breakwater** Some superb fish are caught here every summer.
● **Thames Estuary, Herne Bay** Offers some excellent-sized fish for boat anglers.
● **Holyhead, Anglesey** Sandy beaches with many 4-5lb (1.8-2.3kg) bass.
● **Brighton and Newhaven, Sussex** Rocky beaches with 4-7lb (1.8-3.2kg) fish.
South-west Ireland A popular place for visiting anglers. Some of the best known hotspots include Dingle Bay, the estuary of the Kenmare River and Bantry Bay. Many of the smaller bays and inlets also make this area the shore angler's paradise.

Slow-maturing fish

Spawning occurs in May or June. Unlike cod, which shed all their eggs at once, female bass lay their eggs in batches. The eggs drift in shallow water and hatch into larvae in four to seven days. The fry head for the shelter of estuaries and feed on plankton and other small organisms. As they grow, they form shoals and feed on small fish and a fairly wide variety of crustaceans.

Since bass take four to six years to mature (much slower than cod), they are prone to overfishing. At this stage of their life they are only 30-35cm (12-14in) long. Using gill nets, commercial fishermen have decimated bass populations in many areas, taking many fish before they had a chance to spawn. EEC restrictions have now been imposed, and bass have a more optimistic future – though stocks are still exceedingly low.

The warm coastal waters of southern England, Ireland and Wales have scattered populations of bass. In particular, you can find them near estuaries, power station outflows, surf beaches, harbours and rocky headlands. Structures in deeper water such as reefs, off-shore sandbanks and wrecks also have large populations. If the water temperature is high enough in the summer months, bass move into the North Sea, but this is rare. Few are caught off northern England and Scotland, for they are not a cold-water species.

Bass are attracted to warm, freshwater feeding areas during the summer, and they swim up brackish rivers. The warmer water helps them to digest food at a much higher rate. When winter draws near, however, they retreat to the deeper waters of the Atlantic – swimming as far south as the Canary Islands.

Overfishing

Because of the popularity of bass fishing, new restrictions have been introduced to preserve future stocks. The Ministry of Agriculture, Fisheries & Food (MAFF) imposes a minimum landing size of 36cm (14in) throughout Britain. The Ministry also prohibits angling from a boat in 34 designated bass nursery areas. Full details are given in the MAFF publication *Bass: Nursery Areas and other Conservation Measures.*

TYPICAL BASS FEEDING AREAS

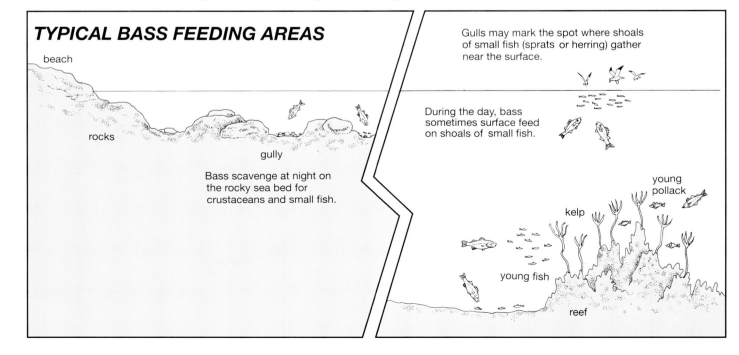

beach

rocks

gully

Bass scavenge at night on the rocky sea bed for crustaceans and small fish.

Gulls may mark the spot where shoals of small fish (sprats or herring) gather near the surface.

During the day, bass sometimes surface feed on shoals of small fish.

young pollack

kelp

young fish

reef

Thick-lipped mullet

The thick-lipped grey mullet has a distinctive feeding method, so it doesn't usually compete with other fish for food. Learning about its feeding habits may help you to be more effective against this wary fish.

Record mullet

● The British boat-caught record is a 10lb 1oz (4.56kg) specimen caught off Portland, Dorset in 1952 by P. C. Libby.
● The British shore-caught record mullet is much larger. R. S. Gifford caught a 14lb 2oz (6.42kg) fish off the Leys, Aberthaw, Glamorgan, Wales in October 1979.
● The Irish record is a 7lb 10oz (3.5kg) mullet taken from Killybegs, Donegal, on 8 June 1972 by Kevin Boyle.

There are three species of mullet around the coasts of Britain and Ireland – the thick-lipped, thin-lipped and golden-grey. The thick-lipped is the most widespread.

It has four to seven silver-grey bands spanning its streamlined flanks and two small dorsal fins along its grey-blue back; the front fin has four stiff spines. The mullet's underside is white, and its tail is forked.

An unmistakable identification feature of this fish is its thick front lips which contain sensitive nerve projections (called papillae) which may help it locate food.

Great survivors

The grey mullet can survive in places where other fish would soon perish. For example, it can withstand pollution, low levels of

Distribution

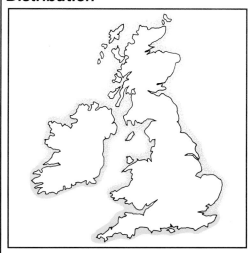

Mullet move inshore in spring/summer and are found along British and Irish coasts. In winter they move to deeper, warmer waters off southern England.

salinity (in estuaries) and oxygen-depleted waters.

The thick-lipped grey mullet stays in deep, warmer waters in winter and moves inshore as late spring approaches. In summer it can be found in estuaries, but it doesn't travel as far up river as the thin-

Vital statistics
Scientific name: *Chelon* (or *Mugil*) *labrosus*
Maximum weight: 15lb (6.8kg)
Average weight: 3lb (1.4kg)
Maximum length: 35in (88cm)

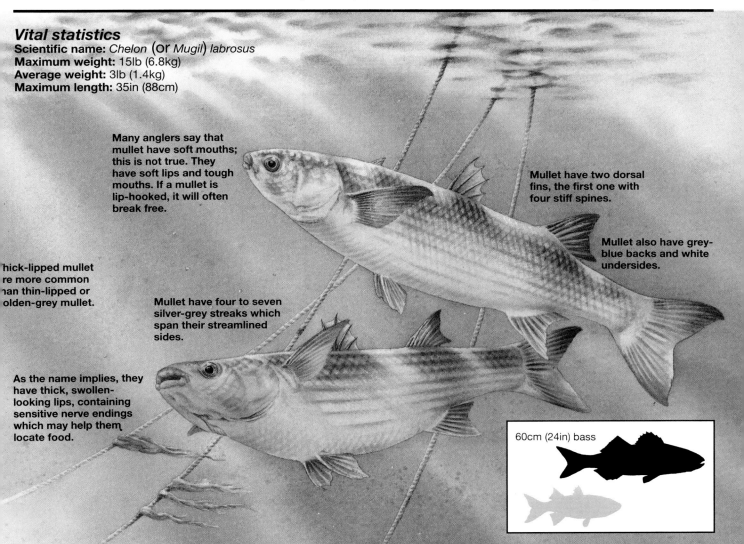

Many anglers say that mullet have soft mouths; this is not true. They have soft lips and tough mouths. If a mullet is lip-hooked, it will often break free.

Mullet have two dorsal fins, the first one with four stiff spines.

Mullet also have grey-blue backs and white undersides.

Thick-lipped mullet are more common than thin-lipped or golden-grey mullet.

Mullet have four to seven silver-grey streaks which span their streamlined sides.

As the name implies, they have thick, swollen-looking lips, containing sensitive nerve endings which may help them locate food.

60cm (24in) bass

▲ *An angler displays a fine thick-lipped grey mullet. It isn't considered a good table-fish in Britain – perhaps because of their mud-sucking feeding habits.*

Ever-filtering mullet

The mullet also feeds by filtering food particles through its gill rakers. Mud and debris are expelled while the edible matter is quickly coated with a layer of mucus and then swallowed.

The fish has yet another method of feeding: it skims the surface of the water, sucking algae or whatever edible food is available. Rocks, ropes and stanchion pier posts covered with algae also receive attention from the mullet.

You can catch it with a variety of baits including bread, mussels, ragworms, or small cubes of mackerel. The lips of a mullet are soft, but its mouth is hard, and it fights well. You need to play the fish firmly but patiently. Bullying it often causes the line to break or the hook to pull free.

Life-cycle

The thick-lipped grey mullet spawns in the spring near the coast. Numerous eggs are shed and then fertilized. After about a week the eggs hatch, and the young begin to feed on plankton, swimming farther inshore for safety reasons. You can sometimes see them stranded in rock pools. After one year the young are 3in (7.5cm) long. They mature in four to five years, growing quickly in the warm coastal waters.

Top thick-lipped mullet areas

Although mullet are found along the coasts of Britain and Ireland, these are some the better known venues.
● **Ley's Lagoon (South Wales)** An excellent venue. Many large fish are taken here every year.
● **Weymouth Breakwater or Harbour, Dorset** Many smaller mullet.
● **Dover Breakwater** Regularly produces 4-5lb (1.8-2.3kg) mullet.
● **Lowestoft Pier, Suffolk** An excellent venue in the summer for medium-sized fish.
● **Southampton Harbour, Hampshire** Another harbour which seems to attract populations of mullet.
● **Brighton Marina** Many 5lb (2.3kg) mullet are taken here regularly.
● **Thames Estuary** Large numbers of mullet feed here in summer.

lipped mullet. Harbours, bays and shallow, rocky shorelines usually have substantial numbers. Overall, it prefers relatively sheltered areas – away from strong tides.

A distinctive difference

A mullet doesn't usually compete with other fish for food. Its diet consists mainly of diatoms (a form of plankton), plants, algae, tiny crustaceans and small worms and molluscs. It is also thought that, given the opportunity, it will eat sewage. Holiday-makers in tourist areas drop bits of chips or bread into the sea, providing another source of food for mullet.

A mullet feeds in unique ways. In one method (ingestion) it finds a muddy bottom, points its head and mouth downwards (its body rising up towards the surface) and sucks and swallows a mouthful of mud and tiny organisms. Many studies suggest that about 15-20% of what a mullet takes in is edible plant or animal life. The rest (80-85%) is mud or sand.

To cope with eating all this mud, it has a gizzard-like stomach. This thick-walled, muscular stomach (along with the mud and small stones) helps to grind up the food particles. The mullet also has an exceptionally long intestine which makes absorption of nutrients and disposal of waste materials much easier. A 12in (30cm) fish, for example, has an intestine about 6-7ft (1.8-2.1m) long. As the cold winter approaches, a mullet tends to stop feeding until the water warms up again.

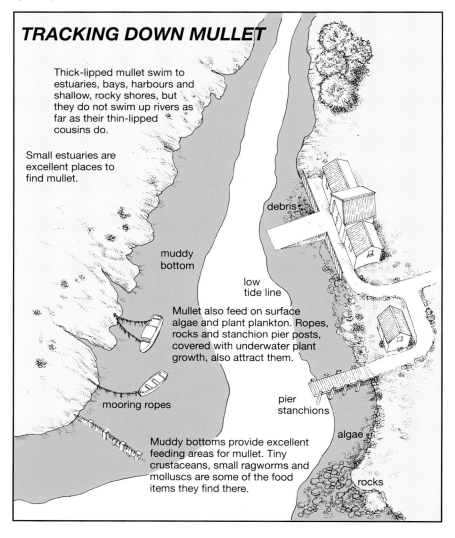

TRACKING DOWN MULLET

Thick-lipped mullet swim to estuaries, bays, harbours and shallow, rocky shores, but they do not swim up rivers as far as their thin-lipped cousins do.

Small estuaries are excellent places to find mullet.

muddy bottom

debris

low tide line

Mullet also feed on surface algae and plant plankton. Ropes, rocks and stanchion pier posts, covered with underwater plant growth, also attract them.

mooring ropes

pier stanchions

algae

Muddy bottoms provide excellent feeding areas for mullet. Tiny crustaceans, small ragworms and molluscs are some of the food items they find there.

rocks

Ballan wrasse

A popular fish among holiday-makers, ballan wrasse are quite prolific around rocky shorelines. Fun and easy to catch on light tackle, they make powerful first runs.

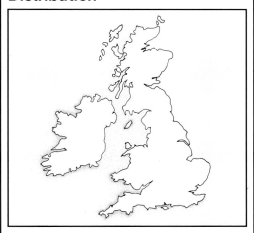

Distribution

Ballan wrasse are mostly found on the western shores of Britain and Ireland. They prefer deep, rocky shorelines to shallow surf beaches.

Record wrasse

● The British boat-caught record wrasse is 9lb 6oz (4.25kg). Mike Goodacre caught it while fishing off the Eddystone Gulley on 21 October 1981.
● R.W. LePage has the British shore-caught record – 8lb 6oz (3.8kg) – from Bordeaux Beach, Guernsey on 14 September 1976.
● The Irish record (9lb 8oz /4.3kg) was caught by B. Kron off Clogher Head in 1983.

With their stocky bodies, rows of thick, protective scales and wide tails, wrasse are perfectly suited to their rocky environment. Colouring varies considerably. Some wrasse have bright orange bellies with pale white flecks, reddish-brown flanks and black backs. Others can be just as spectacular with white undersides and blackish-green tinges to their flanks, dappled with crimson rings.

Many inexperienced anglers can testify to the wrasses' sharp teeth and powerful jaws. Their lips are thick – an unmistakable feature – and their eyes are large.

Feeding habits

Wrasse feed primarily by sight and are affected by the tide movement like most sea fish – they usually feed when the water is high. But if you toss a juicy lugworm in among a group of wrasse, you can tempt them to feed at any time during the day.

Wrasse usually stay in one area, preferring not to move too far out when the tide drops. Only when the weather is extremely cold in mid-winter do they move out to

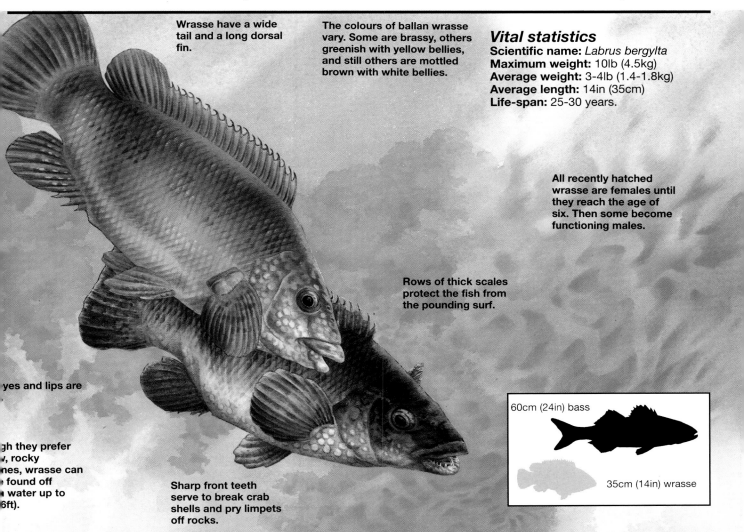

Wrasse have a wide tail and a long dorsal fin.

The colours of ballan wrasse vary. Some are brassy, others greenish with yellow bellies, and still others are mottled brown with white bellies.

Vital statistics
Scientific name: *Labrus bergylta*
Maximum weight: 10lb (4.5kg)
Average weight: 3-4lb (1.4-1.8kg)
Average length: 14in (35cm)
Life-span: 25-30 years.

All recently hatched wrasse are females until they reach the age of six. Then some become functioning males.

Rows of thick scales protect the fish from the pounding surf.

...yes and lips are

...gh they prefer ..., rocky ...nes, wrasse can .. found off .. water up to 6ft).

Sharp front teeth serve to break crab shells and pry limpets off rocks.

60cm (24in) bass
35cm (14in) wrasse

deeper, warmer water. Extreme cold for long periods of time can drastically reduce wrasse populations.

Wrasse have powerful pharyngeal teeth which enable them to eat peeler and hardback crabs, mussels, shrimps and molluscs. They also feed on razorfish, barnacles, small worms and fry.

Fishing for them at night is futile – a peculiar feature of the fish is that they sleep at night between rock crevices or in kelp forests. Divers have actually picked up sleeping wrasse at night!

Rough and rocky

Wrasse are commonly found along the rocky (granite) coastlines of western Britain and Ireland – in water up to a maximum depth of 20m (66ft). Anglers beware – wrasse are renowned for making tremendous first runs, retreating into the safety of their crevices and more than likely breaking your line. You must not be bullied by the hooked fish; otherwise, you'll lose it. Reefs and gullies also provide suitable habitat, but shallow surf and silty beaches don't .

A toothy smile!

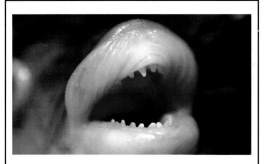

Wrasse have long sharp front teeth under their thick lips. They can pry limpets off rocks with these teeth. They also have powerful pharyngeal (throat) teeth which can crush hard food items such as crabs.

◄ *Ballan wrasse can vary enormously in colour. This 4lb (1.8kg) specimen was taken on crab bait. Using light tackle is one of the most enjoyable ways to fish for wrasse.*

Life-cycle

Another feature of ballan wrasse is that they are one of the few fish which build nests before they spawn. Using kelp, oarweeds and other seaweeds, wrasse build small nests in rock crevices. The nest is then coated with a thin mucus lining.

When wrasse are about six years old, they become sexually mature. In June or July the females deposit numerous eggs in their nests. When the eggs hatch, the fry – which are all female – swim to shallow waters where they feed on plankton.

After several seasons of producing eggs, some of the female wrasse (aged five to seven years) change sex and become functioning males – though there always seems to be more females in a shoal than males. The exact reason for this change is not known but it is thought that having more females in a population means that more offspring are produced.

Top areas for finding wrasse

Anglers are advised to use caution when fishing along the steep western shorelines which have slippery rocks.
● **Portland Bill, Dorset (especially Pulpit Rock)** supports a large wrasse population and has thick kelp forests and a fast tide. Plenty of 5-6lb (2.3-2.7kg) fish.
● **Falmouth to Penzance, Cornwall** Some of the best wrasse fishing in Europe. Many 5-8lb (2.3-3.6kg) fish along the steep, rocky shorelines.
● **Wadebridge, Cornwall to Barnstaple, Devon** Unparalleled wrasse fishing. Float fishing with lugworm works well.
● **Swanage, Dorset (Anvil Point to the southern edge of Swanage Bay)** Provides good wrasse fishing with fish of 3-4lb (1.4-1.8kg).
● **Brixham, Devon (Barry Point)** Many large catches of 3-5lb (1.4-2.3kg) fish.

TRACKING DOWN WRASSE

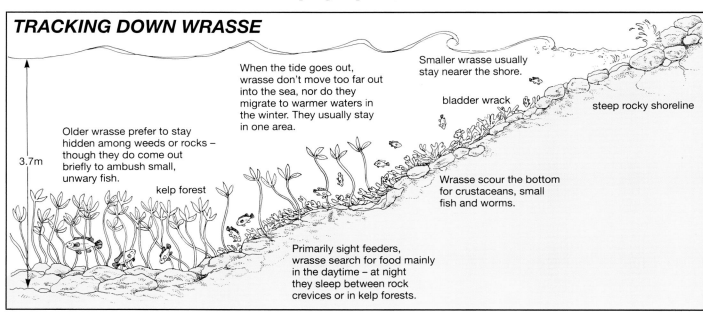

When the tide goes out, wrasse don't move too far out into the sea, nor do they migrate to warmer waters in the winter. They usually stay in one area.

Smaller wrasse usually stay nearer the shore.

bladder wrack

steep rocky shoreline

Older wrasse prefer to stay hidden among weeds or rocks – though they do come out briefly to ambush small, unwary fish.

3.7m

kelp forest

Wrasse scour the bottom for crustaceans, small fish and worms.

Primarily sight feeders, wrasse search for food mainly in the daytime – at night they sleep between rock crevices or in kelp forests.

Common skate

Brian Swinbanks, charter boat skipper from the Isle of Mull, Scotland, looks at the common skate, a unique bottom-dwelling fish.

British record common skate

● The British boat-caught record is a 227lb (103kg) common skate caught by Reg Banks in July 1986 off Tobermory, Isle of Mull, on Brian Swinbanks' boat *Laurenca*.

● R. Knight has the shore-caught record – a 138lb (62kg) skate. He was fishing from the pier, Breasclete, Loch Roag, Isle of Lewis, in 1989.

Common skate are one of the largest fish in European waters. They have wide, flat bodies, 'wings' and long tails lined with sharp spines. The colour of skate varies – some have brownish-grey upperparts; others are dappled with white or grey blotches. The undersides are greyish white.

The eyes are on the top of the head while the huge mouth – filled with rows of small teeth – is on the underside.

Holes just behind the eyes (called spiracles) allow water to be taken in. Without them, the fish would have to breathe through the mouth like most other fish. With rays and skate which lie flat on the sea bed, this would be a problem, for they'd get a mouthful of sand or gravel every time they tried to breathe!

Preferred terrain
Skate prefer gravel, shingle bottoms, rough, rocky ridges and huge boulders.

Distribution

Once widespread all around Britain, the common skate can only be found around northern and western Scotland, the Shetland and Orkney Islands and western Ireland.

They are often located near underwater cliffs. In the winter and spring they lie in deep water – 90-150m (300-500ft). In May, June and July they move into water about 45-75m (150-250ft) deep.

Common skate were once found all

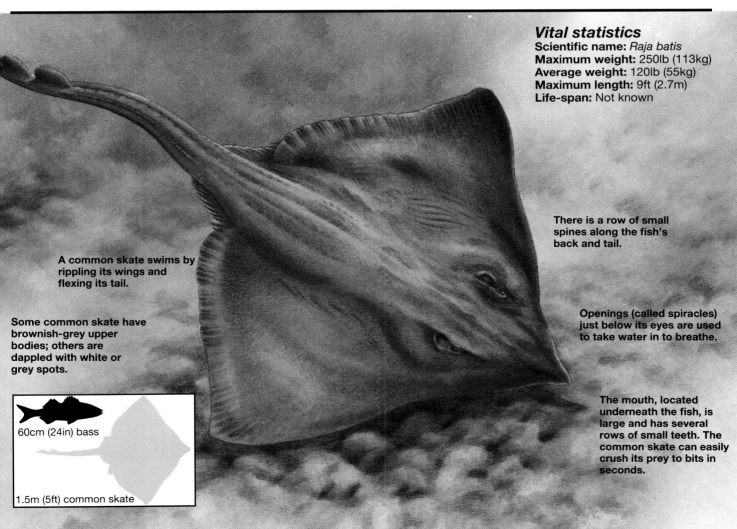

Vital statistics
Scientific name: *Raja batis*
Maximum weight: 250lb (113kg)
Average weight: 120lb (55kg)
Maximum length: 9ft (2.7m)
Life-span: Not known

A common skate swims by rippling its wings and flexing its tail.

Some common skate have brownish-grey upper bodies; others are dappled with white or grey spots.

There is a row of small spines along the fish's back and tail.

Openings (called spiracles) just below its eyes are used to take water in to breathe.

The mouth, located underneath the fish, is large and has several rows of small teeth. The common skate can easily crush its prey to bits in seconds.

60cm (24in) bass

1.5m (5ft) common skate

▲ *Trevor Housby battles with a large common skate. It is said that pulling up a common skate is like trying to bring aboard a Volvo estate car!*

▶ *This skate was caught off Tobermory, Isle of Mull, Scotland. Because they are so rare, they should be returned to the sea.*

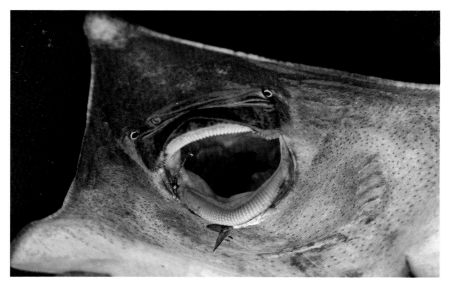

around the British Isles, but overfishing has now greatly reduced populations of these magnificent fish. Only a few areas have sufficient numbers of skate – the west coast of Ireland, the Orkney and Shetland Islands and the north and west coasts of Scotland.

Feeding habits

Many boated skate have regurgitated large crabs, spurdogs and thornback rays. Skate also prey upon pollack, coalfish, cod and lobster. Concealed by their dark, flat bodies, skate lie motionless on the sea bed during a strong tide, waiting for unwary fish to swim near. The voracious predators then pounce upon their quarry.

Because the eyes are on the top of the body and the mouth is on the bottom, common skate sometimes miss their prey. If that happens, they trap the victim under a 'wing' and then manoeuvre it toward their large mouths.

Skate can also feed in mid-water, chasing pilchards, herrings, coalfish and pollack from above.

Fishing for skate requires simple but heavy tackle. Usually size 8/0-12/0 hooks, baited with coalfish or mackerel, are sufficient. Use either heavy monofilament or wire traces; the big fish aren't spooked by heavy traces and often greedily devour two or three baits before an angler can set the hook.

Life-cycle

Common skate are members of a family of fish which have skeletons of cartilage, not bone. They are a bit like flat sharks. In spring and summer skate move into shallow water to mate. Females deposit numerous egg cases along rocky or gravel bottoms. After about five to six months young skate emerge from their cases in search of food – small crustaceans and fish.

▲ *The mouth of a common skate is huge. It has immensely powerful jaws and rows of small teeth.*

 Tagged local residents

The Glasgow Museum, Department of Natural History and The Irish Fisheries Department determined from various tagging programmes that skate populations are extremely localized. Many of the fish are caught again and again within a few miles of their release point. Tagged skate off Tobermory have been caught two and even three times.

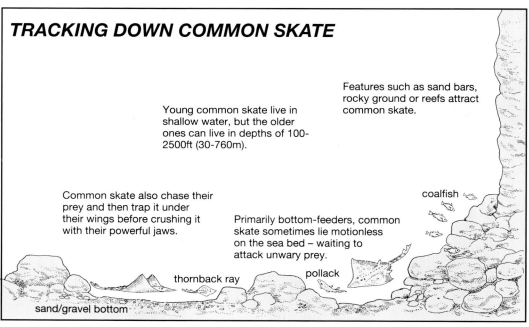

TRACKING DOWN COMMON SKATE

Young common skate live in shallow water, but the older ones can live in depths of 100-2500ft (30-760m).

Features such as sand bars, rocky ground or reefs attract common skate.

Common skate also chase their prey and then trap it under their wings before crushing it with their powerful jaws.

Primarily bottom-feeders, common skate sometimes lie motionless on the sea bed – waiting to attack unwary prey.

coalfish

thornback ray

pollack

sand/gravel bottom

Herring

Once, whole communities depended on catching herring. Now, because of constant overfishing, the population of these 'silver darlings' is a mere shadow of its former self.

Record-breaking herring

● The boat-caught record is held by Brett Barden, for a fish caught off Bexhill-on-Sea, East Sussex in 1973. It weighed 1lb 1oz (0.481g).

A record claim has been put forward by Mr G. Dalton for a 1lb 3¼oz (0.54kg) herring caught off Exmouth, Devon in April 1991, but this has yet to be ratified.

● No-one holds the shore-caught record, which has a qualifying weight of 1lb (0.45kg) – fish this size live in much deeper water.

The herring is such an everyday fish – every high street fishmonger has trays of these shiny, silvery fish with reddish gills – that few of us give it a second glance. This familiarity can sometimes cause problems when an angler catches a herring – the gleaming blue-backed fish with golden tints does not look like the dead fish on the fishmonger's slab.

More errors are made distinguishing young herring from sprats and shads than almost any other fish. All members of the herring family have slender bodies, a short dorsal fin, distinctly forked tail and no lateral line. Their oily flesh makes them an ideal bait food for many bigger species. The edge of the herring's upper jaw is rounded and unlike the shad there is no notch in the midline. The dorsal fin starts in front of, or above, the base of the pelvic fins – in the sprat it is behind the pelvics. The sprat and

Distribution

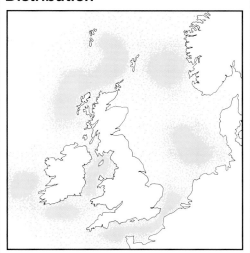

Adult herring are found offshore around most of the British Isles, though not throughout the year because of their migration patterns. The young can be found in estuaries and most coastal waters.

shad both have a row of sharp scales on the belly, but the herring does not.

Free swimming

Herring live in the open sea down to depths of 250m (820ft). They swim in shoals which

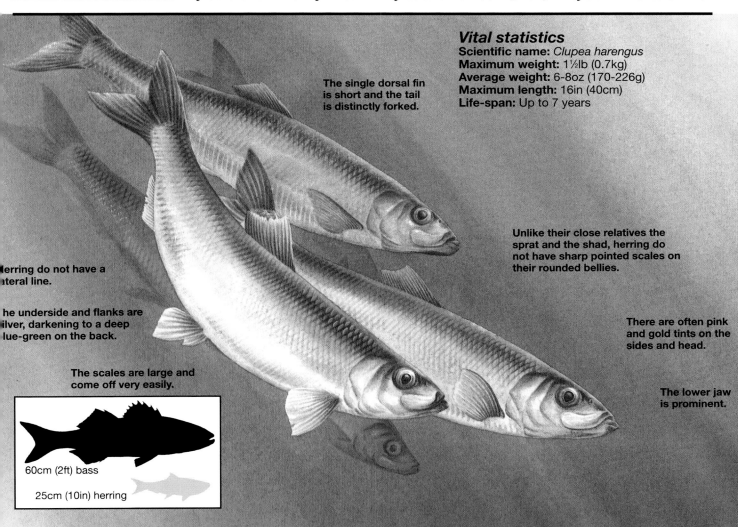

The single dorsal fin is short and the tail is distinctly forked.

Vital statistics
Scientific name: *Clupea harengus*
Maximum weight: 1½lb (0.7kg)
Average weight: 6-8oz (170-226g)
Maximum length: 16in (40cm)
Life-span: Up to 7 years

Unlike their close relatives the sprat and the shad, herring do not have sharp pointed scales on their rounded bellies.

Herring do not have a lateral line.

The underside and flanks are silver, darkening to a deep blue-green on the back.

There are often pink and gold tints on the sides and head.

The scales are large and come off very easily.

The lower jaw is prominent.

60cm (2ft) bass

25cm (10in) herring

Herring aid

Heavy overfishing in the 1950s and 1960s led to a drastic decline in herring stocks. By 1975 the population was less than 10% of what it had been. Bans were imposed in 1977-8 in the North Sea and to the west of Scotland to counteract this.

Although these bans have since been lifted, herring stocks haven't risen, partly because small herring are still being caught for the fish-meal industry. These days only boats from Scotland go fishing for herring; most of those in England and Wales have hung up their nets.

sometimes contain thousands of tons of fish. In European waters several different races of herring exist – each with separate spawning grounds, feeding habits and migration patterns. At one time herring were abundant, but overfishing on the part of various countries has reduced numbers greatly. This in turn led to the disappearance of blue fin tuna in the North Sea – a species which relied heavily on herring shoals for food.

There are still plenty around, but nothing like the millions of fish that once seasonally passed along British coasts, and certainly not enough to be of much commercial value.

One of the best known migrations was in the North Sea – after spawning, the herring travelled southwards in an anti-clockwise direction to end up off the Kentish coast.

Follow the plankton

The shoal follows food to the surface at night, moving to deeper water at dawn. Unlike many plankton-feeding fish, the herring does not simply swim around with

▲ This herring was caught using attractor beads. Because they are plankton feeding fish and have a small mouth they are not real quarry for sea anglers.

its mouth open, but selects food items by sight. It occasionally eats small crustaceans, shrimps and large numbers of young fish.

Life-cycle

Most of the herring groups around the British Isles spawn in autumn – spring spawners are found too but their numbers are relatively small. Each shoal returns to the same spawning ground year after year. Most fish that feed at the surface also lay their eggs there, but the herring differs by spawning close to the sea bed. The female lays up to 50,000 eggs which sink to the bottom, forming a carpet up to 20 eggs deep over the sea bed.

The eggs hatch a fortnight later as scaleless, transparent larvae, and swim towards the surface to float among the plankton. Within a few weeks they reach a length of 5cm (2in) and drift with the current into estuaries and coastal waters. They form huge shoals along with young shad – known collectively as whitebait.

The young fish remain inshore for up to a year before moving into deeper water. It is not until they are sexually mature at two to three years old that they join the adult shoals and begin the annual migration to their birthplace.

TRACKING DOWN HERRING

trawler

During a 24 hour period, herring shoals may move up and down a vertical column of several hundred feet in search of plankton.

The biggest predator of herring is the commercial fisherman.

150m

Herring spend the day in deeper water, coming to the surface at night.

Herring live in the open sea, far from the shelter of rocks or wrecks, so they form huge shoals to gain some protection.

Flounder

Happy living in both fresh and sea water, the flounder is the only flatfish to be so adaptable.

Many anglers still confuse flounders, dabs and plaice – but though they are all members of the 'right-eyed' flatfish family, they do have distinguishing features that set them apart. Plaice are smooth-bodied with a series of bony bumps between the eyes, and bright red/orange spots, while the dabs feel rough all over when rubbed from tail to head. The flounder is easily identified by the prickly region that runs along its lateral line and round the base of its dorsal and anal fins. It also has a square-cut tail, while in most other flatfish the tail is rounded.

Chameleon colouring

Like all flatfish, the flounder can adapt its mottled brown colouring to match that of the sea bed – each cell changes shape to vary the amount of pigment visible, so changing the colour of its skin.

Spending most of its day buried in the sand or mud of estuaries and coastal waters, the flounder becomes active at night, moving nearer the shore to feed at high tide, then retreating as it falls.

Distribution

Flounders are widespread around the coasts of Britain and Ireland. They are abundant in estuaries during the winter months.

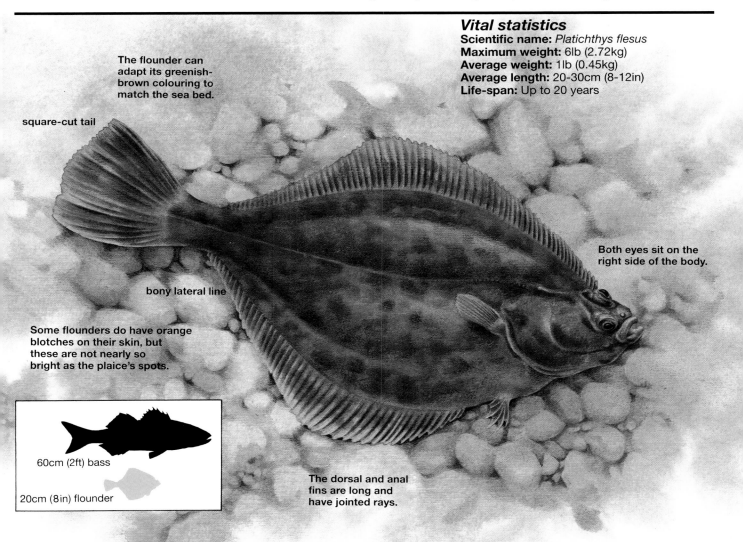

The flounder can adapt its greenish-brown colouring to match the sea bed.

square-cut tail

bony lateral line

Some flounders do have orange blotches on their skin, but these are not nearly so bright as the plaice's spots.

60cm (2ft) bass

20cm (8in) flounder

The dorsal and anal fins are long and have jointed rays.

Both eyes sit on the right side of the body.

Vital statistics
Scientific name: *Platichthys flesus*
Maximum weight: 6lb (2.72kg)
Average weight: 1lb (0.45kg)
Average length: 20-30cm (8-12in)
Life-span: Up to 20 years

Fresh/sea water homes

The flounder is unique among British flatfishes in that it is able to live in both fresh and sea water. Although some venture upstream into completely fresh water, most are found in the brackish water of estuaries, attracted by the vast worm populations on which the mature fish feeds.

However, the fish cannot move very quickly between these two contrasting environments; it needs time to adjust physically to the point where its blood is neither diluted by too much freshwater nor dehydrated by salt water.

Large volumes of inland rainfall and melting snow reduce the salinity and temperature of the water, providing problems for the slow-changing flounder. The angler can take advantage of this as the fish tends to be most abundant – and vulnerable – in late autumn/winter when these problems are most likely to occur.

During this period the mature flounder feeds heavily to prepare itself for reproduction and to help see it through any cold snaps – and is therefore more likely to take an angler's bait.

All change

In spring, the flounder moves out to the open sea to spawn; the female lays between half and two million eggs in depths up to 50m (165ft). These float on the sea's surface, before hatching one week later as tiny, round fish.

The young flounder then moves to shallow coastal waters, feeding on microscopic plants and animals before moving on to molluscs, polychaete worms and soft-shelled crabs. (Unlike the plaice, it does not have the ability to crush tough shellfish.)

Anglers usually find that peeler crab is one of the best baits for catching this fish.

As with plaice and dabs, a dramatic change takes place when the young flounder reaches a length of about 1.5-3cm (½-1in) – the fish's body flattens and the left eye moves to sit alongside the right. The dorsal fin grows forwards along the edge of the head, and the young flounder now swims with its (eyeless) left side downwards. Sexual maturity is reached when the male is only 12cm (5in) long and the female 18cm (7in).

Recommended hotspots

The following are good waters for flounders.
● **River Kent Estuary, Lancs/Cumbria border** Many locations, the best being Arnside.
● **Magilligan Strand, N. Ireland** Plenty of medium-sized fish from this open shore location.
● **Portsmouth, Chichester & Langstone Harbours** All produce a good amount of fish.
● **Silloth, Cumbria** The inner Solway has plenty of average-sized fish.
● **Southampton Water, Hants** Consistently good numbers of fish.
● **Teign Estuary, Devon** Without doubt the country's most prolific producer of specimen flounders.
● **Wexford Harbour, Co. Wexford, Republic of Ireland** Many good specimens here.

◄ *This fine brace of winter flounder, weighing in at 2lb (0.9kg) apiece, were caught off the beach at Dawlish Warren in Devon.*

Able to adapt their colouring to match the sea bed, they range from dull grey to brown.

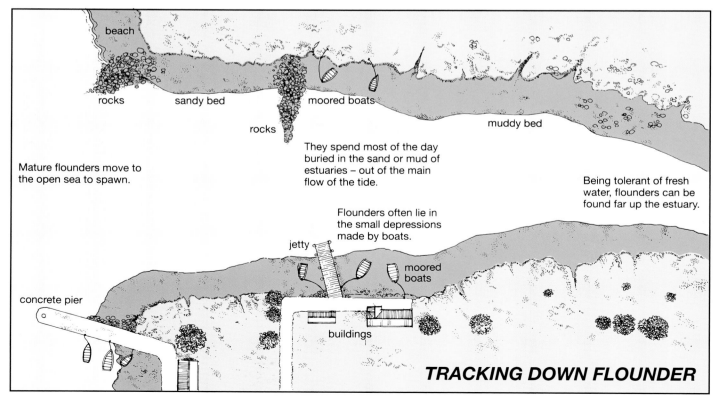

beach

rocks   sandy bed

rocks

moored boats

muddy bed

Mature flounders move to the open sea to spawn.

They spend most of the day buried in the sand or mud of estuaries – out of the main flow of the tide.

Being tolerant of fresh water, flounders can be found far up the estuary.

Flounders often lie in the small depressions made by boats.

jetty

moored boats

concrete pier

buildings

TRACKING DOWN FLOUNDER

Porbeagle

Although not for the inexperienced, the porbeagle (or mackerel shark) offers the best opportunity for anglers to enjoy big-game fishing in European waters.

Distribution

Porbeagles can be found all round the British Isles, though they are distinctly less common in the eastern English Channel and the North Sea than they are in the western approaches or the Atlantic coast.

Record boat-caught porbeagle

● The British boat-caught record is held by J. Potier, who caught a 465lb (210.9kg) fish off Padstow, Cornwall in 1976.
● There is no holder of the British shore-caught record, which has a qualifying weight of 40lb (18.143kg).

Shore caught fish are unlikely as it is rare to find porbeagles less than 300m (330yd) from the coast.

For the British angler porbeagles are the most exciting of all the sharks because of their size, power and relative abundance. They belong to the same family as the mako and the great white shark. However, the great white has never been reported in British seas and the mako is rare – both are less tolerant of cold water than porbeagles. Nevertheless, there is some risk of confusion between porbeagles and makos.

Porbeagle versus mako

You can distinguish the porbeagle from the mako by the position of the second dorsal fin. In the porbeagle it is opposite the anal fin, while in the mako it is in front. The porbeagle also has keel-like ridges on each side of its tail, and a bluntly rounded snout. The mako has no tail ridges and its snout is sharp.

The conclusive way of telling the two apart is by the shape of their teeth. In the porbeagle these are pointed with cusps on either side – these cusps are absent in the

Vital statistics
Scientific name: *Lamna nasus*
Maximum weight: 500lb (227kg)
Average weight: 50lb (22.7kg)
Maximum length: 10ft (3m)
Life-span: Possibly up to 25 years

The porbeagle's deep, barrel-shaped body is grey/blue on the back and sides, and its underbelly is white.

Its snout is much more rounded than that of its close relative the mako.

The small second dorsal fin is positioned opposite the anal fin.

The porbeagle is able to grow replacement teeth, so two or three rows can be present at any one time.

There are keel-like ridges on either side of the tail.

e tail is crescent-aped, with a long, tched upper lobe.

Like all members of the shark family, the porbeagle has five uncovered gill slits.

2.4m (8ft) porbeagle

60cm (2ft) bass

▲ *With its large, powerful body, the porbeagle offers an exciting challenge for the experienced British angler.*

mako. (Don't be too hasty in using this method to tell the difference between the two – often what looks like a dead shark is very much alive!) Sharks also grow replacement teeth and two or three rows can be mature at any one time.

Like most sharks, porbeagles are blue on their sides and back, and have a white underbelly which helps them to merge into their surroundings.

Ever decreasing circles

Porbeagles are fast swimmers and spend their lives on the trail of schooling fish, such as mackerel (hence the nickname mackerel shark), herring and pilchard, hunting them for food. They swim fairly close to the surface in small groups, and are occasionally caught up in the nets of trawlers.

Unfortunately, because of the over-fishing of mackerel and herring, porbeagles are much scarcer than they once were. The Norwegians fish for porbeagles intensively, making use of their flesh and massive oil-filled livers. They work mainly off the west coast of Ireland, each boat using several floating long lines.

Like all sharks, porbeagles are slow-growing and take several years to reach sexual maturity. They bear their young live, producing one 'pup' at a time when the females are small and up to four when they are fully grown.

The embryos lie free in the mother's uterus, and when they have absorbed their own yolk sac – they are about 6cm (2.4in)

long at this point – they feed on any unfertilized eggs. The young are 60cm (24in) long when born. Porbeagles are unlikely to breed every year and this low productive rate is another reason for their ever-decreasing numbers.

A-hunting we will go

Waters off the south-west of England and west of Ireland are ideal places to go hunting for these barrel-like fish. They often come fairly close inshore in summer in their search for food, and follow the mackerel back to deep water offshore in winter.

This is not an everyday fish for the sea angler, but a catch to make with strong, good quality tackle. Use rubby dubby to attract the porbeagle to your boat, then mackerel or herring bait. This monster will fight long and hard, and is not a quarry for inexperienced or solitary anglers.

▶ *You need good quality, robust tackle to land a hard-fighting porbeagle. A large hook – size 10/0 or 12/0 – attached to a 60-90cm (2-3ft) wire trace, plus several hundred yards of 50lb (22.7kg) b.s. line is ideal.*

Tub gurnard

No-one really knows why, but the tub (or saphirine) gurnard makes grunting sounds by vibrating its swim bladder – it's the noisiest fish in British coastal waters.

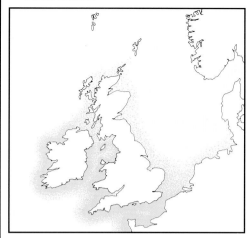

Distribution

The tub gurnard has been reported all round the British coast, but is less common in the northern North Sea and north of the Isle of Man.

Record tub

● C.W. King holds the boat-caught record with a fish weighing 11lb 7oz (5.195kg) from Wallasey, Merseyside in 1952.
● The British shore-caught record is 12lb 3oz (5.528kg), caught by G.J. Reynolds in 1976 from Langland Bay, Wales.
● The Irish record is held by R. Seaman for a 12lb 3oz (5.528kg) tub caught off Bullsmouth, Achill in 1973.

With their huge 'armour-plated' heads, raised, bulbous eyes and tapering bodies, the gurnards are odd-looking fellows, though easily identifiable. It is not so easy, however, to distinguish between the six different species found in British waters. The piper is a deep-water fish living at depths of at least 300m (985ft), while the long-finned gurnard is rare. The remaining four species – tub, red, grey and streaked gurnards – are more abundant.

Multi-coloured tub

The tub gurnard is the most common. It is large, being the only one of the six species to

▶ *The brilliant blue edging only shows when the tub's fins are spread out.*

Vital statistics
Scientific name: *Trigla lucerna*
Maximum weight: 12lb (5.4kg)
Average weight: 3lb (1.4kg)
Maximum length: 30in (76cm)
Life-span: 7-8 years

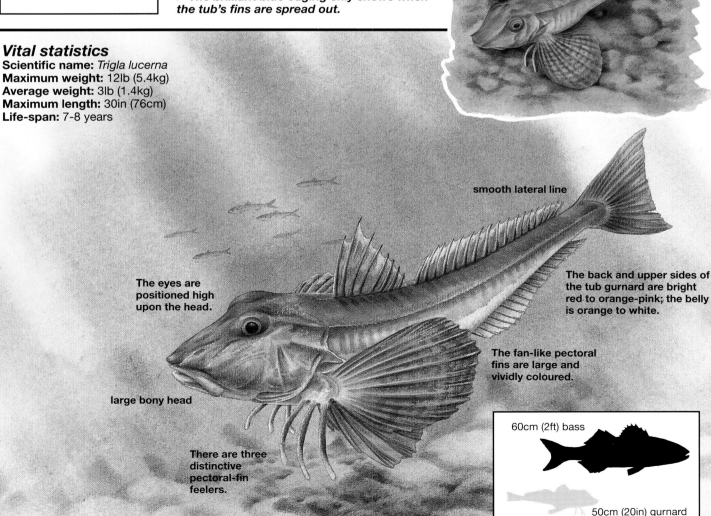

smooth lateral line

The eyes are positioned high upon the head.

The back and upper sides of the tub gurnard are bright red to orange-pink; the belly is orange to white.

large bony head

The fan-like pectoral fins are large and vividly coloured.

There are three distinctive pectoral-fin feelers.

60cm (2ft) bass

50cm (20in) gurnard

weigh in at more than 4½lbs (2kg). Colour is important too – in the tub the pectoral fins can be either blue or green, edged with either red or bright peacock blue (when the fins are spread out these colours are uppermost). In other gurnards these fins are not nearly so well developed nor so brightly coloured.

No-one is certain what the brilliant pectoral fins are for – but they are probably used either as a defence mechanism to deter predators or for attracting a mating partner. Many other animals have bright colours which can suddenly be revealed to startle an oncoming predator. They also make the creature seem much larger than it really is. The degree to which bright colouring is developed in the tub is perhaps a response to its rather solitary life-style.

Its body colouring is variable and can range from red/pink (making it easy to confuse with the red gurnard) to yellow and brown. Its eye tends to be smaller than that of either the red or grey gurnard and its lateral line scales are small and smooth (not large and spiny as in the grey).

Going solo
The tub lives on muddy or sandy bottoms at depths of up to 50m (165ft). Common around Britain, it is more widely dispersed than either the red or grey gurnard. In parts of the North Sea grey gurnards are caught in their hundreds, and in western parts of the English Channel the same is true of red gurnards; but in both areas the tub is only caught in ones and twos, preferring a more solitary life-style than that of its cousins. Being a larger fish, the tub can afford to spread out, while smaller species form schools for protection.

Feeling for food
The gurnard has a unique way of searching for food – its pectoral fins are so well developed that the first three rays have become separate feelers which are covered in sensitive taste buds. It uses these finger-like rays to 'walk' along the sea bed probing for crabs,

▶ *The tub's vividly coloured pectoral fins are probably used to deter predators or to attract a mating partner.*

The 'singing' gurnard

The gurnard is unusual in being able to grunt – it does this by vibrating the muscles along the sides of its swim bladder. It is known to be especially noisy during the spawning season – possibly to warn off competitors or aggressors. These growling, squawking or grunting sounds can often be heard at night from a quiet boat in shallow waters.

▼ *Like all gurnards, the brightly coloured red uses its feelers to probe the sea bed for food.*

shrimps and bottom-living fish such as gobies, sandeels and young flatfish. The tub is a fast swimmer so it can catch sand smelts and pilchards.

The gurnard reaches sexual maturity after three years, and moves to shallow waters between spring and early summer to spawn. The eggs hatch after about ten days and the larvae feed on plankton until they are big enough for life on the sea bed.

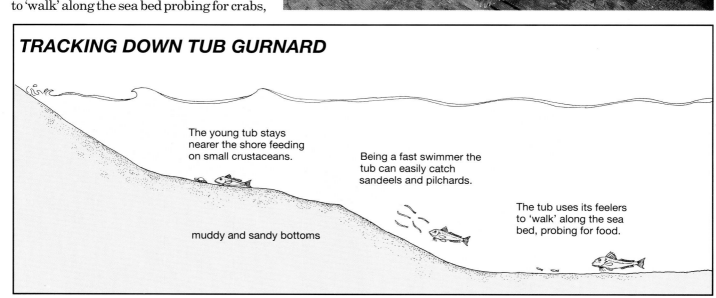

TRACKING DOWN TUB GURNARD

The young tub stays nearer the shore feeding on small crustaceans.

Being a fast swimmer the tub can easily catch sandeels and pilchards.

The tub uses its feelers to 'walk' along the sea bed, probing for food.

muddy and sandy bottoms

Tope

Tope are one of Britain's best loved and most abundant sharks. Caught from shore or a boat, they fight courageously and make long and often unstoppable runs.

The tope belongs to the same family as blue sharks and the notorious man-eating tiger sharks. Like all sharks, a tope is a powerful fish, capable of swimming at high speeds. Its body is a streamlined, blue-grey (sometimes sandy grey) mass of cartilage and muscle. The tail is deeply forked, and the front dorsal fin and pectoral fins are large, helping it to manoeuvre tight angles easily.

Sand and rock resident

Many anglers believe that tope live mostly over sand in the summer months; this isn't entirely true. Though sand and gravel are good places to look for tope, boulders and even very rough ground (where there are rocky reefs or large sand bars) receive attention from the sharks. The prey they hunt plays an important role in where you find tope.

Distribution

In summer tope move inshore and are found in the Channel, the Irish Sea and as far north as Iceland. In winter tope migrate to deep water off southern Ireland.

Solitary? Sometimes

Tope are reputed to be a solitary fish – and this is in fact the case most of the time. What can appear to be a shoal is probably little more than a loose pack of fish over a favoured feeding area – though in a few places, such as the Lancashire

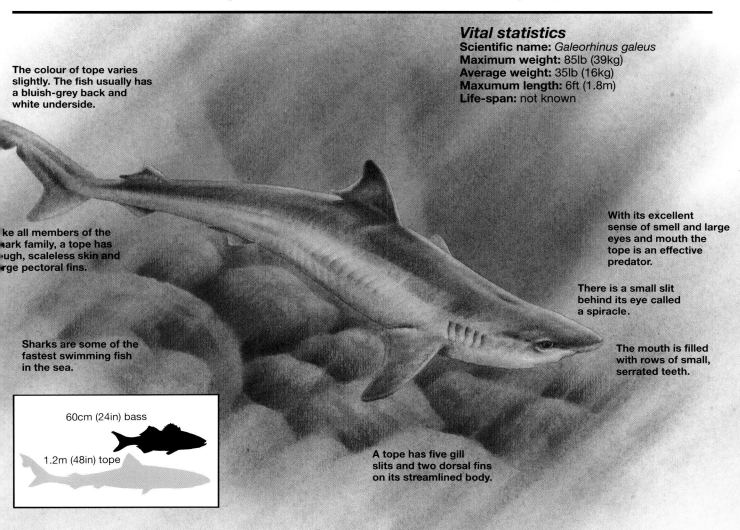

Vital statistics
Scientific name: *Galeorhinus galeus*
Maximum weight: 85lb (39kg)
Average weight: 35lb (16kg)
Maxumum length: 6ft (1.8m)
Life-span: not known

The colour of tope varies slightly. The fish usually has a bluish-grey back and white underside.

...ke all members of the ...ark family, a tope has ...ugh, scaleless skin and ...rge pectoral fins.

Sharks are some of the fastest swimming fish in the sea.

With its excellent sense of smell and large eyes and mouth the tope is an effective predator.

There is a small slit behind its eye called a spiracle.

The mouth is filled with rows of small, serrated teeth.

A tope has five gill slits and two dorsal fins on its streamlined body.

60cm (24in) bass

1.2m (48in) tope

▲ *Female tope give birth to about 20 'pups', small tope about 15in (38cm) long. The pups form schools and live in shallow waters.*

▲ *This healthy-looking 50lb (23kg) tope was caught off Beachy Head.*

▲ *The tope's golden eye is enormous. Tope are exceptional predators – their eyesight and sense of smell are excellent.*

coast and parts of the Hampshire coast, anglers see vast numbers of tope inshore together. In most areas, however, the shark is solitary.

Follow the feeding
Efficient hunting and killing machines with a superb sense of smell and rows of serrated teeth, tope take a back seat only to porbeagle sharks as ambush artists. Tope prey mainly on whiting, mackerel and pouting. Crabs, eels and small flatfish such as flounder and dabs are also part of a tope's diet. Along parts of the Cumbrian coast big tope are regularly taken over rocky ground on large peeler crabs. On the east coast anglers use eel sections, also an effective bait.

The key to successful tope fishing is plenty of rubby dubby and ultra fresh hook bait.

Life-cycle
Sharks reproduce in a variety of ways. Some lay cased eggs while others – like the tope – bear live pups. The gestation period

of tope pups is about ten months to a year. Mature female tope move inshore in early summer and give birth to about 20 pups in shallow water. The small fish – about 15in (38cm) long – form schools and remain in shallow water, feeding on small crustaceans, fish and worms.

Handle with care
Tope need to be handled gently. Without the support of the sea to help contain the weight of the vital organs within the body cavity, small blood vessels can rupture. Badly treated fish can bleed to death. Only the best fish should be brought carefully into the boat for weighing on a scale fitted with a cradle (something which is similar to the scale used by carp anglers).

Top tope areas – shore and boat

● **Bradwell, Essex** Most of the biggest tope on record have come from this part of the Thames Estuary.
● **Baggy Point, Devon** Shore fishing is excellent for big tope.
● **Luce Bay, Scotland** Boat fishing from Drummore. Many big 50-60lb (23-27kg) tope.
● **Aberdovey, Wales** Many tope are taken off here.
● **Blackpool, Lancashire** Early summer fishing is the best. Many medium-sized tope.
● **Aberystwyth, Wales** Large numbers of 40-50lb (18-23kg) fish.

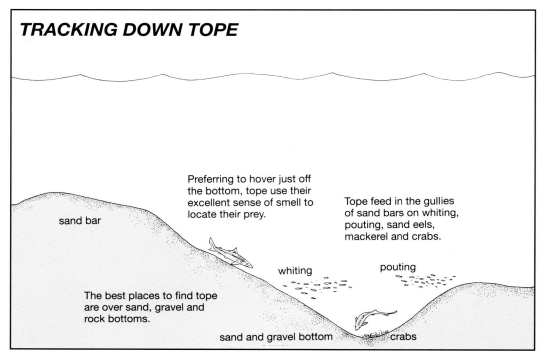

TRACKING DOWN TOPE

sand bar

Preferring to hover just off the bottom, tope use their excellent sense of smell to locate their prey.

Tope feed in the gullies of sand bars on whiting, pouting, sand eels, mackerel and crabs.

whiting

pouting

The best places to find tope are over sand, gravel and rock bottoms.

sand and gravel bottom

crabs

Sole

Much prized as a food fish for its fine flavour, the sole – also called the Dover sole – can be found all round the coasts of Britain.

Where to fish

Summer/autumn fishing for sole is good all round the south coast of England and Wales, especially off Ramsgate, Seabrook, Bognor Regis, the Isle of Wight and the Channel Islands, and in the Irish Sea.

Sole records

- **Boat-caught** S. Brice for a 3lb 12oz 4dm (1.708kg) sole, Isle of Wight, 1980.
- **Shore-caught** N.V. Guilmoto for a 6lb 8oz 10dm (2.966kg) fish, Alderney, 1991.

The Dover sole is probably one of the best known of the flatfishes living in British seas. Its long oval shape is characteristic – a fact its name acknowledges since *sole* is the Latin for sandal or slipper.

Not so lonely

There are, of course, other members of the sole family in British seas but none is as large (average length 30cm/12in) or as numerous as the Dover sole.

Of the others, the tiny solenette, less than 13cm (5in) long, has a dark bar along every fifth or sixth ray in its dorsal and anal fins; the thickback sole has five regular broad brown bands across its back; and the rare sand sole, 36cm (14in) long, has a hugely swollen, rosette-like front nostril on the underside of the head.

Any sole lacking these features must be a Dover sole. (The lemon sole isn't a sole at all – it's a relative of the dab.)

Distribution

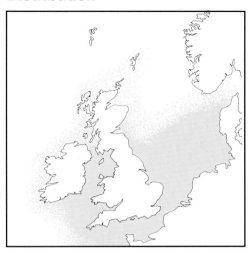

The sole is most common in the southern half of the British Isles; it occurs fairly frequently in Scottish waters. The whole distribution pattern is obscured by over-fishing and bad management of the resource.

Sea bed life-style

Strongly associated with sandy coastlines and offshore to a depth of 100m (330ft), the sole also occurs on muddy bottoms or mud mixed with sand or stones. It burrows in the surface of the sand, lying hidden with just

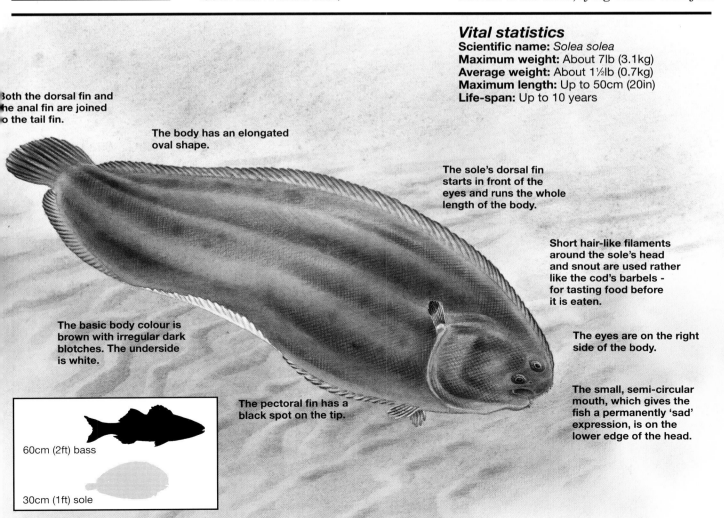

Vital statistics

Scientific name: *Solea solea*
Maximum weight: About 7lb (3.1kg)
Average weight: About 1½lb (0.7kg)
Maximum length: Up to 50cm (20in)
Life-span: Up to 10 years

Both the dorsal fin and the anal fin are joined to the tail fin.

The body has an elongated oval shape.

The sole's dorsal fin starts in front of the eyes and runs the whole length of the body.

Short hair-like filaments around the sole's head and snout are used rather like the cod's barbels - for tasting food before it is eaten.

The basic body colour is brown with irregular dark blotches. The underside is white.

The eyes are on the right side of the body.

The pectoral fin has a black spot on the tip.

The small, semi-circular mouth, which gives the fish a permanently 'sad' expression, is on the lower edge of the head.

60cm (2ft) bass

30cm (1ft) sole

its eyes showing. Most soles live like this throughout the day, perfectly concealed, the colour of their upper side matching the sea bed. At twilight and during the night they become active, scouring the bottom for food, and even swimming in mid water or near the surface.

The fish's food consists almost entirely of bottom-living invertebrates – small crustaceans, worms and molluscs and occasionally fish such as sand gobies and sandeels. These are almost all burrowing animals which the sole locates by using complex sensory organs on the underside of its head. These show up as a mat of short protrusions literally packed with sensory cells including taste buds.

Migratory movements

The sole spawns in spring or early summer – as late as June in deep northern waters. The eggs float near the surface, as do the young fish which are about 3-4mm long on hatching. At a length of about 18mm (¾in) the young become bottom-living and look like miniature soles.

However, between hatching and becoming bottom-living, enormous changes take place in these minute fish. At hatching, the sole is similar to other fish with an eye on each side of its head and a symmetrical mouth. By the time it is living on the sea bed, the left eye has migrated through the head tissue to lie close beside the right eye, the mouth has changed shape and the sense organs around the mouth on the eyeless side have developed.

It is a nicely timed sequence of events which is co-ordinated with a total change in life-style – from a tiny translucent fish swimming in mid water to a bottom-living fish coloured on one side only to match the sea bed.

While these changes are taking place, post-larval sole migrate inshore to shallow water. This movement in the first weeks of

life brings them into the breakers on sandy shores. From here they spread out into deeper water until they are sexually mature and then migrate to the spawning grounds by coming up near the surface and 'hitching a lift' on the surface currents flowing in the right direction.

▲ *This specimen sole was caught from Salcombe Estuary in Devon. Sole do venture into river estuaries with large sandbanks, but not as far upriver as flounders – they can't tolerate low salinity.*

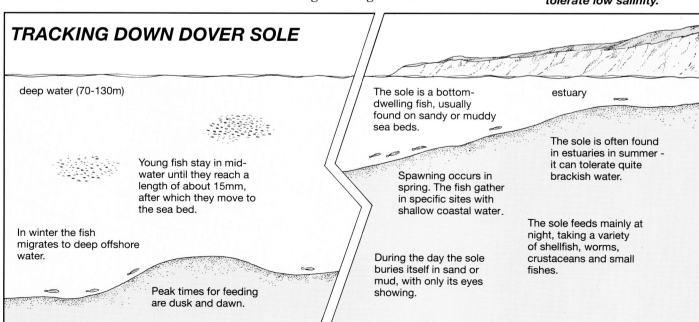

TRACKING DOWN DOVER SOLE

deep water (70-130m)

Young fish stay in mid-water until they reach a length of about 15mm, after which they move to the sea bed.

In winter the fish migrates to deep offshore water.

Peak times for feeding are dusk and dawn.

The sole is a bottom-dwelling fish, usually found on sandy or muddy sea beds.

Spawning occurs in spring. The fish gather in specific sites with shallow coastal water.

During the day the sole buries itself in sand or mud, with only its eyes showing.

estuary

The sole is often found in estuaries in summer - it can tolerate quite brackish water.

The sole feeds mainly at night, taking a variety of shellfish, worms, crustaceans and small fishes.

Pouting

Although small, the pouting is a greedy fish – it eats anything and everything small enough to fit in its mouth, including your bait.

Distribution

Pouting are found all round the British Isles, though they are most common off the coasts of southern England and Ireland.

Record pouting

● The rod-caught record from a boat is held by R.S.Armstrong for a 5lb 8oz (2.494kg) fish caught off Berry Head, Devon in 1969.

● The shore-caught record stands at 4lb 9oz (2.1kg) for a fish caught by R. Andrews off Pembroke, Guernsey, in 1991.

The pouting (also known as bib, pout and whiting pout) is a small member of the cod family. Though not seriously fished for commercially, it is still an important member of the underwater food chain.

You can recognize the pouting by its colouring – the body is dark copper with three or four lighter pink/golden bands running vertically down the flanks. These bands fade as the fish matures.

The pouting also has a noticeable black dot at the base of the pectoral fin and like all members of the cod family, it has large, black pupils. Anglers should handle the pouting with care since its scales are small and easily dislodged.

It is easy to confuse the pouting with its close relative the poor cod because they share many physical similarities. However, the poor cod is a uniform copper colour and is much smaller than the pouting, so they can usually be distinguished in this way. Small haddock can also be mistaken for pouting, but on closer inspection can be identified by a black thumbprint mark on their sides.

Vital statistics

Scientific name: *Trisopterus luscus*
Maximum weight: 5½lb (2.5kg)
Average weight: 1lb (0.45kg)
Maximum length: 24in (60cm)
Life-span: 6-8 years

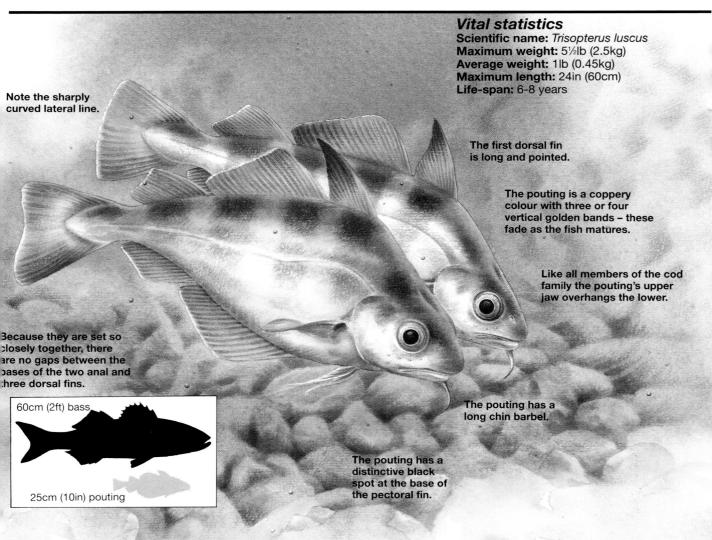

Note the sharply curved lateral line.

The first dorsal fin is long and pointed.

The pouting is a coppery colour with three or four vertical golden bands – these fade as the fish matures.

Like all members of the cod family the pouting's upper jaw overhangs the lower.

Because they are set so closely together, there are no gaps between the bases of the two anal and three dorsal fins.

The pouting has a long chin barbel.

60cm (2ft) bass

25cm (10in) pouting

The pouting has a distinctive black spot at the base of the pectoral fin.

Forever feeding

The hungry pouting is always on the look-out for food; it is not a fussy eater, and feeds on anything it happens to find that is small enough, including whelks, mussels, hermit crabs and shrimps. However, it is wary of clear water, and tends to feed with more confidence at night or in water that is murky enough to hide it.

Such a voracious fish grows rapidly, and reaches maturity when just one year old. It spawns between March and April at depths of up to 70m (230ft), and at temperatures above 8°C (46°F). The eggs float on the surface of the water, and hatch after about ten days; the larvae then spend their first few weeks living among the plankton.

The young fish lives in fairly shallow water, feeding on small shore crabs and shrimps. As it matures it moves into deeper water and is known to roam up to depths of 300m (960ft), preferring a sea bed of mixed sand and rock. The young pouting is not at all shy, even swimming close up to divers in its quest for food; however, the older pouting is less adventurous, and spends most of its time hiding in the nooks and crannies provided by wrecks and reefs.

Never safe

Because of its small size, the young pouting forms large shoals, though this is not enough to protect it from predatory fish. Cod in particular eat vast numbers of them.

The pouting is of little economic value because of its size and soft flesh – those that are caught usually end up as fish meal.

Unfortunately, pouting, along with poor cod and small whiting, often get caught up in the nets of trawlers fishing for larger species, and by the time they get dumped

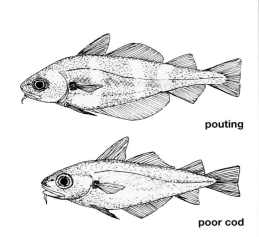

Pouting or poor cod?

The pouting and poor cod are often confused – in both, the upper jaw overhangs the lower, the fins are set very closely together, and both have a long chin barbel. If the stripes on the pouting have faded, the two can only be distinguished by size. The poor cod is slim bodied with an average length of 15-20cm (6-8in), whereas the pouting has a deep body and is usually 25-30cm (10-12in) long.

Both species live in small shoals around British coasts.

pouting

poor cod

back overboard they are usually dead.

The pouting is an important fish for the shore match angler; if you can latch on to a pouting in a competition you can be sure there will be plenty more to follow. Larger specimens, however, are mostly caught by boat anglers from deep water marks, using leger or paternoster tackle. They also make good live bait for conger and bass.

▼ *Because of its lack of size, the brightly coloured pouting forms large shoals for protection.*
However, this does not stop large numbers of them being eaten by predatory fish, especially cod.

TRACKING DOWN POUTING

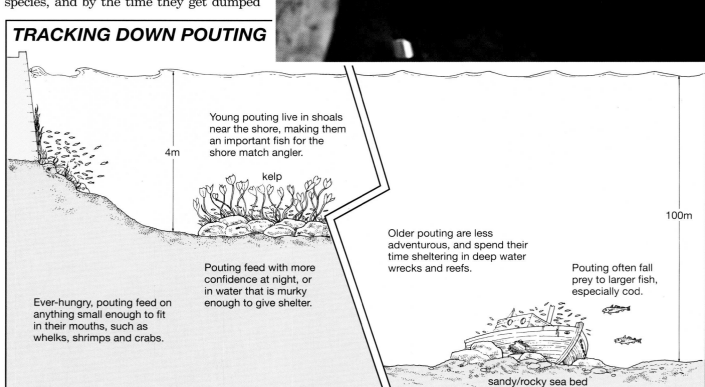

Young pouting live in shoals near the shore, making them an important fish for the shore match angler.

4m

kelp

100m

Older pouting are less adventurous, and spend their time sheltering in deep water wrecks and reefs.

Pouting feed with more confidence at night, or in water that is murky enough to give shelter.

Pouting often fall prey to larger fish, especially cod.

Ever-hungry, pouting feed on anything small enough to fit in their mouths, such as whelks, shrimps and crabs.

sandy/rocky sea bed

Haddock

Haddock are one of the smaller members of the cod family but an important commercial fish in Britain. But because of overfishing numbers are dwindling and trawlers are having to venture far afield to find them.

Members of the cod family include numerous look-alike species, for example poor cod, pouting and Norway pout, or coalfish and pollack. But one that's distinct from any other family member is the haddock.

The dark thumbprint on either side of the haddock's back between the lateral line and the pectoral fin is the most obvious feature – in young fish this blotch is often ringed with white. The story goes that the marks were made by St. Peter's finger and thumb when he plucked the fish from the sea. The black lateral line also makes the haddock easy to identify.

The fish has three dorsal fins, the first being high and pointed; it also has two anal fins. There is a minute barbel on the chin and the prominent snout juts over a rather short lower jaw.

Follow the feeding

The underslung mouth shows that the haddock picks up most of its food from the sea bed. It feeds on brittlestars (relatives of the starfish) which, in many areas, are the most numerous inhabitants of the ocean floor. Other food items include ragworms, molluscs and small sea urchins.

On some offshore fishing grounds haddock feed on encrusting sponges which have a very unpleasant smell. As a result, the fish have to be gutted as quickly as possible after being caught or their flesh becomes tainted.

In at the deep end

The haddock has a northerly distribution, ranging from the Arctic seas, Iceland and the north-eastern coasts of North America down to the British North Sea. It is not common in the shallower English Channel or in the southern half of the North Sea, although once in a while substantial numbers are caught there. In the western Channel there is always the chance of catching a very large fish.

They are found offshore in depths of 40-300m (130-990ft) over a sandy or muddy

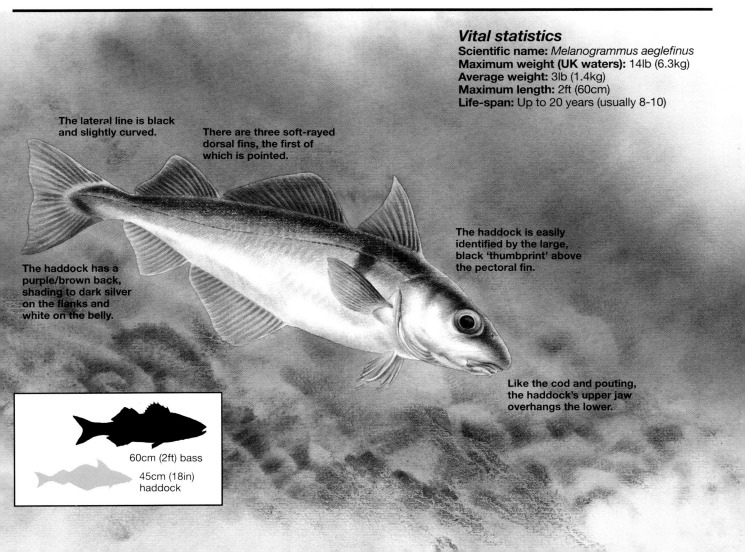

Vital statistics
Scientific name: *Melanogrammus aeglefinus*
Maximum weight (UK waters): 14lb (6.3kg)
Average weight: 3lb (1.4kg)
Maximum length: 2ft (60cm)
Life-span: Up to 20 years (usually 8-10)

The lateral line is black and slightly curved.

There are three soft-rayed dorsal fins, the first of which is pointed.

The haddock has a purple/brown back, shading to dark silver on the flanks and white on the belly.

The haddock is easily identified by the large, black 'thumbprint' above the pectoral fin.

Like the cod and pouting, the haddock's upper jaw overhangs the lower.

60cm (2ft) bass

45cm (18in) haddock

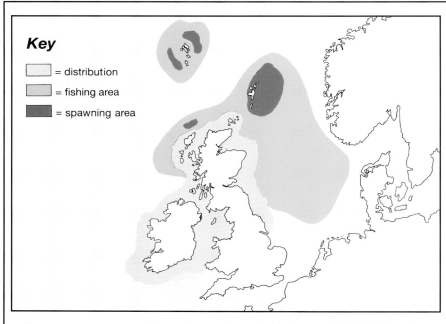

Key

▢ = distribution

▢ = fishing area

▢ = spawning area

Distribution: spawning and fishing grounds

Up until the beginning of the 1970s, haddock were common in inshore waters around the British Isles. In Scotland this was particularly true – the deep sea lochs were once carpeted with fish.

Unfortunately, along with stocks of cod and herring, haddock populations have fallen dramatically because of overfishing. Now that all inshore stocks of haddock are depleted, fishermen have to take their boats out farther to catch enough fish to make a living.

Consequently, haddock are being taken from their spawning grounds in the northern North Sea, west of Orkney and off the Faroe Isles, reducing numbers even more.

Despite this, haddock are still second only to cod as a commercial fish in Britain. Between 200,000-300,000 tons are caught annually, mainly by Scottish boats.

bed, though shoals are sometimes discovered in mid-water. Haddock used to be plentiful inshore, especially in sea lochs, until constant overfishing depleted stocks.

Spawning sites

Haddock spawn in specific areas to the north of the British Isles – in the North Sea, to the west of Orkney, around the Faroe Isles and off southern Iceland.

The sexually mature fish move to these grounds during the winter and spawn between late February and May. Courtship between the sexes includes grunting sounds as well as a visual display. The eggs float to the water's surface and are widely spread by ocean currents.

Strange hiding place

Young haddock are frequently found drifting in the shelter of surface-living jellyfish – a habit they share with juvenile whiting. This gives them some protection from predatory fish and birds.

After about seven months – when they have reached a length of 5cm (2in) – the fry move down to the sea bed. Growth depends on the amount of food available to them, but in average conditions a year old fish is about 18cm (7in) long.

Because of the heavy commercial fishing for haddock, few fish live for more than ten years. Without such heavy fishery pressure the haddock might well live for much longer. Large fish weighing over 30lb (13.5kg) and measuring 1m (3ft) long are caught off Iceland and could well be over 20 years old.

▶ *Boat fishing at least a mile from the shore is the only way an angler can find haddock these days – this one was caught in Kilalla Bay, Ireland. The haddock has a very soft mouth, so always use a net to land the fish, otherwise it may pull free of the hook.*

Angler fish

The adaptable angler fish can change the colour of its skin to match the sea bed – it's the perfect disguise for fooling prey lured close by its waving 'fishing rod'.

Record anglers

● **Boat-caught** S. Neill holds this record for a massive 94lb 12oz (42.98kg) fish caught in Belfast Lough, Northern Ireland in 1985.
● **Shore-caught** This record has stood since 1967 when H. Legerton caught a 68lb 2oz (30.89kg) angler fish off Canvey Island, Essex.

With its bizarre body shape, menacing looks and unusual life-style, the angler fish is unmistakable. It's one of the ugliest fish in the sea – and not one you'll see since it spends most of its time hidden on the sea bed, lying in wait for prey to pass by.

Like such sea bed dwellers as skates and rays, the angler has a wide, flattened body that tapers gradually to the tail. Its semi-circular mouth is enormous, stretching from one side of its head to the other, and is equipped with long, unevenly spaced, backward-pointing teeth that prevent prey from escaping its clutches.

Fringe benefits

Camouflage is the key to the angler's life-style – it can change the colour of its skin to

Distribution

Angler fish are found over sandy, gravelly and rocky sea beds in water up to 100m (330ft) deep. Fairly common, they are more frequent off the south and western coasts of Britain and Ireland.

match the natural background of any hiding place. Waving fronds of skin break up the fish's large outline and help to conceal it even further. The underside of its body is pure white, except for the tips of the pelvic fins which are black.

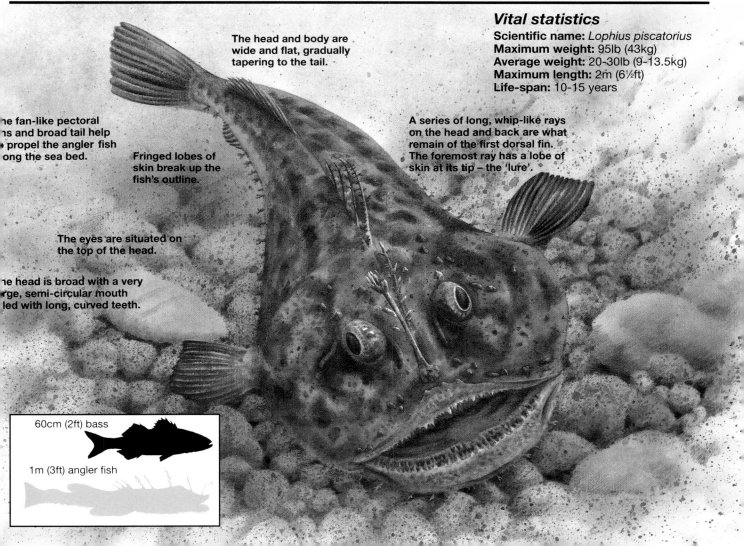

The head and body are wide and flat, gradually tapering to the tail.

Vital statistics
Scientific name: *Lophius piscatorius*
Maximum weight: 95lb (43kg)
Average weight: 20-30lb (9-13.5kg)
Maximum length: 2m (6½ft)
Life-span: 10-15 years

The fan-like pectoral ns and broad tail help propel the angler fish ong the sea bed.

Fringed lobes of skin break up the fish's outline.

A series of long, whip-like rays on the head and back are what remain of the first dorsal fin. The foremost ray has a lobe of skin at its tip – the 'lure'.

The eyes are situated on the top of the head.

he head is broad with a very rge, semi-circular mouth led with long, curved teeth.

60cm (2ft) bass

1m (3ft) angler fish

Related species

● **The black-bellied angler** is the common angler's closest relative, but it lives in deep water off the south and western coasts of England and is rarely seen.
● **The Atlantic football fish**, sometimes caught by trawlers off western Ireland, is literally the size and shape of a football. It is also easily identified by its luminous 'glow in the dark' lure.
● *Ceratias holboeli* is another deep-water species found off parts of western Britain. Unique among vertebrates, the tiny male is parasitic upon the much larger female for its entire life.

◄ *Caught using a mackerel bait in deep water off Plymouth, this angler fish weighed in at a hefty 54lb (24.3kg).*

What's in a name?

There's confusion over what to call the angler. Sea fishermen know it as the angler fish, but it's sold in restaurants and fish-and-chip shops as 'monkfish' – a name that belongs to a member of the shark family.

A series of long, separate rays down the head and back is all that remains of the angler's first dorsal fin. The first – and longest – ray is topped by a leafy flap of skin, at the base of which is a worm-like feature. This 'rod and lure' set-up is used by the angler fish to tempt prey towards its mouth. The large pectoral and tail fins help the angler propel its body through the water on the rare occasions when it ventures out for a swim.

Highly adaptable, the angler can live on most types of sea bed. Sand and gravel are its typical habitat, but it is sometimes found on the edge of reefs or rocks where sand patches offer a chance to hide. It is occasionally captured in muddy estuaries.

Going fishing

The most remarkable aspect of the angler's life is its technique of fishing for food with its 'rod and lure'. As a potential victim approaches, the angler raises its first dorsal ray above its back and bends it forwards, sometimes jerking the fleshy tip up and down to entice prey closer. The obvious parallel with this technique and that of an angler fishing is how this extraordinary fish came by its name. It is also called the fishing frog.

The prey does not even have to be all that close: when the angler opens its cavernous mouth and throat, the rapid in-rush of water so created carries the victim straight inside.

It feeds on almost any type of fish and bottom-living animal; there are even a few reports of it attacking sea birds sitting on the surface!

Life-cycle

Spawning takes place in late spring/early summer in deep water well offshore. The female sheds her eggs in huge ribbon-like, gelatinous sheets, usually one egg thick. These sheets can be up to 9m (30ft) long and 3m (10ft) wide, but they are soon broken up by the waves and widely distributed by the current.

The newly hatched fish stay near the sea surface, kept afloat by the large surface area of their long fin rays. Once they have reached a length of about 8cm (3in) they take up the bottom-living life-style of their parents.

TRACKING DOWN ANGLER FISH

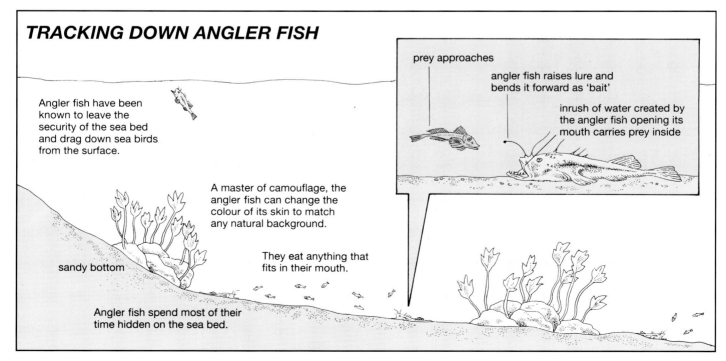

Angler fish have been known to leave the security of the sea bed and drag down sea birds from the surface.

A master of camouflage, the angler fish can change the colour of its skin to match any natural background.

sandy bottom

They eat anything that fits in their mouth.

Angler fish spend most of their time hidden on the sea bed.

prey approaches

angler fish raises lure and bends it forward as 'bait'

inrush of water created by the angler fish opening its mouth carries prey inside

Dab

Over twenty species of flatfish are found in British seas – and while the largest is the halibut, one of the smallest is the dab, a reliably abundant inshore fish.

Record dabs

● **Boat-caught** R. Islip holds the record for a 2lb 12oz (1.25kg) dab at Gairloch, Wester Ross, Scotland in 1975.
● **Shore-caught** In 1936 M.L. Watts caught a 2lb 9oz (1.17kg) fish at Port Talbot, Glamorgan, Wales.
● **Irish record** Paul Beglin caught a 2lb ⅓oz (0.92kg) dab at Dunmore East, Co. Waterford, in 1989.

C ommon all around the British Isles, the dab is easily distinguished from other right-eyed flatfish by its sharply curved lateral line and by finely serrated scales that feel rough when rubbed from tail to head. Another species, the long rough dab is a close relative, but it is fairly rare and has a straight lateral line.

The upper side of the dab is a sandy brown colour, which helps it to blend in well with its surroundings. Some fish may have a few orange speckles, but these are not as well developed as those of the plaice. Like most other flatfish, the dab's anal and dorsal fins are long with jointed rays.

Sandy shores

The type of sea bed determines whether or not dabs are to be found. They appear from the shore down to 150m (490ft), but sandy ground up to 40m (130ft) is their favoured

Distribution

Dabs are common in the coastal waters all around the British Isles and are particularly abundant in the North Sea. They are usually found over a sandy sea bed at depths of 20-40m (65-130ft).

habitat. Sandbanks, bays and generally flat ground attract them in their thousands, and they're often found in the mouths of estuaries, though they cannot tolerate as much fresh water as flounders. Their habitat is also dependent on food supply – they

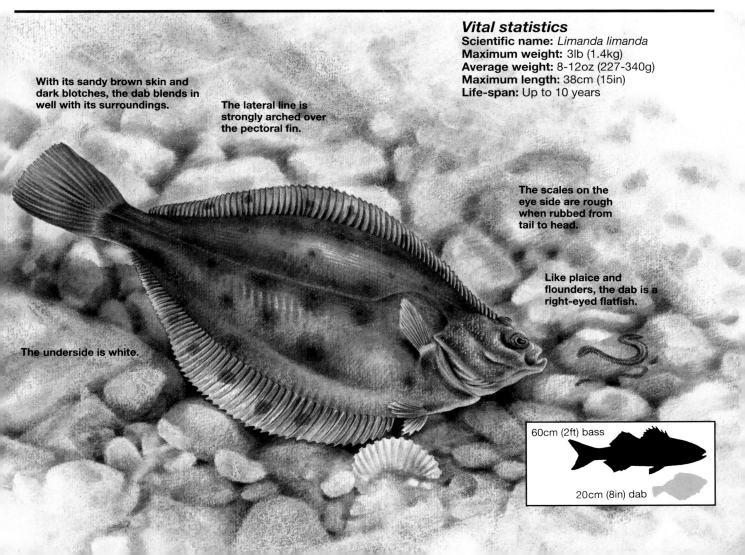

With its sandy brown skin and dark blotches, the dab blends in well with its surroundings.

The lateral line is strongly arched over the pectoral fin.

The underside is white.

Vital statistics
Scientific name: *Limanda limanda*
Maximum weight: 3lb (1.4kg)
Average weight: 8-12oz (227-340g)
Maximum length: 38cm (15in)
Life-span: Up to 10 years

The scales on the eye side are rough when rubbed from tail to head.

Like plaice and flounders, the dab is a right-eyed flatfish.

60cm (2ft) bass

20cm (8in) dab

eat anything that is small enough. Sandeels are plentiful around banks and this is their main food source.

The dab – and also the sole – has a curious way of feeding. The fish raises its head and the front part of its body and then waits for a worm or shellfish to emerge. Then it strikes rapidly, biting down on its prey. Dabs fatten up during summer and autumn and then move to deeper offshore marks with the onset of winter.

When and where

Sometime between January and June, according to the water temperature, mature fish of three years and older are ready to spawn. Those around Britain and Ireland do so in March and April. Unlike some species, dabs do not have specific spawning sites. The female lays 50,000-150,000 eggs, after which the adult fish move in towards warmer coastal waters to feed.

Twisted bodies

The eggs float near the sea's surface and hatch after a week or two. Once they have absorbed their yolk sac, the fry feed on the plankton around them. When they reach a length of 12mm (½in) they begin to move down to the sea bed. Here they change from being round-bodied fry to flatfish – the body flattens and the left eye migrates to sit next to the right. Although it is not unusual to find left-eyed flounders, dabs reversed like this are quite rare. Because of this unusual metamorphosis, flatfish have earned the name heterosomata, meaning twisted body.

Although dabs are not as commercially important as plaice or halibut, they are often taken incidentally in a trawl, where a minimum size limit of 20cm (8in) applies.

▲ *Small shellfish, worms and shrimps are all good baits for catching dabs. A tiny sliver of mackerel belly is also excellent. The best way to catch dabs is either using a small hook from a paternoster at anchor, or a long trace with a spoon and beads on the drift.*

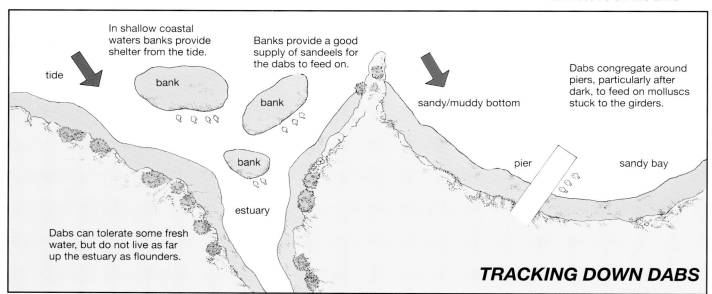

In shallow coastal waters banks provide shelter from the tide.

tide

bank

Banks provide a good supply of sandeels for the dabs to feed on.

bank

bank

estuary

sandy/muddy bottom

Dabs congregate around piers, particularly after dark, to feed on molluscs stuck to the girders.

pier

sandy bay

Dabs can tolerate some fresh water, but do not live as far up the estuary as flounders.

TRACKING DOWN DABS

Coalfish

Whatever you choose to call it, the coalfish can give you a good run for your money – if you're lucky enough to get a big one on the end of your line it's a thrill under any alias.

Distribution

The coalfish, ranging from the Arctic southwards to Britain, is most abundant off the northern coasts of England, the North Sea, Scottish waters and the Irish Sea.

Record coalies

Many big coalies come from the western channel and off the south western Irish coast.
● **Boat-caught** A 37lb 5oz (16.923kg) fish caught over a wreck, south of Eddystone in 1986 by D. Brown.
● **Shore-caught** A 20lb 6oz (9.214kg) fish caught at Flycellers, Newquay, Cornwall in 1982 by D. Cook.

The coalfish has possibly more names than any other fish except salmon. Depending where you are you will hear it called coalfish, saithe, lythe or billet. To the fishmonger it is coley and if you fish on the North Atlantic coast of America you find it goes by the name of pollock.

It is not just the names which tend to be confusing with the coalfish. Sometimes its identification causes problems too. The reason is that it is a close relative of our pollack and looks very similar to it.

Same difference

Both coalfish and pollack are members of the cod family and have the typical three dorsal fins and two anal fins. They are both a dark greeny-brown above and lighter on the belly, and have relatively large eyes.

The two species may be similar in appearance, but if you look closely there are several clear-cut features which identify the coalfish for certain.

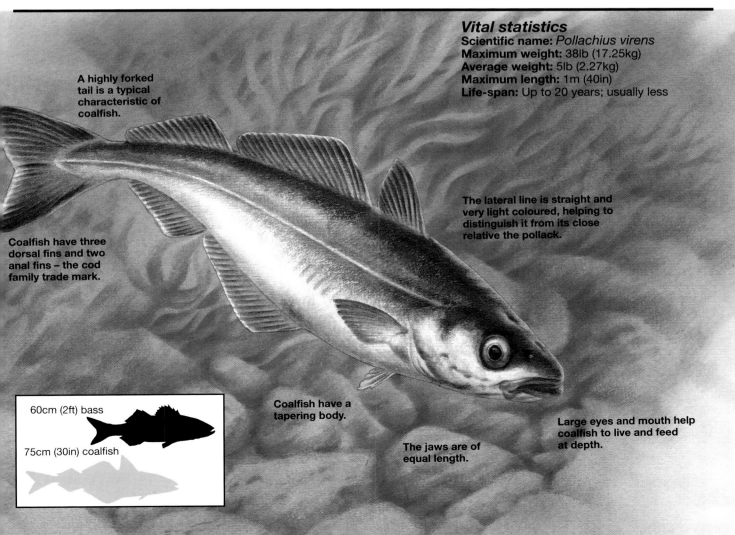

A highly forked tail is a typical characteristic of coalfish.

Coalfish have three dorsal fins and two anal fins – the cod family trade mark.

Vital statistics
Scientific name: *Pollachius virens*
Maximum weight: 38lb (17.25kg)
Average weight: 5lb (2.27kg)
Maximum length: 1m (40in)
Life-span: Up to 20 years; usually less

The lateral line is straight and very light coloured, helping to distinguish it from its close relative the pollack.

60cm (2ft) bass

75cm (30in) coalfish

Coalfish have a tapering body.

The jaws are of equal length.

Large eyes and mouth help coalfish to live and feed at depth.

The jaws are of equal length but in big specimens the lower jaw is slightly longer than the upper – in pollack the lower jaw is much longer.

The lateral line is straight and creamy coloured, running directly from the gill covers to the tail – in pollack it is dark and strongly curved over the pectoral fin.

The sides are dull and silvery and the transition to the back colouring is sharp – in pollack the sides are golden and the colouring merges with the back.

Life-cycle

Coalfish are mid-water predators and typical shoaling fish, often found around reefs, wrecks or rocky ground, or swimming above the kelp forest.

Large fish tend to live in big schools in open water, although you might get a big solitary fish inside a wreck or gully.

In contrast the young, during their first two years of life, live in very shallow water among rocks and weeds. In northern Britain young coalfish even inhabit shore pools – but they are small fish, from 10-15cm (4-6in) in length. These young fish eat small crustaceans and other young fish, but as they grow they increasingly become fish-eaters. Sandeels, sprats, herring, poor cod and bib all go to feed the coalfish. Many of these food fish have been heavily commercially overfished – something that will affect future coalie numbers.

The coalfish becomes sexually mature at five to ten years old and spawns from January to April in depths of 100-180m (330-600ft). It spawns in places of high salinity and a temperature of 6-8°C (43-47°F).

The most important breeding areas are in the northern North Sea, off Norway and the Faroes. Small numbers breed off our coasts.

The eggs and larvae float in the upper 27m (90ft) of the sea, and the young fish are carried inshore by currents – into nursery ground waters of a few feet deep.

▲ *This specimen coalfish, which weighed in at nearly 20lb (9kg), was caught on an Eddystone eel. Note the distinctive straight, light-coloured lateral line.*

Catching coalies

A European cold water species, the coalfish ranges from the Arctic southwards to the British Isles.

They are a favourite quarry of boat anglers. In winter, specimen hunters head for the deep-water wrecks off our coasts which hold hundreds of big coalfish – they can put up quite a fight on sporting tackle.

Commercial fishermen also target the coalie, catching them mainly in open water of 40-180m (130-600ft), by net, trawl and long line.

Coalfish hotspots

● **Boat fishing** Mid-channel wrecks yield big coalies. Boats out of West Country ports such as Plymouth, Newquay and Brixham take many specimens.
● **Shore fishing** Plenty of sport with smaller coalies right round the northern coast. Peel Breakwater, Isle of Man, Greystones in County Wicklow, Ireland, and the north-east coast between Berwick and Whitby are good spots.

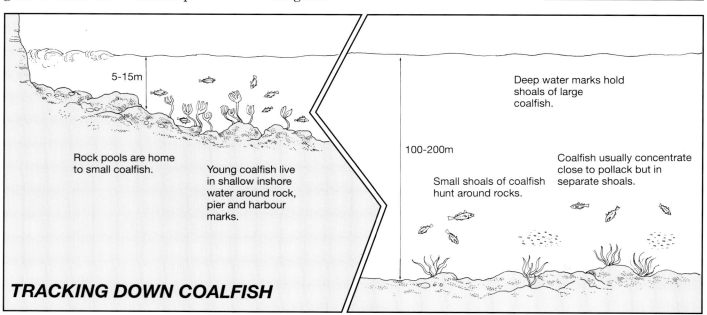

5-15m

Rock pools are home to small coalfish.

Young coalfish live in shallow inshore water around rock, pier and harbour marks.

Deep water marks hold shoals of large coalfish.

100-200m

Small shoals of coalfish hunt around rocks.

Coalfish usually concentrate close to pollack but in separate shoals.

TRACKING DOWN COALFISH

Greater and lesser weever

Beware the weever fish – it spends the day half-buried in the sand and, when alarmed, raises its poison-tipped first dorsal fin.

No sea angler deliberately sets out to catch either the lesser weever or its bigger relative, the greater weever. But, since they are sometimes accidentally caught by anglers, it's important to know what they look like – they are two of the few dangerous fishes found in British seas.

The lesser weever – which reaches up to 15cm (6in) long – is fairly common around the coasts of Britain and Ireland, although distribution is patchy. It lives in shallow water from the tide line down to about 50m (160ft).

During the day the weever burrows in the sand so that its eyes, the top of the head and the back are exposed. Much of its food, particularly crustaceans and small bottom-living fish such as sand gobies and sandeels, is captured as they pass over the

Distribution

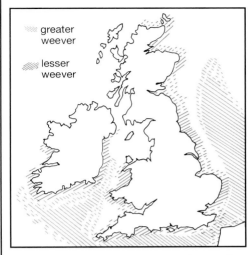

- greater weever
- lesser weever

Lesser weevers are common on the sandy coasts of eastern Scotland and England, Wales and Ireland. Greater weevers are found on sandy offshore marks off Scotland, in the North Sea and the English Channel.

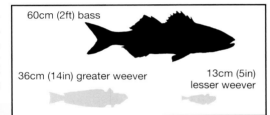

60cm (2ft) bass

36cm (14in) greater weever

13cm (5in) lesser weever

Vital statistics

LESSER (COMMON) WEEVER (*Echiichthys vipera*)
Maximum weight: 4oz (113g)
Average weight: 2oz (57g)
Maximum length: 15cm (6in)
Life-span: Perhaps 3 years

The spines of the first dorsal fin are grooved to provide a channel for the poison.

In both fish the spines of the first dorsal fin and on the gill covers are poisonous, with a venomous gland at the base of each one.

The greater weever has two or three non-venomous spines between the eyes.

Both fish have long bodies and deep, compressed heads.

GREATER WEEVER

Both the second dorsal and anal fins are long.

The greater weever's body is yellowish brown with darker mottling on the head and back.

The lesser weever's pectoral fins are rounded, but those of the greater weever are more squarely cut.

The lesser weever has a dark edge to its tail.

The first dorsal fin of the lesser weever is entirely black – the greater weever's is only partly so.

The upward-pointing mouth is useful for attacking prey from below.

The greyish brown colour of the lesser weever is dotted with faint brown markings.

GREATER WEEVER (*Trachinus draco*)
Maximum weight: 2lb (0.9kg)
Average weight: 1lb (0.45kg)
Maximum length: 40cm (16in)
Life-span: Perhaps 5 years

LESSER WEEVER

buried weever. With a rapid lunging movement the weever attacks from underneath, catching its prey with its upward-pointing mouth.

Going with the flow

At night the weever actively forages for food, moving up the shore as the tide advances to feed on dislodged animals. The weever also retreats with the tide, but occasionally becomes trapped in shallow tide pools on the shore.

The burrowing habit is the clue to their local distribution since weevers may be common on one beach and absent on the next. The size of the grains of sand is all-important: burrowing is easier in fairly coarse sand than on a shore where the sand is fine-grained or mixed with mud. Unfortunately, clean sandy shores also attract bathers and shrimpers – and this brings the weever into conflict with man.

Lying in wait

Both species of weever have two dorsal fins – the first, short-based one is armed with four strong spines. There is also a stout spine on each gill cover. All these spines have venom glands at the base. The weever lies buried in the sand and raises its dorsal spine if disturbed. Somebody stepping on the fish is instantly stabbed by the spines, which then inject venom into the wounds.

Anglers and shrimpers are also at risk – when picking up their catch they can be stabbed by the gill cover spines as well as by those on the dorsal fin. Holding the fish by its tail is no solution either, since it swings itself from side to side and stabs the back of your hand.

The protein-based venom is incredibly painful and the affected area rapidly swells up. The pain usually subsides within 12 hours, giving credence to the old fisherman's tale that the effects last until the tide

returns to the height it was when the injury occurred! Although the sting is not directly fatal, it is serious – due in large part to shock and to secondary infections that may occur (keep the wound clean).

Big brother

The greater weever, at 40cm (16in) long, is up to three times the size of the lesser weever. Fortunately it lives offshore over sandy ground in depths of 10-100m (30-330ft) and is not frequently caught by anglers.

Apart from size and habitat, you can distinguish the two species by looking at the first dorsal fin – this is entirely black in the lesser weever but only partly so in the greater. Similarly, the lesser weever has smoothly rounded pectoral fins, while those of the greater are more squarely cut. The greater weever is often caught in trawls, particularly over known sole fishing grounds, and is turned into fishmeal. On the Continent it is reckoned to be excellent for eating.

Little is known about the life-cycle of either species, other than that they spawn inshore between June and August. The eggs are free-floating.

▲ *You can clearly see the four sturdy spines on the first dorsal fin of this weever. If you catch one while fishing, treat it with extreme care – try not to hold it directly if you want to unhook it.*

Alternatively, cut your line and let the fish go without handling it at all.

⚠ Ouch! Watch your step

Take all weever stings seriously and seek medical attention at once. First aid is simple and effective – soak the affected part in water as hot as can be tolerated until medical help arrives. The heat destroys the protein-based venom and renders it inactive.

TRACKING DOWN WEEVERS

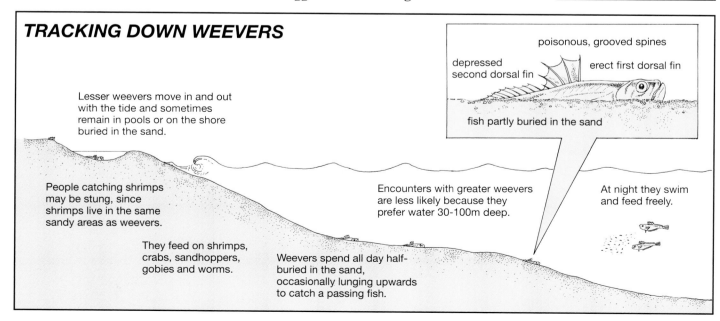

Lesser weevers move in and out with the tide and sometimes remain in pools or on the shore buried in the sand.

People catching shrimps may be stung, since shrimps live in the same sandy areas as weevers.

They feed on shrimps, crabs, sandhoppers, gobies and worms.

Weevers spend all day half-buried in the sand, occasionally lunging upwards to catch a passing fish.

Encounters with greater weevers are less likely because they prefer water 30-100m deep.

At night they swim and feed freely.

poisonous, grooved spines

depressed second dorsal fin

erect first dorsal fin

fish partly buried in the sand

Cuckoo ray

Despite being taken in large numbers commercially, little is known about the life of the cuckoo ray – one of the smallest rays in British waters.

The cuckoo ray is most abundant in the western English Channel, the Irish Sea, and the western coasts of Ireland and Scotland. It also occurs on the eastern coast of northern Scotland.

Record cuckoos

● **Boat-caught** This record is held by V. Morrison for a 5lb 11oz (2.579kg) fish caught off Causeway Coast, Northern Ireland in 1975.
● **Shore-caught** C. Wills took a 4lb 10oz (2.097kg) fish from North Cliffs, Cornwall on a session in January 1981 to claim this record.

Rays as a group are often fairly difficult for the average angler to identify, but the cuckoo ray is the exception to this rule. Along with the undulate ray, it is one of the two British species that are so clearly marked that its identification is both certain and immediate.

Spot the spots

The cuckoo ray belongs to the small group of 'round-winged' rays in which the edges of the wings are smoothly curved. Its short snout is also rounded, with a small up-turned tip.

Except for a smooth patch on each wing, the skin on the back is covered with prickles, making it feel rough. The underside of the snout is also rough to the touch.

There are four rows of curved, closely packed spines running along the tail, but not down its midline. The two central lines also extend up the back but become irregular. The back is a blotchy light brown in colour, the underside white or grey.

In the middle of the wings are two conspicuous black and yellow round marks. It is these spots that give this ray its scientific

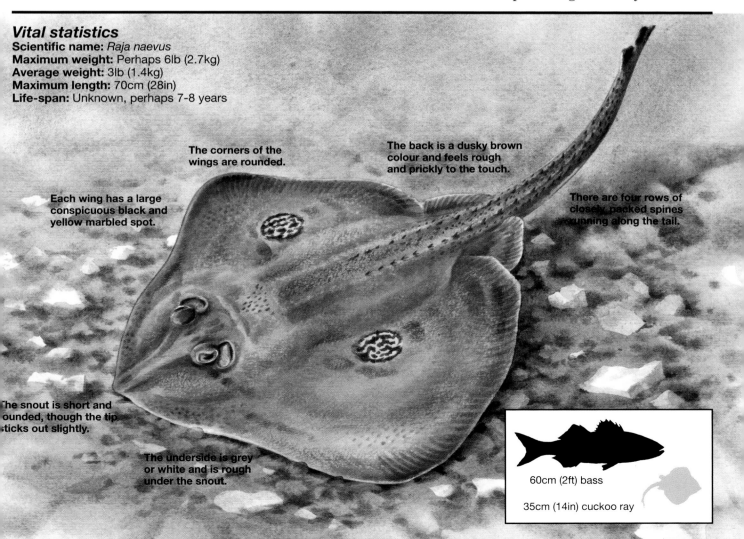

Vital statistics
Scientific name: *Raja naevus*
Maximum weight: Perhaps 6lb (2.7kg)
Average weight: 3lb (1.4kg)
Maximum length: 70cm (28in)
Life-span: Unknown, perhaps 7-8 years

The corners of the wings are rounded.

The back is a dusky brown colour and feels rough and prickly to the touch.

Each wing has a large conspicuous black and yellow marbled spot.

There are four rows of closely packed spines running along the tail.

The snout is short and rounded, though the tip sticks out slightly.

The underside is grey or white and is rough under the snout.

60cm (2ft) bass

35cm (14in) cuckoo ray

name *Raja naevus* – naevus is Latin for a birthmark. Why it is a 'cuckoo' ray is inexplicable; it certainly does not make a noise like the bird.

Deep water dwellers

Like most rays, this is a bottom-living fish. It is most abundant in deep water between 70-100m (230-330ft), but can be found in water as shallow as 20m (66ft). Because it lives in fairly deep water it is not often caught by anglers, but it is taken in large numbers by commercial fishermen.

As with many rays, details of its biology are unknown. For example, no studies have been made of its diet. Our knowledge is therefore based on isolated notes made on just a few specimens. When young it eats mainly small crustaceans and worms. Larger cuckoo rays eat fish of various kinds, particularly those that live near the sea bed such as sandeels, gobies and dragonets.

They are also reported to eat large numbers of herrings and sprats. If this is so, it means they are feeding well off the bottom. Certainly the rather long pointed teeth of the cuckoo ray suggest that it is adapted to catching and eating fast-moving prey like these mid-water shoal fish.

Breeding habits

The cuckoo, like all rays, lays its eggs in tough horny cases, called 'mermaid's purses'. They are light brown (though they can be almost transparent) and rather small – about 6cm by 4cm (2¼in by 1½in) excluding the horns at each corner. The forward pair of horns are longer than the rear pair which have in-curving tips.

Newly hatched rays are only 12cm (4¾in)

long. Each mature female produces some 90-100 eggs which she lays throughout the year. In aquarium conditions the eggs hatch in about 240 days, though in the sea, where the temperature is generally lower, they may take longer.

▲ *C. Wills proudly displays his British record shore-caught cuckoo ray – a splendid specimen of 4lb 10oz (2.097kg). He caught it in Northern Ireland in 1975.*

▼ *The distinctive black and yellow marbled spots are clearly seen in this picture. Be careful of that spiny tail.*

Black bream

Black bream (also known as old wives and porgies) spend their lives hiding among rocks and wrecks on the sea bed – they even spawn down in the depths, in gravel nests dug by the male. The male then guards the nest from danger.

Distribution

Black bream have been reported virtually all round the coast, but they are only common in the English Channel, Irish Sea, and off southern Ireland. Even then they are only localized within these areas.

Record black sea bream

● **Boat-caught** The record is held by J.A. Garlick for a 6lb 14oz (3.125kg) fish caught over a wreck off the coast of Devon in 1977.

● **Shore-caught** This record is held by D.P. Bohan, who in 1984 caught a 4lb 14oz (2.232kg) fish from Natural Arch, Alderney, C.I.

Sea bream are mainly found in the tropics and temperate waters of the world. There are numerous species in the Mediterranean and off the Portuguese coast. However, they are much scarcer in Britain's chilly waters, and although we do see about eight species, only the red and black breams are at all common.

The black bream is a deep-bodied fish with a small head. The mouth is small and doesn't reach back to the level of the eye. It is filled with numerous curved teeth, all of them the same size and shape.

The fish has a grey back and silvery flanks, often with six or seven vertical dark bars across the body, though these fade with age. Breeding males are particularly dark in colour and have a humped shoulder – a feature not possessed by the females. Like all members of the sea bream family, the black bream has a long single dorsal fin and a large forked tail.

Vital statistics

Scientific name: *Spondyliosoma cantharus*
Maximum weight: 7lb (3.2kg)
Average weight: 3lb (1.4kg)
Maximum length: 20in (51cm)
Life-span: Up to 10 years

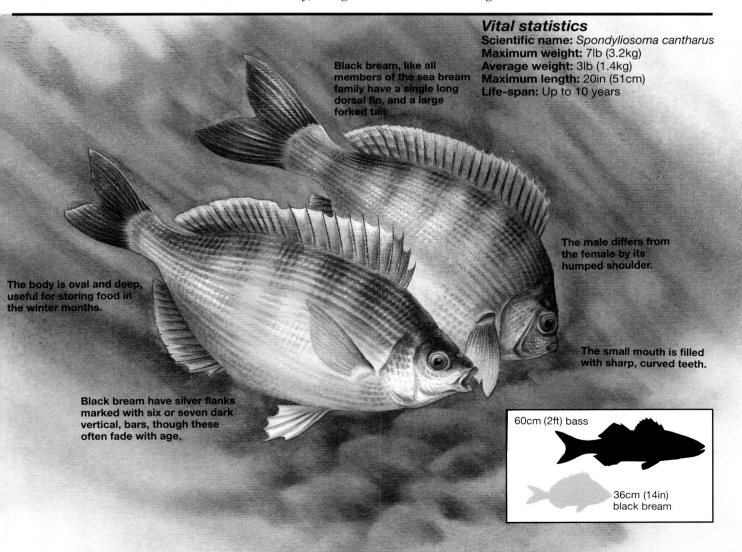

Black bream, like all members of the sea bream family have a single long dorsal fin, and a large forked tail.

The body is oval and deep, useful for storing food in the winter months.

Black bream have silver flanks marked with six or seven dark vertical, bars, though these often fade with age.

The male differs from the female by its humped shoulder.

The small mouth is filled with sharp, curved teeth.

60cm (2ft) bass

36cm (14in) black bream

Local distribution

Although black bream have been caught all around the coasts of the British Isles, they are only really common on the south and western coasts. They are also locally distributed, so that they may be common in one area, but rarely seen in neighbouring regions. The reason they are occasionally captured in northern areas seems to be that the young fish and adults disperse after breeding.

The eastern Channel is the best known region for catching black bream – the local sea bed conditions there are ideal spawning grounds. These consist of fine gravel patches between rocky ledges, or close to reefs and wrecks, which protect the fish from strong currents.

On guard

These fish take two to three years to become sexually mature. Unlike other sea bream, black bream lay their eggs in a hollow made in the gravel by the male. The male then guards the nest, and later the young fish, protecting them from predators or other black bream trying to build nests in the same area.

Their habit of breeding in relatively restricted locations has proved unfortunate in the past. In the 1950s and 1960s, the spawning grounds off the Sussex coast were fished so heavily by boat parties that populations dropped dramatically, and the species became quite scarce.

All change

Large numbers of males were caught because this species is one of the few that changes sex as it matures. In this case all black bream begin life as females, then turn into males at between six or seven years old. As the males are the larger fish and confined to guarding the nests, it followed that they were more easily and frequently captured.

Fortunately, the species has recently made a comeback. However, they will thrive only if well-known spawning grounds are left well alone. Even if fish are caught and then put back, it is stressful for the adult fish and the young are left vulnerable to predators.

▲ *A fine brace of black bream caught on mackerel strip. They vary in colour from light silver to grey – males tend to be darker than females, especially before spawning.*

TRACKING DOWN BLACK BREAM

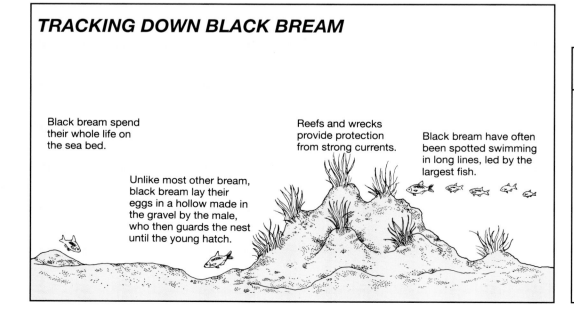

Black bream spend their whole life on the sea bed.

Unlike most other bream, black bream lay their eggs in a hollow made in the gravel by the male, who then guards the nest until the young hatch.

Reefs and wrecks provide protection from strong currents.

Black bream have often been spotted swimming in long lines, led by the largest fish.

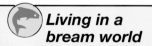 **Living in a bream world**

Although black sea bream are making a comeback in the eastern Channel, anglers and boat skippers must ensure that they return most of the fish they catch.

If you do go fishing for black bream, keep away from any known spawning grounds. Avoid going between March and June, so the fish have a chance to breed in peace.

Cuckoo wrasse

There's no mistaking cuckoo wrasse – females are dusky rose pink, the males a brilliant blue and yellow. Such difference in colour between the sexes is unusual among fish.

Distribution

Cuckoo wrasse are found off rocky coasts around the western and southern coasts of Britain and Ireland. They are particularly common in the English Channel and off western Ireland and Scotland.

Record-breaking cuckoo wrasse

● **Boat-caught** A. Welch holds this record with a 2lb 3oz (1kg) fish caught in Lyme Bay, Devon in 1990.

● **Shore-caught** In 1984 A.J. Smart hooked a 1lb 12oz (0.796kg) cuckoo wrasse off Goat Island, Alderney, Channel Islands to claim the shore record.

Although the cuckoo wrasse is widely distributed and fairly common, it is little known to anglers when compared with the more abundant ballan and corkwing wrasse. One reason for this is its solitary life-style – it doesn't form schools but keeps to its own territory.

The cuckoo, at 35cm (14in), is one of the larger species of wrasse in British waters – only the ballan (40cm/16in) is bigger – and is easily identified by its body shape and colouring. The head and jaws are elongated and its large, thick-lipped mouth is packed with teeth. The dorsal fin is long with a spiny part of 16-18 spines and a soft rear section with 11-14 branched rays. However, there's no need to count the rays when the fish's colour is so striking.

Multi-coloured fish

Female cuckoo wrasse, and the young of both sexes, are pink/orange on the back with a paler underside. They also have three large black blotches on the back – the first and second on either side of the back

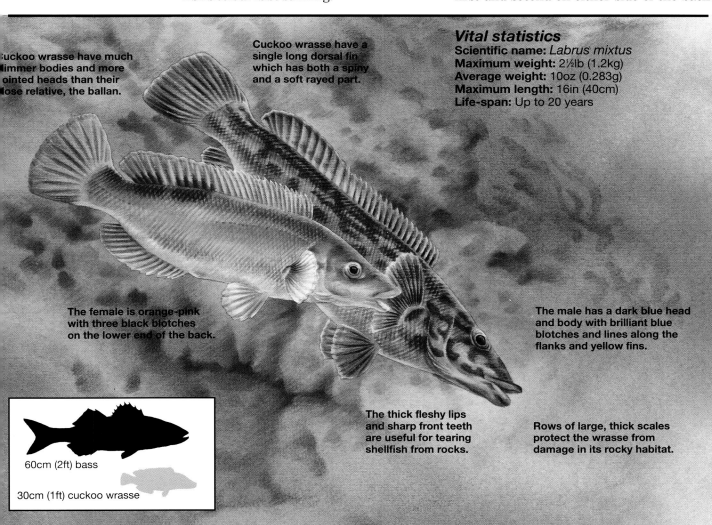

Cuckoo wrasse have much slimmer bodies and more pointed heads than their close relative, the ballan.

Cuckoo wrasse have a single long dorsal fin which has both a spiny and a soft rayed part.

Vital statistics
Scientific name: *Labrus mixtus*
Maximum weight: 2½lb (1.2kg)
Average weight: 10oz (0.283g)
Maximum length: 16in (40cm)
Life-span: Up to 20 years

The female is orange-pink with three black blotches on the lower end of the back.

The male has a dark blue head and body with brilliant blue blotches and lines along the flanks and yellow fins.

The thick fleshy lips and sharp front teeth are useful for tearing shellfish from rocks.

Rows of large, thick scales protect the wrasse from damage in its rocky habitat.

60cm (2ft) bass

30cm (1ft) cuckoo wrasse

half of the dorsal fin and the third on the tail. Mature males have a brilliant blue head, the blue continuing on to the body and back. The remainder of the male's body and fins is yellow or orange.

Cuckoo wrasse migrate locally, coming into rocky inshore waters in the summer where they can be caught in as little as 10m (30ft) of water. In winter they move offshore to escape the colder shallow water. They are sensitive to cold temperatures and a severe winter can cause fatalities.

The geographical distribution of the species confirms this: the fish ranges throughout the Mediterranean and along the North African coast, but extends no farther north than the Shetland Isles.

Shell-crushers

Like all wrasse, the cuckoo has a formidable set of conical teeth used for prising molluscs off rocks. It sucks in prey through its fleshy lips and then crushes it with powerful pharyngeal teeth at the back of the throat. In addition to molluscs, it eats crustaceans, including squat lobsters and swimming crabs.

The cuckoo wrasse is active during the day but seeks refuge in rock crevices and dense weed at night.

Ritual dances

Spawning takes place in early summer. The male attracts the female with an elaborate 'dancing' display, during which its whole head may blanch to a pure white then back to blue every few seconds. Having been won over, the female builds a nest by jamming pieces of seaweed and debris into a rock crevice. Males are highly territorial and fiercely drive away rivals that come too

TRACKING DOWN CUCKOO WRASSE

Cuckoo wrasse feed by sight, so they are most active during the daytime.

At night they take refuge in rock crevices or hide in kelp jungles.

They are highly territorial fish and usually remain in one area.

30m

They feed mainly on shellfish, which they prise from the rocks.

kelp

reef

close while the female is laying her eggs.

Strangely, all cuckoo wrasse are female for the first few years of life – the reasons for this are not really known. They are slow-growing and take about six years to become sexually mature. Some remain female for the rest of their life but about half change sex at 7-10 years old.

▼ *Lugworms or the flesh of crustaceans, for example mussels and crabs, are ideal for catching cuckoo wrasse. The best time to fish for them is in daylight hours on the incoming tide when they are feeding.*

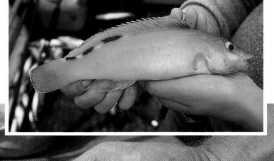

▼ *Startling changes of colour occur when some female cuckoos become functioning males. This specimen is so vivid, it might have been dipped in a pot of brilliant blue paint!*

Red mullet

Recent warm summers have made the red mullet a more frequent visitor to the southern coastline of Britain. But it is still a scarce fish in most of the seas of northern Europe.

It isn't certain whether the red mullet exists as two varieties of one fish, or as two distinct species. *Mullus surmuletus,* 30cm (1ft) or more in length, is the species we recognize living in the waters off the south coast of Britain. The very similar *Mullus barbatus,* on the other hand, a smaller fish known to reach only 20cm (8in) long and lacking the yellow bands of the larger fish, does not reach the British coastline. Some people think that these two are just variations of one species.

Colour changes

The red colour distinguishes the red mullet from other mullet in British waters (such as the golden grey, the thick-lipped grey and the thin-lipped grey), as does its steep forehead and the two large barbels hanging from its lower jaw.

A beautifully coloured fish, the red mullet is reddish brown during the day with four to five yellow stripes and a darker stripe running from eye to tail. At night the stripes break up into an indistinct marbled pattern. Below a depth of about 15m (50ft) the fish stay a deep red.

Moderately slender, the red mullet has a

Distribution

The greatest numbers of red mullet occur around the Channel Islands and the south coast of England. Although it can be found all round Great Britain and Ireland, it is never a common fish.

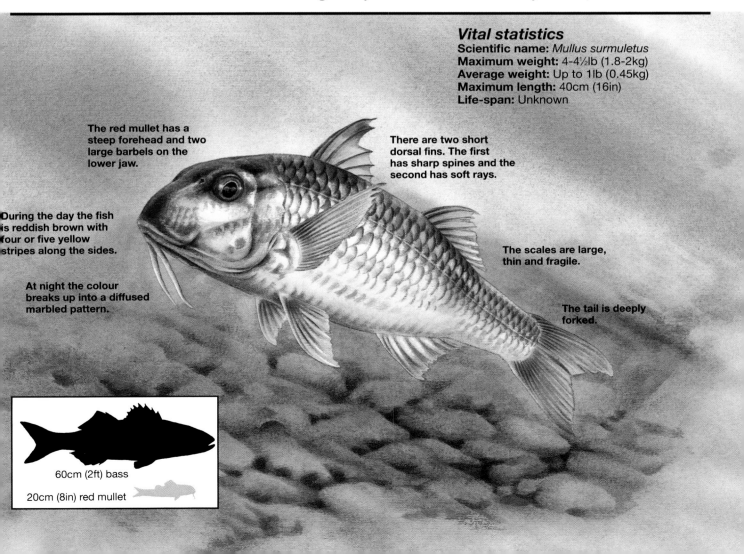

Vital statistics
Scientific name: *Mullus surmuletus*
Maximum weight: 4-4½lb (1.8-2kg)
Average weight: Up to 1lb (0.45kg)
Maximum length: 40cm (16in)
Life-span: Unknown

The red mullet has a steep forehead and two large barbels on the lower jaw.

There are two short dorsal fins. The first has sharp spines and the second has soft rays.

During the day the fish is reddish brown with four or five yellow stripes along the sides.

The scales are large, thin and fragile.

At night the colour breaks up into a diffused marbled pattern.

The tail is deeply forked.

60cm (2ft) bass

20cm (8in) red mullet

blunt snout and large, thin, fragile scales. There are two short dorsal fins, the first spiny with a dark trailing edge and the other soft.

The lateral line is continuous and the tail is deeply forked. The eyes are moderate in size – with a colour reminiscent of the eyes of a teddy bear. The teeth, which occur in two rows on the lower jaw, are blunt and not very strong. There are no teeth on the upper jaw, but some are located on the palate.

The two barbels under the chin, usually in constant motion, can be laid back into a groove along the sides of the lower jaw. The fish uses them to search for food. They are covered in sensory pores which detect prey as the fish forages along the muddy sea bed, catching and eating molluscs, shrimps and worms. Sometimes the fish excavates a small pit to reach its target.

Migratory movements

Red mullet migrate northwards during the summer. It is not known where British populations spawn, but in the Mediterranean Sea the female sheds her eggs on the sea bed in 10-55m (33-180ft) of water.

The eggs, with a diameter of 0.8-0.9mm, are pelagic. The larvae hatch in three to four days, and can be recognized by the yolk sac which projects forwards, well in advance of the head. An oil globule is sited at the extreme end of the yolk sac.

The young fish live among the plankton, near the sea surface. At this stage they have a blue back and silvery sides.

Living in small schools on sandy or muddy sea beds from 3-9m (10-30ft) deep, the adult red mullet is a highly prized food fish. It isn't common enough in British waters, though, to make it viable for commercial fishing.

Fabulous prices are said to have been paid for this fish in ancient times. It was one of the favourite dishes of the Romans and is still sought after today by gourmets for its wonderful taste.

▲ *There's no mistaking the red mullet with its two long barbels hanging down from the lower jaw. It is a prime food fish, best eaten as fresh as possible – perhaps barbecued, baked or grilled.*

Where to fish

The red mullet is never numerous enough in British waters to be commercially exploited, and it is not often fished for, usually being caught by rod and line anglers who are fishing for other species.

● **The Channel Islands** are by far the best place to find red mullet in any numbers.

● **The Solent** (between Southampton and the Isle of Wight) can produce some good red mullet.

● **Chesil Beach, Bournemouth Pier** and **Dover** can produce a few fish from time to time – a 2lb 3oz (0.992kg) specimen red mullet was landed at Dover for the first time in 1991.

TRACKING DOWN RED MULLET

They root about in soft mud or sand, using their sensitive barbels to find small prey animals.

Red mullet are bottom dwellers. Adult fish can be found at depths from 3m down to about 90m.

Red mullet live in small schools of up to 50 fish, though they also live and feed singly.

The fish swim slowly over the sea bed, constantly flicking their barbels in search of food.

sandy or muddy bottom

Blue shark

Every summer schools of blue sharks turn up off Britain's south and south-west coasts, brought in with the North Atlantic Drift. But where they go afterwards to breed is a mystery.

Distribution

Blue sharks are found in tropical and temperate waters world-wide. In summer they are found off south-west Britain and the southern and western coasts of Ireland.

Record blue shark

● The boat-caught British record for a blue shark is a long-standing one. It is held by N. Sutcliffe for a massive 218lb (98.878kg) fish, caught off Looe, Cornwall in 1959.
● No-one holds the shore-caught record to date. The qualifying weight is 40lb (18.14kg).

Before the late 1940s the blue shark was only known to live in British seas from occasional specimens caught in the western English Channel. They were found tangled in the drift nets set for pilchards. Apart from the nuisance value – they rolled themselves in the nets and it took a long time to untangle them, and even longer to repair the nets – they were regarded as rather rare fish in British waters.

However, just after the end of World War II Brigadier J.A.L.Caunter began to explore the possibility of catching blue sharks from his boat off Looe, Cornwall. He found that in summer blue sharks were common off the Cornish coast, and from then on shark fishing out of Looe and other coastal ports became a small industry. (Sadly, their num-

bers have dwindled over the years because of overfishing.)

True blue

The blue shark is easy to recognize – its long, slimline body, large, upper lobe to the

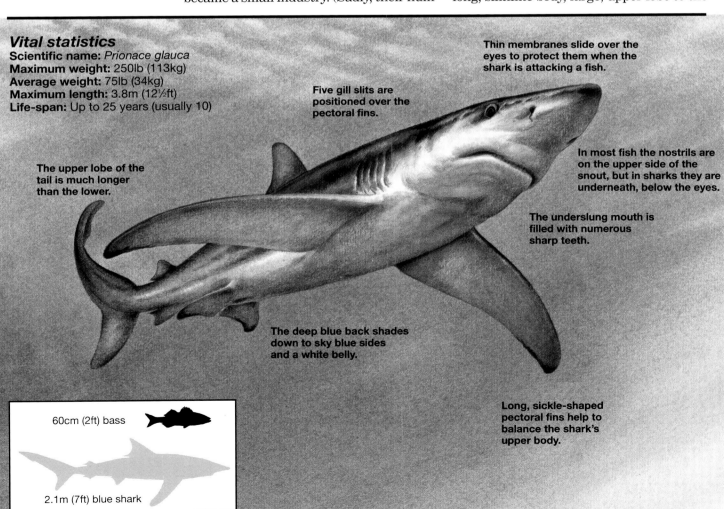

Vital statistics
Scientific name: *Prionace glauca*
Maximum weight: 250lb (113kg)
Average weight: 75lb (34kg)
Maximum length: 3.8m (12½ft)
Life-span: Up to 25 years (usually 10)

Five gill slits are positioned over the pectoral fins.

Thin membranes slide over the eyes to protect them when the shark is attacking a fish.

In most fish the nostrils are on the upper side of the snout, but in sharks they are underneath, below the eyes.

The upper lobe of the tail is much longer than the lower.

The underslung mouth is filled with numerous sharp teeth.

The deep blue back shades down to sky blue sides and a white belly.

Long, sickle-shaped pectoral fins help to balance the shark's upper body.

60cm (2ft) bass

2.1m (7ft) blue shark

tail and immensely long, sickle-shaped pectoral fins are characteristic. The back is deep blue, the sides a brilliant blue and the belly translucent white. This vivid, distinctive colouring fades to a dull grey soon after death.

Mainly a surface-dwelling shark, it lives to depths of 150m (500ft). Where it occurs is dictated mainly by temperature: it prefers water that is between 7-16°C (45-61°F), but can tolerate temperatures up to as much as 21°C (70°F).

As a result, the blue shark only turns up off British coasts from mid June to the end of September – the water is simply too cold for the rest of the year. It is found off the southern and western coasts of Ireland for more or less the same period, and is occasionally encountered off the coast of western Scotland.

Clockwise migration

Tagging blue sharks has shown they make a circum-Atlantic migration. Leaving British coasts at the end of September, they turn southwards, making a huge clockwise sweep into the tropical Atlantic before crossing southwards towards South America. Here they pick up the warm water of the North Atlantic Drift, a strong current flowing north-eastwards across the northern Atlantic. Passing close to the Azores before hitting south-west Britain, they split into two – one branch continuing up the west coast of Ireland, the other turning south to the Bay of Biscay.

In some years the current is stronger and more persistent than usual and this accounts for the presence of blue sharks in the northern North Sea.

Nocturnal feeders

The blue shark feeds mainly at night on various small fish and squid. In British seas its diet consists mainly of pilchards, herring, mackerel, skippers and garfish. It also feeds on offal and rubbish from boats.

Anglers attract sharks by hanging a bag of mashed bits of oily fish – rubby dubby – over the side, then dropping their bait into the scent trail it creates. Sharks can follow scent trails in the water for long distances and, with their acute sense of smell, can detect wounded fish from a considerable distance.

Single-sex schools

The vast majority of sharks around British coasts are immature females – about one in 5000 is male – and very few are mature. Where the sexes meet and mate is still something of a mystery.

Blue sharks are one of the shark species that bear live young. The number of blue shark pups born at any one time varies with the size of the mother – the greatest number recorded is 135, but in British seas litters of between 20 and 30 are usual (though few have been reported). The young are about 38-46cm (15-18in) long at birth.

▲ *It may not look aggressive here, but the blue shark is an extremely voracious animal, feeding on shoals of fish and squid – and even other sharks.*

Where to fish

Blue shark fishing has only just begun to pick up for the first time in 20 years. At the end of 1991 only the following places offered this sport.
● **Mevagissey and Looe** in Cornwall.
● **Courtmacsherry and Kinsale** in Co. Cork, Eire.
● **The Shark Angling Club of Great Britain** can be contacted at: The Quay, East Looe, Cornwall (Tel 05036 2642).

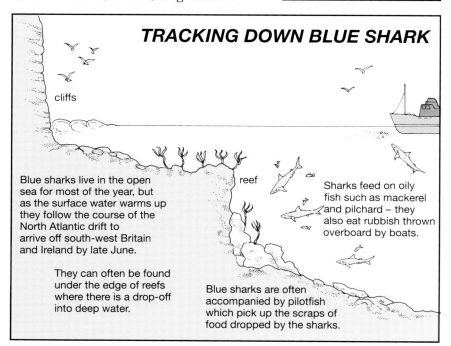

TRACKING DOWN BLUE SHARK

cliffs

reef

Blue sharks live in the open sea for most of the year, but as the surface water warms up they follow the course of the North Atlantic drift to arrive off south-west Britain and Ireland by late June.

They can often be found under the edge of reefs where there is a drop-off into deep water.

Sharks feed on oily fish such as mackerel and pilchard – they also eat rubbish thrown overboard by boats.

Blue sharks are often accompanied by pilotfish which pick up the scraps of food dropped by the sharks.

Spurdog

The most common member of the spiny shark family, the spurdog frequents many Northern European coastal and offshore waters.

Record spurdogs

● **Boat-caught** P.R. Barrett holds this record with a 21lb 3oz 7dm (9.622kg) fish caught in 1977 off Porthleven, Cornwall.

The Irish record is held by John Murnane for an 18lb 12oz (8.5kg) fish caught off Bantry, 1977.

The Welsh record is 17lb 15oz (8.1kg), caught by C. Clayton, Conway in 1980.

● **Shore-caught** For this record R. Legg caught a 16lb 12oz 8dm (7.611kg) fish from Chesil Beach, Dorset in 1964.

In recent seasons spurdog numbers have dropped as a result of commercial overfishing. Vast numbers, taken in nets and on longlines, are skinned, then sold with other dogfish as rock salmon or flake. The spurdog's habit of shoaling in huge numbers, along with its fighting qualities have made it popular with anglers. But now the days of big catches on rod and line appear to be numbered.

Well-named shark

Easily distinguished, the spurdog is the only common shark to have a spine at the front of both dorsal fins. These spines, fairly long, are extremely sharp and can inflict a large wound which takes a long time to heal. It pays to take great care when you are handling a spurdog.

The spurdog is dark grey on the upper half of its slender body, with scattered white spots over the back and sides. The

Distribution

The spurdog is very common all round the British Isles. Largest numbers are found along the southern coastline, throughout the English Channel and the Irish Sea and around the Shetland Isles.

belly is lighter in colour. The snout is pointed and the shark has large eyes and five medium sized gill slits.

The species grows to a maximum length of 1.2m (4ft), but it is more common to find specimens 1m (3ft) long. Females grow

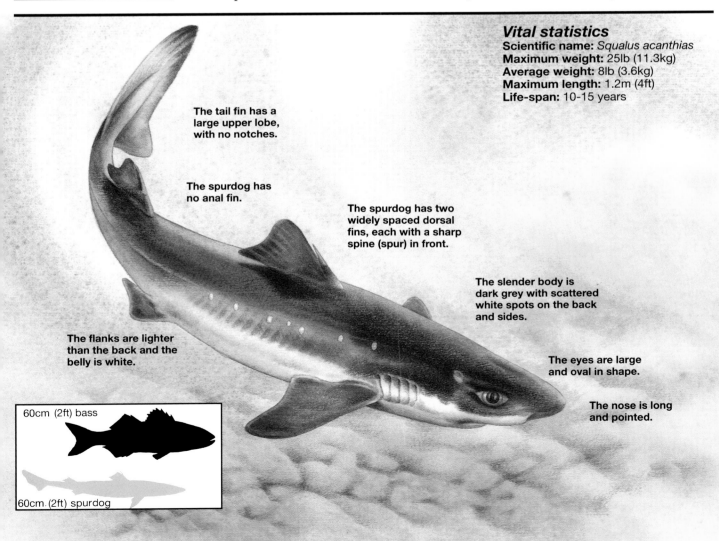

The tail fin has a large upper lobe, with no notches.

The spurdog has no anal fin.

The spurdog has two widely spaced dorsal fins, each with a sharp spine (spur) in front.

The slender body is dark grey with scattered white spots on the back and sides.

The flanks are lighter than the back and the belly is white.

The eyes are large and oval in shape.

The nose is long and pointed.

Vital statistics
Scientific name: *Squalus acanthias*
Maximum weight: 25lb (11.3kg)
Average weight: 8lb (3.6kg)
Maximum length: 1.2m (4ft)
Life-span: 10-15 years

60cm (2ft) bass

60cm (2ft) spurdog

larger than males, with a maximum weight of over 20lb (9kg). Good specimen targets to aim for are 10-12lb (4.5-5.4kg) from a boat and 6-8lb (2.7-3.6kg) from the shore.

Follow the feeding

The spurdog is generally found on or near the sea bed – especially where the terrain is sandy or muddy – at depths of 10-100m (33-330ft). But it has been contacted by trawls at depths of 950m (over 3000ft) and also right at the surface.

It is thought to approach the surface at night to feed. Schooling fish such as whiting, herring, sprat, pilchard, sandeel and even garfish are the mainstay of the spurdog's diet. However, it doesn't appear to be too fussy in its eating habits, and consumes various bottom-living species such as flatfish, dragonets and cod. It also takes crabs and squid.

Growing up in the sea

This species of shark bears its young live. Litters range from three to eleven pups. The eggs have large yolks and are enclosed in a thin membrane which breaks down as the pups grow. The pups vary in size from 20-33cm (8-13in) long at birth. Both the number of the pups carried and their length at birth depend on the size of the mother.

Females mature at 75-80cm (30-32in) long, but males mature much smaller, at 55-60cm (22-24in). The large size the female must reach before breeding, and the long gestation, greatly affect numbers.

Population controls

Early this century the spurdog was sought after for its large oil-bearing liver. It was also considered a pest by many because

▲ A sleek 10lb (4.5kg) spurdog – an excellent boat-caught specimen. It has the long, streamlined shape typical of most members of the shark family.

huge foraging packs damaged nets, while others caught large quantities of fish.

However, recent levels of exploitation have taken their toll and careful regulation is now needed if stocks are to be maintained at reasonable levels.

Fishing tackle

Since the spurdog favours sandy/muddy sea beds, your tackle should be light to medium so you can enjoy the fish's fighting qualities. Uptiding, for example, is a sporting method which can produce good numbers; a 15-30lb (6.8-13.6kg) downtide set-up also works well. Squid seem to account for many of the specimens landed.

Fewer spurdogs are caught from the shore, but standard beachcasting outfits should deal with any you encounter.

Spurdog hotspots

WHERE TO FISH: BOAT
● **English Channel marks,** off Folkestone, Kent.
● **Goodwin Sands,** off Ramsgate, Kent.
● **Llantwit Major** and **Porthkerry,** off South Glamorgan, South Wales.
● **Nab Tower grounds,** off the Isle of Wight.
● **The Needles,** off the Isle of Wight.
● **Shambles sandbanks,** off Portland Bill, Dorset.

WHERE TO FISH: SHORE
● **Atherfield Bay,** Isle of Wight.
● **Chesil Beach,** Dorset.
● **Loch Etive,** Strathclyde, Scotland.
● **Sowley Beach,** Hants.

TRACKING DOWN SPURDOGS

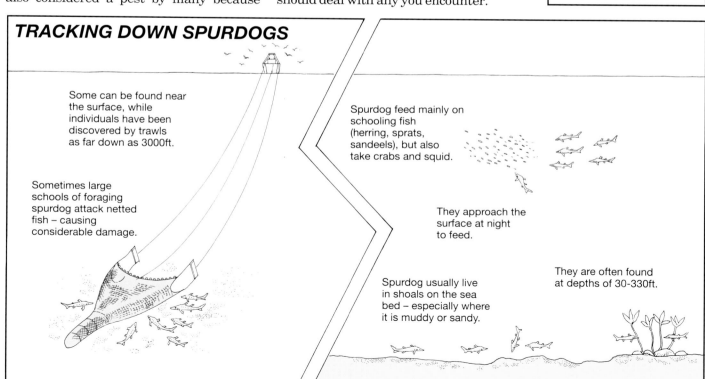

Some can be found near the surface, while individuals have been discovered by trawls as far down as 3000ft.

Sometimes large schools of foraging spurdog attack netted fish – causing considerable damage.

Spurdog feed mainly on schooling fish (herring, sprats, sandeels), but also take crabs and squid.

They approach the surface at night to feed.

Spurdog usually live in shoals on the sea bed – especially where it is muddy or sandy.

They are often found at depths of 30-330ft.

Turbot

The turbot, rated as one of the tastiest of all sea fish, fetches a good price at market since there are not too many of them about.

With its tasty flesh, the turbot is highly sought after by anglers and commercial fishermen alike. As one of the largest members of the flatfish family, the turbot can attain weights of up to 55lb (25kg), with all of the largest specimens being female. However, a 15lb (6.8kg) fish from a boat can be considered a good specimen. Shore specimens are much smaller.

The turbot is a left-eyed flatfish. It has a broad, almost circular body and a large mouth containing numerous pointed teeth. The first few rays of the dorsal fin are branched with just the tips remaining free from the membrane, but it does not have the untidy frill-like appearance seen in the brill.

Spotty skin

The turbot's skin colour varies to match the conditions of the sea bed; generally though, it is sandy brown with a heavy smattering

Distribution

Although found all around the coasts of Britain and Ireland, the turbot is at the northern extreme of its range in European waters. Therefore, it is commonest off the south and south-west coasts of England.

of darker spots. These spots extend on to the tail fin. The body is scaleless, but carries large, bony tubercles irregularly strewn over its back – their presence is the easiest method of telling this fish from the brill.

Although it can be found all around the

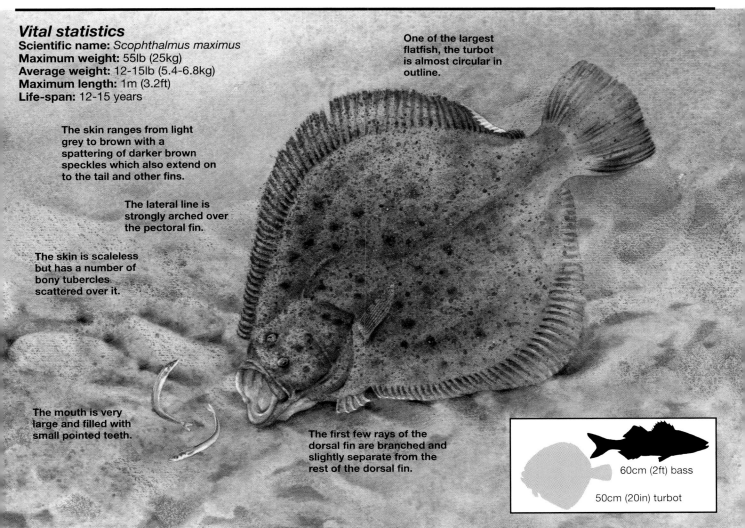

Vital statistics
Scientific name: *Scophthalmus maximus*
Maximum weight: 55lb (25kg)
Average weight: 12-15lb (5.4-6.8kg)
Maximum length: 1m (3.2ft)
Life-span: 12-15 years

The skin ranges from light grey to brown with a spattering of darker brown speckles which also extend on to the tail and other fins.

The lateral line is strongly arched over the pectoral fin.

The skin is scaleless but has a number of bony tubercles scattered over it.

The mouth is very large and filled with small pointed teeth.

The first few rays of the dorsal fin are branched and slightly separate from the rest of the dorsal fin.

One of the largest flatfish, the turbot is almost circular in outline.

60cm (2ft) bass

50cm (20in) turbot

coasts of Britain and Ireland, the turbot is at the extreme of its range here. Before the 1970s most specimen fish came from traditional sandbank marks in the English Channel – until they became overfished.

Record-breaking turbot

With wreck fishing trips in their infancy in the 1970s, skippers soon discovered that when they were blown off their mark, turbot were found on the sand scours built up alongside wrecks. This soon meant that the rod and line turbot record jumped several times in the next decade, reaching a weight of 32lb 4oz (14.5kg) in 1976.

Since those heady record-breaking days, the number of rod and line specimens has decreased. Never sufficiently abundant to satisfy demand, the turbot is one of the more promising species being researched for intensive culture fish-farming for future generations.

Life-cycle

Spawning takes place on specific sites during the spring and summer months. Turbot in northern European waters breed over gravel in depths of 10-40m (30-130ft). The female produces up to 10 million eggs which hatch within a week to ten days. Both the eggs and larvae are pelagic (living in the upper layers of the sea). At the larval stage the fish carries a distinctive swim bladder which it loses when it begins life on the sea bed.

The pelagic stage may continue for four to six months; this helps the young fish disperse from their few restricted spawning grounds. Having drifted into shallow water, young turbot eat planktonic crustaceans, but once settled on the sea bed they feed mainly on the young of other fish species – haddock, whiting, pouting, sandeels and dragonets.

Relatively speaking

Three other relatives of the turbot are found around Britain.
● **Scaldfish** have a bony tubercle between the eyes and are found in deep water in the North Sea.
● **Megrim** have long, slender bodies and are found in the Atlantic.
● **Topknots** have a dark spot behind the lateral line and are generally found in shallow water.

► *Predominantly fish eaters, turbot can be caught on mackerel strip, sandeels and herring. Most are caught in the summer months.*

▼ *With strong teeth, a large mouth and efficient camouflage, the turbot is an effective predator.*

Where to fish

Between May and October, offshore banks are ideal places for turbot fishing. Here are a few for you to try.
● **Manacles**, Falmouth, Cornwall.
● **Needles**, Isle of Wight.
● **Shambles**, Weymouth, Dorset.
● **Skerries**, Dartmouth, Devon.
● **Varne Bank**, off the Kentish coast.

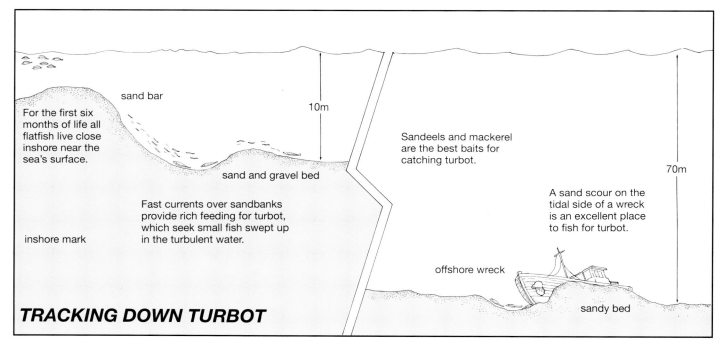

For the first six months of life all flatfish live close inshore near the sea's surface.

sand bar

sand and gravel bed

10m

inshore mark

Fast currents over sandbanks provide rich feeding for turbot, which seek small fish swept up in the turbulent water.

Sandeels and mackerel are the best baits for catching turbot.

A sand scour on the tidal side of a wreck is an excellent place to fish for turbot.

70m

offshore wreck

sandy bed

TRACKING DOWN TURBOT

Blonde ray

Blonde rays are one of the largest of the rays caught in British seas, only the skate and the rare bottle-nosed ray being bigger.

Record-breaking blonde rays

● **Boat-caught** This record is held by H.T. Pout for a 37lb 12oz (17.12kg) fish caught off Start Point, Devon in 1973. (Alwyne Wheeler has little doubt that the current British record boat-caught thornback – 38lb/17.236kg – caught in 1935, was a misidentified blonde. No pictures exist so this can't be confirmed.)
● **Shore-caught** C.M. Reeves caught a 32lb 8oz (14.74kg) blonde ray off the south-east coast of Alderney, Channel Islands in 1986 for this record.

There is always some uncertainty when identifying rays, although the size of the blonde ray is a help. The only two bigger than the blonde (which reaches up to 1.2m/4ft) are the skate (2.4m/8ft) and the bottle-nosed (2m/6½ft). Both are longer-snouted than the blonde.

A prickly customer

Features to look out for on the blonde ray include a fairly short snout and right-angled corners to the wings. The entire back is prickly and the body is disc-shaped. There is a row of large spines down the mid-line of the tail. Large females sometimes have an interrupted line of spines at the sides of the tail.

Young fish have a central row of spines along the tail; their skin is smooth, lacking the prickles on the rear of the disc of their parents.

The clinching feature is the blonde ray's

Distribution

Blonde rays are relatively common in the English Channel, the southern part of the Irish Sea and the Bristol Channel. They occur with decreasing frequency as far as northern Scotland.

colour. The back is light brown with scattered creamy blotches and small, dense dark spots extending to the very edges of the wings and on to the tail. (Those of the smaller spotted ray, which otherwise looks much like the blonde, don't reach so far.)

Vital statistics

Scientific name: *Raja brachyura*
Maximum weight: 40lb (18kg)
Average weight: 15lb (6.8kg)
Maximum length: 1.2m (4ft)
Life-span: Uncertain, perhaps 15 years

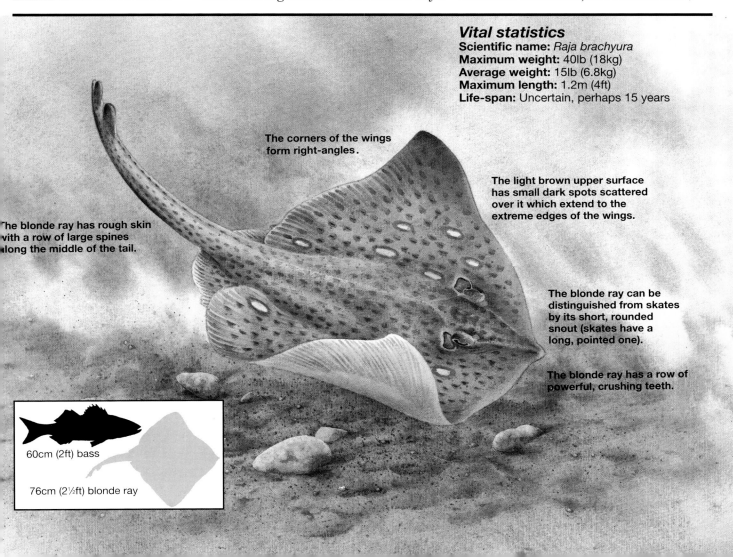

The corners of the wings form right-angles.

The light brown upper surface has small dark spots scattered over it which extend to the extreme edges of the wings.

The blonde ray has rough skin with a row of large spines along the middle of the tail.

The blonde ray can be distinguished from skates by its short, rounded snout (skates have a long, pointed one).

The blonde ray has a row of powerful, crushing teeth.

60cm (2ft) bass

76cm (2½ft) blonde ray

TRACKING DOWN BLONDE RAYS

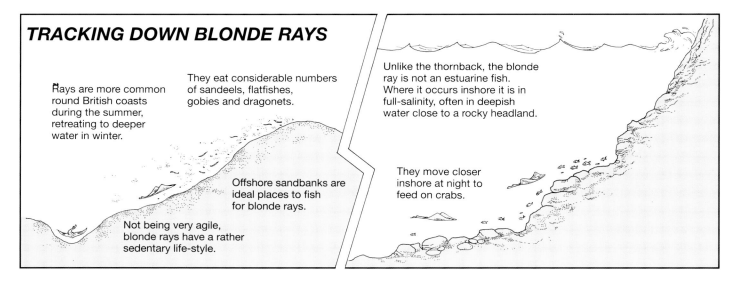

Rays are more common round British coasts during the summer, retreating to deeper water in winter.

They eat considerable numbers of sandeels, flatfishes, gobies and dragonets.

Not being very agile, blonde rays have a rather sedentary life-style.

Offshore sandbanks are ideal places to fish for blonde rays.

Unlike the thornback, the blonde ray is not an estuarine fish. Where it occurs inshore it is in full-salinity, often in deepish water close to a rocky headland.

They move closer inshore at night to feed on crabs.

Deep-water dwellers

Blonde rays are commonest offshore and most of the large specimens are caught by boat anglers. They live in water 18-36m (60-120ft) deep over sand, mud, gravel or shingle. Unlike thornbacks, blonde rays are not found in estuaries. Where they are caught close to the shore it is in full salinity, usually in deep water close to a rocky headland. Younger fish are found in shallower water.

Although blonde rays are relatively common in the English Channel and off southwestern coasts, they are not nearly as common as thornbacks or spotted rays. However, the three are frequently confused.

Blonde rays feed on the sea bed, eating large numbers of sandeels, flatfishes, gobies, dragonets and crustaceans.

The breeding season is in summer, from April to July. The 'mermaid's purse' egg capsule, moderately large at about 10 by 6.5cm (4 by 2½in), is flat on one side, convex on the other and covered with a mat of coarse fibres. The corners are elongated into 'horns'. Up to 30 egg capsules may be laid at a time – they are sticky and adhere to stones, shells or seaweed. The embryo rays take seven months to develop.

Like other rays, the blonde has become much scarcer in recent years. Intensive trawling along the sea bed means that large numbers are captured, and because of their broad, flattened shape even young fish get caught up in mesh that is perfectly legal for round fish.

▼ *Its light colouring and large size help to identify the blonde ray, as do the dozens of small black spots that extend all over the back and right to the very tip of the wings.*

Where to fish for blondes

Blonde rays are fairly localized, though they are quite prolific in certain areas, such as some marks in Hampshire and Dorset. The best of blonde fishing starts at Selsey Bill, then westwards along the Hampshire, Dorset, Devon and Cornwall coasts, with some taken in the Bristol Channel.
● **Devon** The Skerries off Dartmouth have some big blondes; other noted marks include the bays on either side of Start Point.
● **Dorset** The Kidney Bank off Weymouth produces some big blondes. Better numbers have been appearing off The Shambles Bank.
● **Hampshire** Deep water banks six miles or more beyond The Needles produce excellent blondes. South of Selsey Bill and west beyond Durlston, Dorset can be good.

Stingray

You can't mistake the stingray – it's the only ray in British waters (other than the rare eagle ray) which has a tail spine. Highly poisonous, it needs careful handling when caught.

Stingray records

- **Boat** J. K. Rawle for a 65lb 8oz (29.708kg) fish caught off Bradwell-on-Sea, Essex in 1990.
- **Shore** K. Wyatt for a 54lb 9oz (24.7kg) fish caught at Fairbourne Beach in 1991.

The stingray is the only British representative of a fairly large family of rays that is virtually world-wide in its distribution but whose members are most common in tropical and warm temperate seas. In the cool temperate waters of Britain it is a summer season migrant which returns to the warmer waters of the south in autumn.

It isn't difficult to identify. Like the ordinary rays, it is broad-bodied, with thick, well developed pectoral fins and a tail that is rounded at the base but tapering and whip-like at the end. There is no dorsal fin on the tail, but it has one or two (rarely three) long, serrated, dagger-like spines about halfway down the tail. The skin of the back is smooth but some individuals have a series of small rough-surfaced 'buttons' on the back.

The only other ray with a tail spine is the rare eagle ray, with pointed wingtips, a

Distribution

Stingray hotspots are the Solent and the Thames Estuary (Kent and Essex coasts), and it is relatively common around Wales and England up to the Humber Estuary. It occasionally occurs farther north as well.

head distinct from the body, and a small dorsal fin in front of the spine.

A spiny customer

The spine, serrated (barbed) on both edges, is up to 13cm (5in) long. It is a dangerous

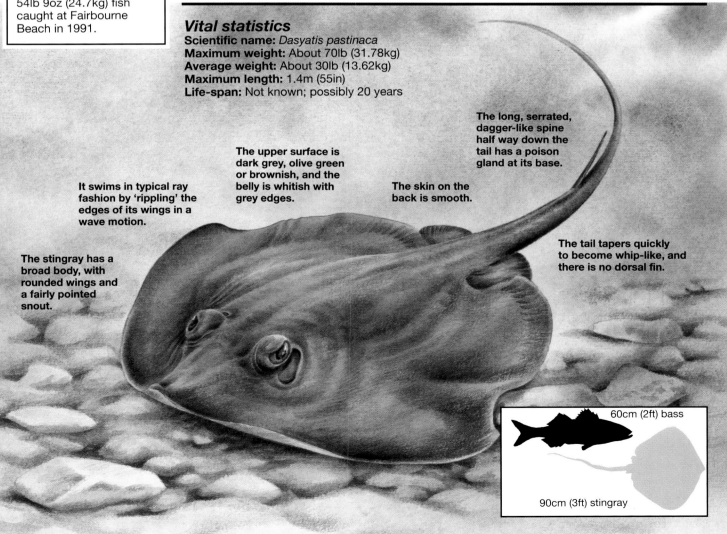

Vital statistics
Scientific name: *Dasyatis pastinaca*
Maximum weight: About 70lb (31.78kg)
Average weight: About 30lb (13.62kg)
Maximum length: 1.4m (55in)
Life-span: Not known; possibly 20 years

It swims in typical ray fashion by 'rippling' the edges of its wings in a wave motion.

The upper surface is dark grey, olive green or brownish, and the belly is whitish with grey edges.

The long, serrated, dagger-like spine half way down the tail has a poison gland at its base.

The skin on the back is smooth.

The stingray has a broad body, with rounded wings and a fairly pointed snout.

The tail tapers quickly to become whip-like, and there is no dorsal fin.

60cm (2ft) bass

90cm (3ft) stingray

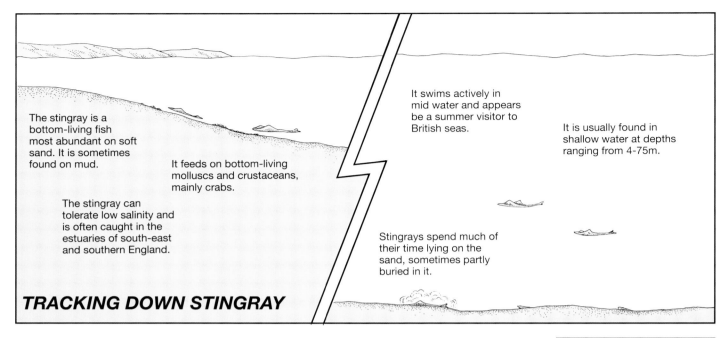

The stingray is a bottom-living fish most abundant on soft sand. It is sometimes found on mud.

It feeds on bottom-living molluscs and crustaceans, mainly crabs.

The stingray can tolerate low salinity and is often caught in the estuaries of south-east and southern England.

It swims actively in mid water and appears be a summer visitor to British seas.

It is usually found in shallow water at depths ranging from 4-75m.

Stingrays spend much of their time lying on the sand, sometimes partly buried in it.

TRACKING DOWN STINGRAY

weapon because the tissue lining the grooves on its sides contains a highly potent venom. Wounds from the sting are both dangerous and very painful. Fortunately, the stingray doesn't live in extremely shallow water and there is little chance of bathers or paddlers being stung, although this is a relatively common event with other spined species in tropical seas.

However, anglers who catch a stingray should handle it with great care. The way it uses its sting is to stab upwards over its back, but the initial slow movement of the tail is deceptive because the final lunge with the sting is lightning-fast. To avoid injury, hold the tail down with your boot placed close to the sting. Cutting the tail off before returning the fish is senselessly cruel, although the ray survives – several tail-less stingrays are caught each year on the Essex coast.

Follow the feeding
The stingray feeds almost exclusively on molluscs and crustaceans, mainly crabs. Most specimens are caught in the major estuaries of the Kent and Essex coasts and in the Solent, both of which regions have large populations of cockles, mussels and even oysters, as well as shore crabs and other crustaceans. The fish can tolerate the lower salinity levels of estuaries.

Summer visitors
A bottom-living fish, the stingray is most abdundant on soft, sandy bottoms or, less often, on mud. It is found at depths of about 4-75m (12-240ft), but does not seem to come very close inshore.

Although it has the classic body form of a bottom-living fish, it swims actively in mid-water. As it seems to be a summertime visitor to British seas, it must be assumed that it swims the several hundred miles needed to get here from somewhere off the French or Spanish coasts. However, it has to be admitted that this is only an assumption because no sustained tagging has ever been attempted to establish exactly where the British stingrays go in winter.

The thickness of the wings shows how well developed the swimming muscles are to enable the fish to make such long-distance migrations.

▶ *A cautious approach is necessary when it comes to handling a stingray.*
This fish swims in typical ray fashion, rippling the edge of its wings in a wave motion that drives it forwards. (This is very different from the eagle ray which beats its heavier, stiffer pectoral fins up and down in bird-wing style.)

▼ *Seen close up, the stingray's spine, lined on both sides with barbs, proves to be a truly formidable weapon.*

A strange way of doing things

The stingray is one of the few fish that gives birth to its young live – the females bear anything from six to nine young pups in a litter.

In the later stages of their development before birth, the embryos are nourished by a 'milky' secretion from their mother's uterine wall – the young are connected to this wall by outgrowths from their gills.

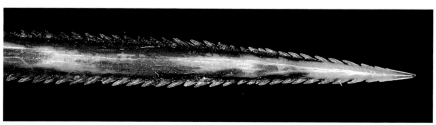

Monkfish

The monkfish is known in some areas as the angel shark, but it is too ugly to be an angel! It's a big, bulky, brutal shark.

Monkfish are cartilaginous fish – like sharks – but are adapted for life on the sea bed and in fact look more like skates and rays. They derive the names monkfish and angel shark from the shape of the head and the enlarged, flattened pectoral fins which give the appearance of a monk's cowl or angel's wings.

Of the 14 different species belonging to the monkfish family, only one lives in British waters, so it is fairly easy to recognize. It may possibly be confused with the angler fish, which has a similar shape, but teeth, jaws, fins and various other features are completely different.

Growing up to 2m (7ft) in length, the monkfish has a broad head and body which quickly tapers down to a much thinner tail. The large nostrils are placed on the top of its

Distribution

These days monkfish are fairly rare in British waters, but they are sometimes found off southern Ireland, the Welsh coast and less commonly off south and south-western England.

head above the eyes and the wide mouth is full of sharply pointed teeth.

Sandpaper skin

The monkfish's skin colour varies depending on its surroundings, but it is generally a

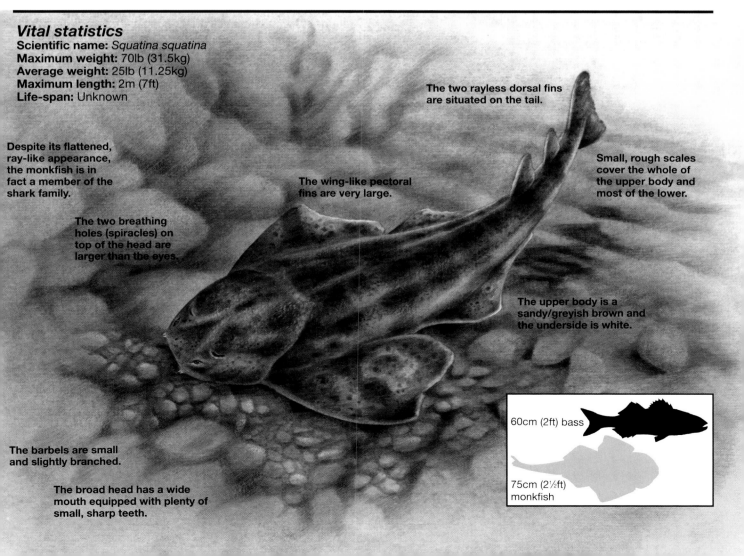

Vital statistics
Scientific name: *Squatina squatina*
Maximum weight: 70lb (31.5kg)
Average weight: 25lb (11.25kg)
Maximum length: 2m (7ft)
Life-span: Unknown

The two rayless dorsal fins are situated on the tail.

Despite its flattened, ray-like appearance, the monkfish is in fact a member of the shark family.

The two breathing holes (spiracles) on top of the head are larger than the eyes.

The wing-like pectoral fins are very large.

Small, rough scales cover the whole of the upper body and most of the lower.

The upper body is a sandy/greyish brown and the underside is white.

The barbels are small and slightly branched.

The broad head has a wide mouth equipped with plenty of small, sharp teeth.

60cm (2ft) bass

75cm (2½ft) monkfish

sandy or greyish brown with finely spotted, darker markings on the upper half of its body. Consequently when it lies half buried in the sand it is very well camouflaged. With its abrasive texture, monkfish skin was once used to polish wood and also to treat some skin ailments.

Best described as a scavenger, the monkfish hunts for food by moving gently over shingle, mud or sandy sea beds, using highly developed barbules under its mouth to feel for prey. It feeds mainly on flatfish, but invertebrates such as crabs, whelks and shrimps are also on the menu.

Live-bearing sharks

Little is known about the breeding habits of monkfish except that, like some other sharks, but unlike rays, they give birth to fully formed young. Anything from 9-16 embryos develop within the mother and the baby fish are about 23cm (9in) when born.

It is not known where monkfish mate but they are not thought to breed in British waters. Essentially warm water fish, they are only found around Britain's coasts in summer, migrating southwards for winter.

Clinging to the sea bed

Although monkfish can swim effectively over long distances, they are not renowned for their fighting abilities on rod and line. Nevertheless, they adhere tightly to the sea bed and hauling them up can take a lot of strength. Unfortunately numbers around Britain are not high because of overfishing in the late 1960s and early 1970s, and few have been landed in recent years.

Tackling a big fish like this needs balanced equipment – a 30lb (13.5kg) class rod and a 4/0 or 6/0 multiplier are ideal.

▲ Despite its flattened, ray-like appearance the hefty monkfish is in fact a shark that is specially adapted to live and feed on the sea bed.

TRACKING DOWN MONKFISH

Although monkfish bear their young in summer, they are not believed to breed in the coastal waters of the British Isles.

In summer they are found inshore in sandy, silty bays.

In winter monkfish migrate southwards, but exactly where they go is still a mystery.

12m

Monkfish feed on other bottom-living fish, molluscs and crustaceans.

pier

Monkfish spend most of the day lying on the sea bed waiting for prey.

sand/gravel

Monkfish spots

Fishing venues are difficult to ascertain, but Westport in Southern Ireland is one of the few places left where you can target this species.

The Welsh coastline, the Needles and the Solent, off the Isle of Wight, and the Sussex coast have all provided a number of monkfish over the years.

Fish weighing 20-25lb (9-11.2kg) from the shore and 35lb (15.7kg) from a boat can be considered very good specimens.

Brill

Though by no means common, brill are not fussy as to what type of sea bed they live on. Happy on sand, gravel, shell or mud – they can adapt their skin colour to match any background.

Distribution

The British Isles are at the northernmost part of the brill's range, so although they can be found all around the coasts of Britain and Ireland they are commonest along the south and south-western coasts.

Record brill

● **Boat-caught** The British record is held by A. Fisher for a 16lb (7.2kg) fish caught off the Isle of Man in 1950.
● **Shore-caught** B. Fletcher caught a 7lb 7oz (3.39kg) specimen in Guernsey, Channel Islands in 1980 to claim this record.

A member of the large, broad-bodied turbot family, the brill can easily be confused with its bigger relative. The most convenient way of telling the two apart is by their skin – the brill has small, smooth scales while the turbot is scaleless and covered in bony tubercles.

The brill is smaller and more rounded in shape than the turbot, though to add to the confusion hybrids between the two are occasionally found, some of them capable of producing offspring of their own.

A left-eyed flatfish (like the turbot and the topknot), the brill is sandy brown to grey on its upper side, with both lighter and darker speckles scattered all over it. Like all flatfish, its skin colour varies depending on the area of the sea bed on which it is found. Each skin cell can expand and contract to vary the amount of pigment visible. Normally the blind side is white but, as in other flatfish, it occasionally has darker

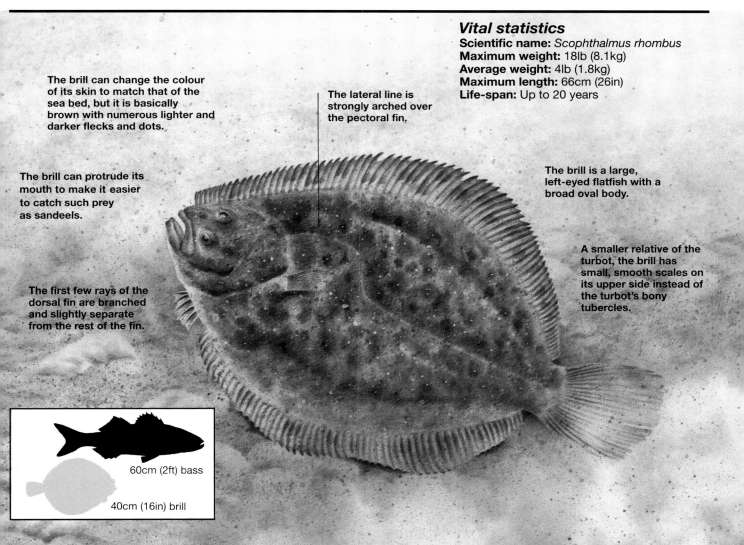

Vital statistics
Scientific name: *Scophthalmus rhombus*
Maximum weight: 18lb (8.1kg)
Average weight: 4lb (1.8kg)
Maximum length: 66cm (26in)
Life-span: Up to 20 years

The brill can change the colour of its skin to match that of the sea bed, but it is basically brown with numerous lighter and darker flecks and dots.

The lateral line is strongly arched over the pectoral fin.

The brill is a large, left-eyed flatfish with a broad oval body.

The brill can protrude its mouth to make it easier to catch such prey as sandeels.

A smaller relative of the turbot, the brill has small, smooth scales on its upper side instead of the turbot's bony tubercles.

The first few rays of the dorsal fin are branched and slightly separate from the rest of the fin.

60cm (2ft) bass

40cm (16in) brill

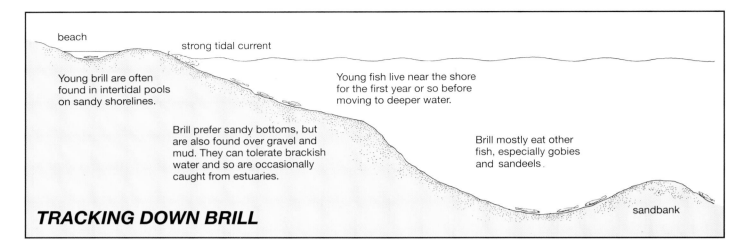

beach

strong tidal current

Young brill are often found in intertidal pools on sandy shorelines.

Young fish live near the shore for the first year or so before moving to deeper water.

Brill prefer sandy bottoms, but are also found over gravel and mud. They can tolerate brackish water and so are occasionally caught from estuaries.

Brill mostly eat other fish, especially gobies and sandeels.

sandbank

TRACKING DOWN BRILL

Brill-iant spots

The following venues are recommended for brill.
● **Channel Islands,** all.
● **Eastbourne,** East Sussex.
● **Lanacombe banks,** off Salcombe, Devon.
● **Nab Tower,** Isle of Wight.
● **Shambles Bank,** Portland Bill, Dorset.
● **Weymouth,** Dorset.

▼ *Sandeels, squid, crabs and mackerel strips are all good baits for catching brill, though being uncommon, not many are caught by rod and line.*

blotches here and there.

Frilly edges

The first few rays of the dorsal fin are branched and partly free from the fin membrane, giving the brill a frilly appearance. The dorsal and anal fins are long, but neither continues around the thick-wristed tail. Another feature is the brill's lateral line which, like that of the turbot, is strongly arched over the pectoral fin.

Any time, any place

Not fussy, brill can be found on sandy, gravelly, shelly and muddy sea beds in water between 10-70m (33-230ft) deep. They are sometimes found around natural reefs and wrecks, and prefer a strong tidal current. Tolerant of brackish water, brill are occasionally found in estuaries too.

Adult fish prey mostly on other fish, especially sandeels. They are active hunters and eat large quantities of whiting, squid, gobies and crustaceans, making easy work of prey with their large, powerful mouth and pointed teeth.

Life-cycle

Brill spawn in early summer in shallow water between 10-20m (33-66ft) deep. The eggs float among the plankton, hatching a week to ten days later. The young fish is symmetrical in shape and stays on the sea surface until it is about 2.5cm (1in) long.

At this point the right eye starts moving over to sit with the left. By the time it has acquired the familiar flatfish shape, the young brill has come to rest on the sea bed. It remains in relatively shallow water for up to two years, often inhabiting intertidal pools on sandy shores while it is still very small.

Although not as commercially important as the turbot, brill are tasty fish. They are more prolific off the south and south-western coasts of the British Isles, but are not at all common anywhere. Unfortunately, numbers seem to be in decline, probably because of trawler overfishing in their limited spawning areas. The minimum legal size brill you can keep is 30cm (12in) long.

Smooth hound and starry smooth hound

Long, slender and sleek in outline, with broad pectoral fins held out stiffly at right angles to the body, the smooth hound and starry smooth hound are typical small sharks.

You can distinguish the smooth hounds from all other British sharks by their teeth. Most sharks (almost by definition) have large, sharp, usually triangular teeth with serrated cutting edges, or else long thin stabbing teeth – but the smooth hounds have flattened blunt teeth in both top and bottom jaws. They are sometimes referred to as 'ray-toothed' sharks – and their jaws do indeed look like the flattened 'pavement' of teeth seen in rays.

Star turn

Apart from their teeth, the smooth hound and the starry smooth hound have all the characteristic features of sharks: a long slender body, a notched, asymmetrical tail, two large dorsal fins, one anal fin and broad pectoral fins which are held out stiffly from the body. There are five gill slits on each side, above the pectoral fin bases, and a conspicuous spiracle (breathing hole) close behind each eye.

Distribution

The starry smooth hound is quite common and can be found all round the British coast, especially in sheltered sandy estuaries.
The smooth hound is uncommon and appears mostly off the southern coasts of the British Isles.

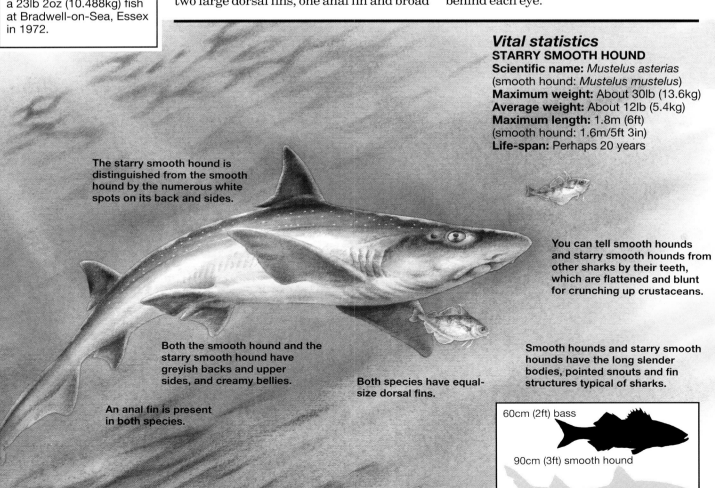

The starry smooth hound is distinguished from the smooth hound by the numerous white spots on its back and sides.

Both the smooth hound and the starry smooth hound have greyish backs and upper sides, and creamy bellies.

An anal fin is present in both species.

Both species have equal-size dorsal fins.

Vital statistics
STARRY SMOOTH HOUND
Scientific name: *Mustelus asterias* (smooth hound: *Mustelus mustelus*)
Maximum weight: About 30lb (13.6kg)
Average weight: About 12lb (5.4kg)
Maximum length: 1.8m (6ft) (smooth hound: 1.6m/5ft 3in)
Life-span: Perhaps 20 years

You can tell smooth hounds and starry smooth hounds from other sharks by their teeth, which are flattened and blunt for crunching up crustaceans.

Smooth hounds and starry smooth hounds have the long slender bodies, pointed snouts and fin structures typical of sharks.

60cm (2ft) bass

90cm (3ft) smooth hound

▲ This fine smooth hound weighed 20lb (9kg). Not much is known of its natural history – like the starry smooth hound, it seems to migrate into shallow water and move northwards during the summer months.

► This isn't the largest starry smooth hound in the world, but you can still see the small spots that give it its name.

Of the two species, the starry smooth hound is far more common. An inshore shark, it is found over sandy or gravelly sea beds up to 70m (230ft) deep.

Getting down to the nitty-gritty

The body scales (dermal denticles) help identify the two species, but the differences are subtle. The denticles are close packed and shield-shaped. In the starry smooth hound each denticle is nearly as wide as it is long and the two ridges nearest its mid-line run down to its tip.

In the smooth hound the denticles are nearly twice as long as they are broad and the ridges fade out before they reach the last quarter of the surface.

Both the smooth hound and the starry smooth hound are greyish on the back and upper sides and creamy on the belly. The starry smooth hound, however, is covered with small white spots, each smaller than the pupil of the eye. These spots resemble the stars that give it its name. The smooth hound does not have white spots.

Vive la difference

It is quite extraordinary that, while the differences in appearance between the two sharks are so subtle that they are difficult to identify, their breeding biology is fundamentally different. Both bear their young live, but the way the pups develop as embryos in the two species is poles apart.

The starry smooth hound is ovoviviparous – the young develop within the mother and are nourished only by the yolk in the egg. Up to 28 pups are produced at a time, each about 30cm (12in) long.

The smooth hound, on the other hand, is viviparous – the young develop inside the mother but, late in development, derive their nourishment directly from her. The yolk sacs establish contact with the mother's uterine wall to form a false placenta. This is very rare in fish. The smooth hound gives birth to litters of up to 15 pups, each about 30cm (12in) long.

The young of both species are born in the summer, after a gestation period lasting about 12 months.

Crunch, crunch, crunch

Both smooth hounds feed almost entirely on crustaceans. Their flattened teeth are designed to cope with a diet of hard-shelled animals. Large smooth hounds tackle hermit crabs in great numbers, not troubling to pick them out of their protective whelk shell but scrunching them up, shell and all. Both species of shark are thought to feed mainly at night.

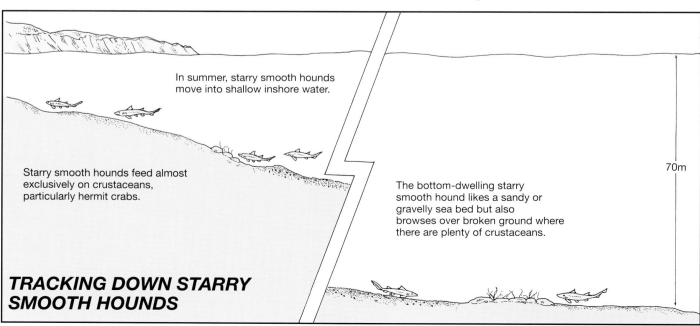

In summer, starry smooth hounds move into shallow inshore water.

Starry smooth hounds feed almost exclusively on crustaceans, particularly hermit crabs.

The bottom-dwelling starry smooth hound likes a sandy or gravelly sea bed but also browses over broken ground where there are plenty of crustaceans.

70m

TRACKING DOWN STARRY SMOOTH HOUNDS

Ling

Six hundred feet down in the murky depths of the sea is a dangerous world for small creatures. There are many large fish lurking among the reefs and wrecks looking for a meal – one of the most voracious being the ling.

The ling is the largest member of the cod family – but, with its elongated body, broad head and wide mouth, it bears a closer resemblance to the conger eel. However, its spineless fins, barbule and tiny scales reveal its relationship to the cod. Its needle-sharp teeth are spread wide in the mouth so that it can secure a good grip on its prey. The body, a mottled green/brown, is covered in slime which gives it a bronze sheen.

Unlike cod, which have three dorsal fins, the ling only has two. The first is short with a dark 'thumbprint' at the rear; the second dorsal fin and the anal fin are long and feathery and extend almost to the tail,

Distribution

Small ling can be caught all around the coasts of the British Isles. Adult ling are abundant in very deep water off Scotland, the south and west coasts of Ireland, south-west England and the English Channel.

rather like those of rockling. Both the dorsal and anal fins are edged with white.

Anything will do

An active predator, the ling eats most species of fish, especially pouting, cod,

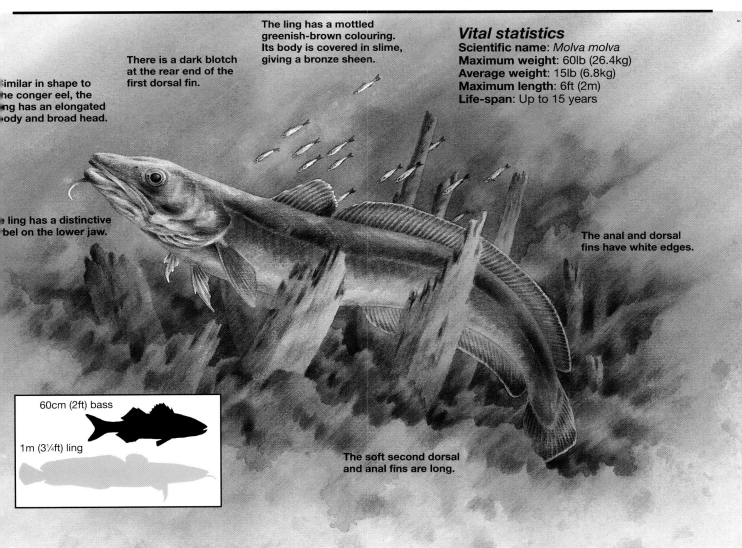

There is a dark blotch at the rear end of the first dorsal fin.

The ling has a mottled greenish-brown colouring. Its body is covered in slime, giving a bronze sheen.

Similar in shape to the conger eel, the ling has an elongated body and broad head.

The ling has a distinctive barbel on the lower jaw.

The anal and dorsal fins have white edges.

The soft second dorsal and anal fins are long.

Vital statistics
Scientific name: *Molva molva*
Maximum weight: 60lb (26.4kg)
Average weight: 15lb (6.8kg)
Maximum length: 6ft (2m)
Life-span: Up to 15 years

60cm (2ft) bass

1m (3¼ft) ling

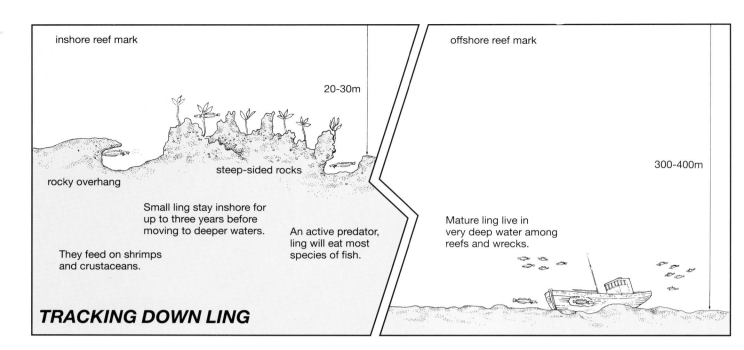

inshore reef mark

offshore reef mark

20-30m

300-400m

steep-sided rocks

rocky overhang

Small ling stay inshore for up to three years before moving to deeper waters.

An active predator, ling will eat most species of fish.

They feed on shrimps and crustaceans.

Mature ling live in very deep water among reefs and wrecks.

TRACKING DOWN LING

whiting, gurnards and flatfish. It also feeds on crustaceans and starfish on occasion, and if an octopus is unlucky enough to be caught in open water, a ling will make short work of it.

In deep water

Adult ling live mainly in very deep water, though young specimens up to 20lb (9kg) are found in depths of 20-30m (60-100ft). The larger fish live in water up to 400m (1300ft) deep. They are usually found hiding among reefs and wrecks and have a particular preference for such features as steep-sided rocks and overhangs.

Life-cycle

The ling lays up to 60 million eggs in order to ensure the survival of the species (many of the eggs provide a rich food source for other hungry fish). They have particular spawning grounds in the North Sea and Icelandic waters, where the female lays her eggs between March and June in depths up to 200m (650ft). Each egg contains a pale green oil globule which helps it to rise to the surface to float among the plankton.

After ten days the eggs hatch and the small fish grow rapidly. Females grow faster than males and can reach up to 20cm (8in) long in their first year. They stay in fairly shallow coastal waters for two to three years before moving offshore.

Ling are of some commercial importance – they are caught on long lines and in trawling nets. Although a small amount is sold fresh, most of the catch is salted and dried and then exported to Southern Europe.

Where to fish

The Scottish coast, the North Sea and wrecks in the English Channel and Irish Sea are ideal places to go fishing for these voracious monsters.

These days large charter boats, using

high-tech navigation, can rapidly reach wrecks well away from port – such locations are the closely guarded secrets of the boat skippers. Echo sounders are a great help in the search for large fish.

▼ *This 34lb (15.3kg) ling was taken from a wreck off the coast at Dartmouth, Devon. The ling is the largest member of the cod family.*

Halibut

Large specimens of this monster of the flatfish tribe are rarely caught nowadays. Miracles of adaptation, they lead a varied life – starting in shallow water and ending up as adults in the depths of the Atlantic.

Distribution

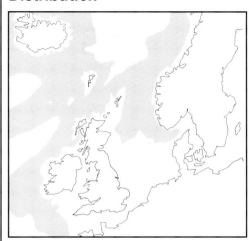

Halibut are found along the western and northern coasts of the British Isles in deep water, as well as northwards to Shetland, Faroe, Iceland and Norway, but they are not nearly as numerous as they once were. They are not found in the English Channel.

Record halibut

● **The boat-caught record** is currently held by C. Booth, for a halibut caught at Dunnet Head off Scrabster, Scotland in 1979. It weighed 234lb (106.136kg).
● **Shore-caught record** This has a qualifying weight of 10lb (4.536kg). There is no British record-holder at present since large halibut only tend to come to the coast close to their spawning grounds off Norway or further north.

The flatfish are one of the most extra-ordinary fish groups in existence. There are something like 540 different kinds worldwide, all of them well adapted to a life on the sea bed.

Halibut go through a series of amazing changes – common to all flatfish – in which they lie on one side while one eye moves over to join the other on the upper side of the head. But no one has ever explained why some species usually have their eyes on the left, while others have them on the right. Flatfish are generally small to moderate sized, but the halibut (a right-eyed flatfish), reaching up to 2.4m (8ft) long, is a giant.

Size says it all

Any really big flatfish caught in British seas can be identified with certainty as a halibut. (The only rival for size it has among flatfish

is the related Pacific halibut). In the case of moderate-sized flatfish, halibut recognition can be confirmed by the thickset body with both eyes on the right side of the fish, a medium sized head and a very big mouth, with large, sharp teeth in both jaws.

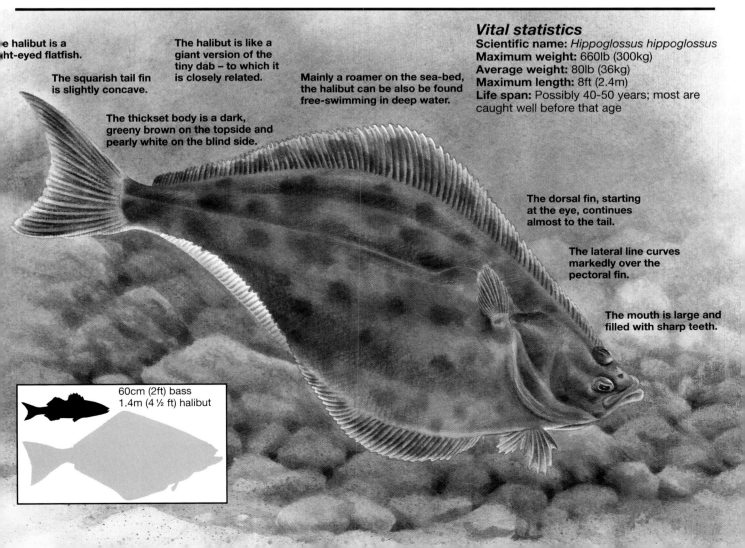

⬤e halibut is a ⬤ht-eyed flatfish.

The squarish tail fin is slightly concave.

The thickset body is a dark, greeny brown on the topside and pearly white on the blind side.

The halibut is like a giant version of the tiny dab – to which it is closely related.

Mainly a roamer on the sea-bed, the halibut can be also be found free-swimming in deep water.

Vital statistics
Scientific name: *Hippoglossus hippoglossus*
Maximum weight: 660lb (300kg)
Average weight: 80lb (36kg)
Maximum length: 8ft (2.4m)
Life span: Possibly 40-50 years; most are caught well before that age

The dorsal fin, starting at the eye, continues almost to the tail.

The lateral line curves markedly over the pectoral fin.

The mouth is large and filled with sharp teeth.

60cm (2ft) bass
1.4m (4 ½ ft) halibut

The dorsal fin starts level with the front edge of the eye and runs almost the entire length of the body; the tail fin is slightly concave at the edge. A good identifying feature is the strong curve in the lateral line over the pectoral fin.

The halibut is usually a dull greeny brown or olive grey (though is sometimes almost black) on the upper (right) side and pearly white on the blind side.

Down in the deeps
A cold water (but not polar) flatfish, the halibut lives down as deep as 1500m (5000ft) but can be caught in just 100m (330ft), or even from the shore in areas where the land drops off steeply into the sea. It inhabits different depths at different times in its life. Young fish are mostly found in shallow water, but are extremely hard to catch. After about the age of four they move into deeper water.

Large males are usually found very deep, even on the edge of the continental shelf. The really big specimen fish are simply huge – fish of 1.8m (6ft) long are sometimes still caught, and there are true records of fish nearly twice that length.

Versatile hunters
The halibut lives on a variety of sea beds from sand and gravel to rocky bottoms. The larger fish probably shelter between pinnacles of rock. However, unlike most flatfish, it is not confined all the time to the sea bed, but hunts actively off the bottom. It feeds on a wide range of near-bottom living fish (haddock, redfish and small skate), squid and some crustaceans. Young fish living in shallower water eat small fish such as herring and sandeels, as well as flatfish and crustaceans, including large prawns.

Elusive breeding
Spawning takes place in late winter and early spring near the sea bed in deep water and close to the edge of the continental shelf. The halibut produces large numbers of eggs (a 200lb/90kg female is estimated to contain more than two million).

Although spawning takes place close to the sea bed the eggs – once fertilized – float up to about 90m (300ft) below the surface. The young fish, about 7mm (¼in) long at hatching, rise towards the surface and are swept shorewards at the same time. By the time they are about 4cm (1½in) long, their eyes have moved over to the right side of the head, and they begin to live on the bottom.

Since the halibut spawns in such deep water and the young fish are difficult to catch, there are many details of their breeding cycle which are not well known. Sadly, the fish is also becoming scarcer.

Good eating
The flesh of the halibut is very tasty and the fish is commercially important. It's marketed fresh, frozen, salted and smoked.

Special halibut nets are used to catch them off the Norwegian coast where they spawn, but they are fairly slow-growing fish and there is a real danger of population decline through overfishing. Now fishing is prohibited at certain times and there is a strict minimum size limit (50cm/20in in Norway).

▼ *This fine halibut would have been regarded as fairly moderate in size in the days before overfishing had taken its toll.*

It is found on both sides of the North Atlantic. On the American coast, it ranges as far south as Cape Cod and northwards to western Greenland.

Mako shark

The mako shark has long had a reputation as a hard-hitting, high-flying game fish. Once fairly common off the south coast of Cornwall, it is now noticeable by its absence.

Distribution

Off the coastlines of Europe the mako is found in the Mediterranean and throughout the tropical and temperate Atlantic Ocean, but it also lives in warm seas all over the world, especially in the waters around Australia and New Zealand

Around Britain it used to appear as far north as Scotland and in the western English Channel, but in recent years it has almost disappeared from these areas. As the seas around Britain warm up, and as shark hunting is restricted, makos may return once more to our waters.

Mako records

● **Boat-caught record**
This stands at 500lb (226.786kg) – a fish caught in 1971 by Mrs J.M. Yallop off Eddystone Lighthouse in the English Channel. With the present scarcity of mako sharks in British waters, this record is unlikely to be bettered for a while.

● **Shore-caught record**
There is no shore record at present. The qualifying weight for a shore-caught fish is 40lb (18.143kg).

Found in seas all round the world, the mako is very much a warm water species. It is an ocean-going fish and likes to live in deep clear water, although the occasional small specimen may venture inshore in pursuit of mackerel or other baitfish. Larger specimens keep well clear of the shoreline.

Though never plentiful around the coasts of Britain, the mako was once found – and caught – fairly regularly. But overfishing, and the decline of prey such as mackerel, herring and pilchard, reduced mako numbers almost to zero. Today the respite from hunting and the warming of British seas mean that numbers may be going up.

Elongated and slimmer in shape than the porbeagle, the mako is a handsome shark.

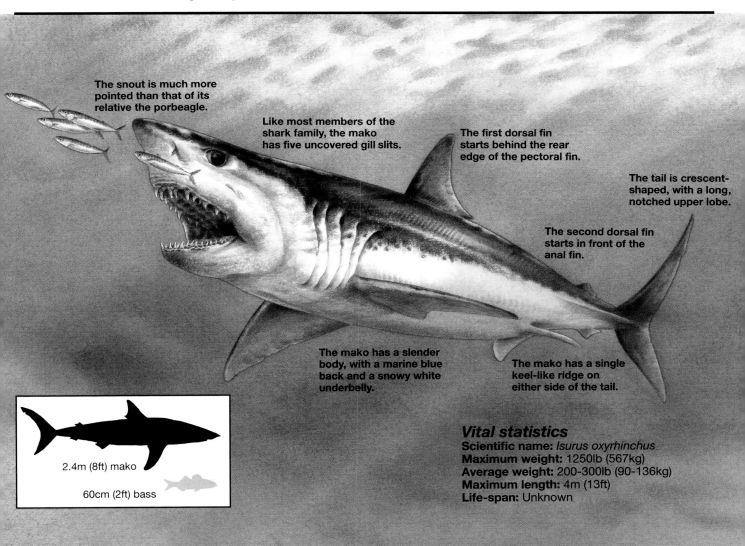

The snout is much more pointed than that of its relative the porbeagle.

Like most members of the shark family, the mako has five uncovered gill slits.

The first dorsal fin starts behind the rear edge of the pectoral fin.

The tail is crescent-shaped, with a long, notched upper lobe.

The second dorsal fin starts in front of the anal fin.

The mako has a slender body, with a marine blue back and a snowy white underbelly.

The mako has a single keel-like ridge on either side of the tail.

2.4m (8ft) mako

60cm (2ft) bass

Vital statistics
Scientific name: *Isurus oxyrhinchus*
Maximum weight: 1250lb (567kg)
Average weight: 200-300lb (90-136kg)
Maximum length: 4m (13ft)
Life-span: Unknown

Don't mix up mako with porbeagle

Several features distinguish the mako from the porbeagle.

The mako's snout is pointed (1), its body slender (2) and its gill slits reach the underside of the body (3). Its first dorsal fin (4) starts behind the rear edge of the pectoral fin, and its second dorsal fin (5) starts in front of the anal fin.

The porbeagle's snout is round (6), its body deep (7). Its gill slits don't reach its underside (8), its first dorsal fin (9) starts behind the base of the pectoral fin and the second dorsal fin (10) starts above the anal fin.

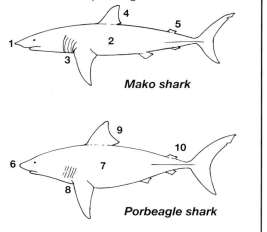

Mako shark

Porbeagle shark

The mako's breeding secrets

Little is known of the mako's breeding habits. The female produces 8-10 pups, each 69-74cm (27-29in) long. They hatch inside their mother, but stay connected to a large yolk which is in turn linked to the mother fish. There is some evidence that the dominant pups may kill and eat their weaker brethren while still inside the mother.

Its body is marine blue, its underparts snowy white. The graceful tail stalk bears a horizontally flattened keel on either side, and the tail fin has a 'crescent moon' shape, with the upper, notched lobe slightly longer than the lower.

The mako is occasionally confused with the porbeagle, but their teeth (if you can get a view of them) show which is which. Those of the porbeagle are large and triangular with a small cusp at each side of the base,

▼ *Sought-after by game anglers because of their superb fighting qualities, mako sharks have become rare in British waters. The rocks and reefs of the south coast of Cornwall used to be mako hotspots.*

but the mako's teeth are long, narrow and irregular with no sign of a basal cusp. Also the lower teeth of the mako hang forward, clear of the lips.

Follow the feeding

Every inch a predator, the mako is active and fast-moving. All those found in British waters have wandered in from the Atlantic.

In the Atlantic the mako lives mainly on tuna, but in British waters it hunts mackerel, herring and pilchard. It is the fastest of all sharks and has no trouble running down fast-moving prey. Very unusually for fish, the mako is warm-blooded – its body temperature is normally 7-10 degrees higher than the surrounding water. The high temperature allows it to respire faster, giving it more energy to maintain the speed needed to overtake virtually any other fish.

Sought-after shark

Running to a top weight of around 1250lb (567kg), the mako is much sought-after as a sporting species. Once hooked, it often resorts to a spectacular display of aerobatics – jumping as much as 9m (30ft). Many anglers think this the highest-jumping species on the game fish list.

Extremely aggressive, the mako has been known to make unprovoked attacks on boats. Once hooked and played out, these fish must be handled with great care. Even experienced commercial shark fishermen take no chances. The largest mako caught in British waters weighed 500lb (226.7kg), but much larger ones have been hooked and lost after marathon battles.

Scad mackerel

One of the most successful predators – despite the fact that its average length is only about 30cm (12in) – the scad mackerel is a fast-swimming shoaling fish.

The scad, or horse mackerel as it is sometimes known, is a frequent visitor to the southern coasts of Britain and Ireland. Its colouring is rather dull and can't be compared with the common mackerel's metallic brilliance. The scad has a drab olive back with hints of blue or grey, and silver sides with greyish bars that span the entire length of the body.

It is also a much smaller fish than the common mackerel and has small dark spots marking the edge of its gill covers. Its first dorsal fin has eight spiny rays; the second fin runs halfway down the body. The curved lateral line is positioned high above the base of the long, sickle-shaped pectoral fins; at the second dorsal fin, it dips downwards, following the centre of the body. Most of the lateral line is unobstructed, increasing the fish's ability to locate prey.

Distribution

Scad mackerel are found mostly along the southern coast of England and the Republic of Ireland. But they also live in the Irish Sea as far north as Scotland.

Mackerel or what?

From its name you might think that the scad is closely related to the common mackerel. Although both appear similar in overall body shape, the scad mackerel isn't really a mackerel at all – but a member of

Vital statistics

Scientific name: *Trachurus trachurus*
Maximum weight: 3½lb (1.6kg)
Average weight: 12oz (340g)
Maximum length: 16in (40cm)

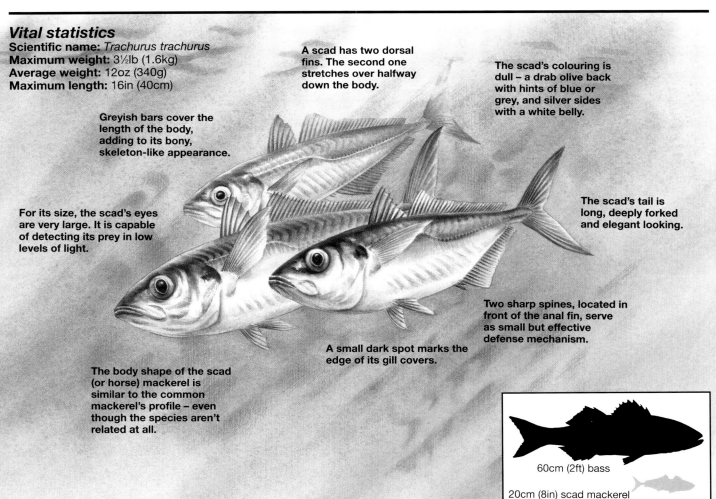

A scad has two dorsal fins. The second one stretches over halfway down the body.

The scad's colouring is dull – a drab olive back with hints of blue or grey, and silver sides with a white belly.

Greyish bars cover the length of the body, adding to its bony, skeleton-like appearance.

For its size, the scad's eyes are very large. It is capable of detecting its prey in low levels of light.

The scad's tail is long, deeply forked and elegant looking.

Two sharp spines, located in front of the anal fin, serve as small but effective defense mechanism.

A small dark spot marks the edge of its gill covers.

The body shape of the scad (or horse) mackerel is similar to the common mackerel's profile – even though the species aren't related at all.

60cm (2ft) bass

20cm (8in) scad mackerel

the Caragidae family which includes the Mediterranean pompano and the heavy-weight amberjack which can grow up to 2m (6 ½ft) long.

Follow the feeding

Scad mackerel come inshore in early summer, following the shoals of sprats, herring, sandeels and other small fish. Look for scad off sandy beaches where they come in close to feed on sandeels.

Stanchion piers attract shoals of fry seeking cover. This is also a good place to look for scad. You can tempt scad by float fishing small slivers of sprat or herring. Light gear is by far the best because the scad come remarkably close to shore during the day – long casts aren't needed. A 12ft (3.6m) float rod with a fixed-spool reel loaded with 5-6lb (2.3-2.7kg) line is suitable gear.

Life-cycle

The female lays 5,000-150,00 eggs just offshore in May and June. After a few days the eggs hatch. At this point, the hatchlings, only 2.5mm long, feed on plankton. Once the hatchlings are 13mm (½in) long, they develop fin rays.

A peculiar trait of young scad (and whiting for that matter) is that many shelter under large jellyfish. You can find young fry, about 5cm (2in) long, close inshore where they tend to form mixed shoals with other small fish.

When winter comes, both adult and young scad move out into the English Channel and off the Republic of Ireland where the water is deeper and warmer. They may live in depths up to 300m (985ft).

Only a few countries such as Spain, France and Portugal fish commercially for scad, making fish meal and various other products from them. Since the fishing pressure isn't too great, there are substantial stocks of fish.

▲ *This fine specimen scad mackerel was taken off the Isle of Wight in mid summer. Look at its eye and mouth – they're huge in comparison with the rest of the body. No wonder then, with this equipment, that the scad is a very successful predator of the open seas.*

Scad in the summer

● **Chesil Beach, Dorset** A popular venue for scad mackerel and common mackerel.
● **Mevagissey, Lizard Point** and **St Ives (Cornwall)** Anglers take many specimen scad here every summer.
● **Ryde Pier, Isle of Wight** Float fishing for scad is superb at this venue.

TRACKING DOWN SCAD MACKEREL

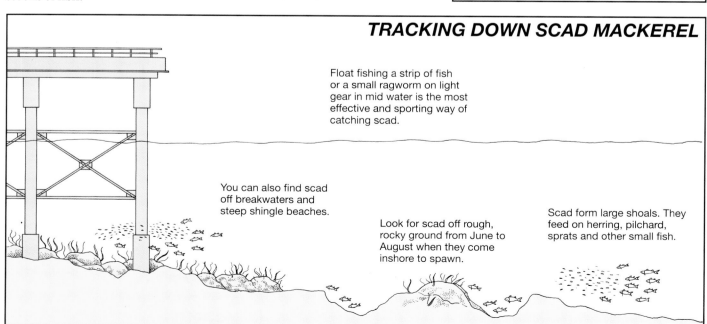

Float fishing a strip of fish or a small ragworm on light gear in mid water is the most effective and sporting way of catching scad.

You can also find scad off breakwaters and steep shingle beaches.

Look for scad off rough, rocky ground from June to August when they come inshore to spawn.

Scad form large shoals. They feed on herring, pilchard, sprats and other small fish.

Index

Page numbers in *italics* refer to illustrations

ACKNOWLEDGEMENTS

Photographs

Chris Clark 58(t), 59; Bruce Coleman (A Purcell) 105(b); John Darling 10, 15, 17(t), 20(b), 21, 22(b), 24(t), 28(b), 30(b), 52(t), 53, 76, 91, 95(br), 96(tr), 114(b), 129(t), 162(b), 170(b), 174(tr), 192; Dave Devine 70; Eaglemoss(Ian Christie) 33, 36(b), (Eric Crichton) 86, 90, (Peter Gathercole) 56, 62(t), 188, (Carl Gedye) 31(c,b), 95(c), 96(tl), 100(c,b), (Trevor Housby) 3, (Neville Kidd) 35, (Patrick Llewelyn-Davies) 26(t), 30(t), 50(l), 72, 84, 131(b), 138(t), (Mike Millman) 83, (Martin Norris) 16, 17(bl,br), 18, 23(r), (Nic Randall) 55, 69(tr), 95(t), 124(b), (Alastair Scott) 137(tl), (Clifford Staley) 32(t), 49, 51, 114(t), (John Suett) 12(l,tr), 13(b), 14(r), 94(b), (Mike Toomer) 97-98; Nick Ferenczy 42, 43, 44(c,b); Jens Ploug Hansen 23(l), 24(b), 25, 28(t), 150, 164(b), 172(b), 202(b); Mike Helliwell 44(t), 81(b), 82; David Houghton 77(b), 108(t); Trevor Housby 6, 11, 12b, 61(t), 62(b), 99(bl), 104(t), 106(bl), 121, 125, 129(b), 162(t), 164(tl), 200, 218; Denis Linley 142; Mike Millman 13(t), 19(t), 20(t), 22(t), 27, 29, 31(t), 38, 45, 46, 47(b), 48, 57(b), 59(b), 63-66, 67, 68, 69(tl,b), 71(b), 73(tl,b), 74(b), 75, 77(t), 78, 79-81(t), 87-89, 92, 93(b), 95(bl), 96(b), 99(tr, br), 100(t), 106(t,c), 107, 110(b), 111, 112(t), 113(b), 115(b), 116(bl), 117, 118(t), 120(b), 122(br), 123(b), 126-128, 130, 132(t), 135(l), 136(t), 137(tr,b), 138(c,b), 139, 148, 152, 154, 156(t), 158, 160, 168, 170(t), 172(t), 176, 190(t), 194(b), 204, 214, 216; Natural Science Photos (P Broadbent) 39, (R Forsberg) 93(t), (Paul Kay) 103(b), (D Smyth) 37, 50(r), (A Spence) 54(b); Oxford Scientific Films 105(t), 122(t), Chris Pledge 36(t), 103(t), 104(b), 118(b), 220; Graeme Pullen 19(b), 32(b), 71(t),110(t); Ken Robinson 52(b); Kevin Smith 14(l), 94(t); Still Pictures (Norbert Wu) 198; Survival Anglia Photo Library 144(b); Swift Picture Library 113(t); Brian Swinbanks 164(tr); Russell Symons 119, 131(t), 132(b), 133(b), 134, 182, 186; Mike Thrussell 61(b); Mick Toomer 85, 120(t), 140, 146, 174(b), 184, 212(t); Bill Howes 180; Ken Whitehead 109(r); Phill Williams 47(t), 57(t), 60, 73(tr), 99(Cr), 106(br), 108(b), 109(l), 112(b), 115(t), 116(t), 122(bl), 123, 124(t), 133(t), 135(r), 144(t), 156(b), 166, 174(tl), 178, 190(b), 194(t), 202(t), 206, 208, 212(b); Alan Yates 26(b), 40, 54(t), 116(br), 196.

Illustrations

Peter Bull 34-5, 42; Mick Loates 141, 147, 149, 151, 153, 155, 157, 159, 161, 163, 165, 167, 169, 171, 173, 175, 177, 179, 181, 183, 185, 187, 189, 191, 193, 195, 197, 199, 201, 203, 205, 207, 209, 211, 213, 215, 217, 219.